The Love Surgeon

D1590747

Critical Issues in Health and Medicine

Edited by Rima D. Apple, University of Wisconsin–Madison and
Janet Golden, Rutgers University–Camden

Growing criticism of the U.S. healthcare system is coming from consumers, politicians, the media, activists, and healthcare professionals. Critical Issues in Health and Medicine is a collection of books that explores these contemporary dilemmas from a variety of perspectives, among them political, legal, historical, sociological, and comparative, and with attention to crucial dimensions such as race, gender, ethnicity, sexuality, and culture.

For a list of titles in the series, see the last page of the book.

The Love Surgeon

A Story of Trust, Harm, and the Limits of Medical Regulation

Sarah B. Rodriguez

Rutgers University Press

New Brunswick, Camden, and Newark, New Jersey, and London

Library of Congress Cataloging-in-Publication Data

Names: Rodriguez, Sarah B., author.
Title: The love surgeon : a story of trust, harm, and the limits of medical regulation /
    Sarah B. Rodriguez.
Description: New Brunswick : Rutgers University Press, [2020] | Series: Critical issues
    in health and medicine | Includes bibliographical references and index.
Identifiers: LCCN 2019040812 | ISBN 9781978800953 (paperback) | ISBN 9781978800960
    (hardback) | ISBN 9781978800977 (epub) | ISBN 9781978800984 (mobi) |
    ISBN 9781978800991 (pdf)
Subjects: LCSH: Burt, James C.,—Health. | Gynecologists—Ohio—Biography. |
    Surgeons—Ohio—Biography. | Generative organs—Surgery—Ohio—History.
Classification: LCC RG76.B87 R63 2020 | DDC 618.10092 [B]—dc23
LC record available at https://lccn.loc.gov/2019040812

A British Cataloging-in-Publication record for this book is available from the British Library.

♾ The paper used in this publication meets the requirements of the American National
Standard for Information Sciences—Permanence of Paper for Printed Library Materials, ANSI
Z39.48-1992.

www.rutgersuniversitypress.org

Manufactured in the United States of America

Sometimes wrong, but never in doubt.

Surgical aphorism

Contents

The Love Surgeon

Janet Phillips, 1981

On November 4, 1981, Janet Phillips went to St. Elizabeth Medical Center in Dayton, Ohio, for a total hysterectomy to remove ovarian cancer. Following surgery, Phillips stayed in the hospital for 11 days and more than once recalled waking up to the sight of nurses around her, visibly upset; their looks of concern scared her. When her physician, James Caird Burt, came to see her, she asked if he removed all the cancer, to which Burt replied, "Don't worry, everything is fine, you are going to be okay."[1]

But for Phillips, everything was not okay. While recovering in the hospital, she was constantly in pain, and she nearly fainted the first time she tried to get out of bed.[2] Even after she left the hospital, she remained in pain and could not control her bladder. When she asked Burt about these problems, he told her he had "tacked up" her bladder and that the muscles needed to "rejuvenate." As a result of her incontinence, Phillips suffered chronic infections and took antibiotics for a year after the surgery. But once she went off the antibiotics, the infections returned, so she went back to Burt, complaining about the infections and that her vagina felt raw.[3] Moreover, she also told Burt she experienced pain during vaginal intercourse, to which she recalled Burt saying her husband "must be bigger than I thought."[4]

Not satisfied with these answers, Phillips asked Burt to recommend a urologist, but he strongly encouraged her against seeing another physician. "I've got you on the road to healing," Phillips remembered Burt saying. He further dissuaded her from seeing another clinician by warning another doctor could tear his surgery, causing severe, possibly life-threatening, hemorrhaging. Phillips recalled appointments when Burt would hug her and pat her on the back, making her feel protected and renewing her belief she would get healthy soon. But he also frightened her into not seeking another doctor's opinion about her condition, so for three years after her surgery, despite continued pain and bleeding during sex—for which Burt told her to "keep trying even if it's painful"— despite her bladder still not functioning properly—she constantly wore pads because she could not control her bladder and frequently urinated without warning—she remained Burt's patient. "I trusted him," she later said, "he was the doctor."[5]

Educated and serving his residencies at prestigious programs, Burt began his medical practice during an era historians often refer to as medicine's "golden age." From the beginning of the twentieth century and extending through at least the late 1960s, physicians in the United States enjoyed unprecedented social esteem and prestige. Medicine was considered a model profession, one Americans consistently told opinion pollsters was one of the most admirable.[6] With this admiration and prestige came the ability for physicians to practice with largely unquestioned authority. Physicians worked under the auspices of a sacred trust. The physician, philosopher Hans Jonas stated in 1969, was "alone with his patient and God."[7] When a reporter later asked Phillips why she didn't question Burt, she answered he "had the degrees on the wall."[8] Phillips, who had never been to a doctor before her first pregnancy, believed that since Burt "was the one in the white coat," she could trust him.[9]

Years after she went to Burt for a hysterectomy, Phillips learned her problems stemmed not from the removal of her uterus and ovaries but from Burt surgically altering her vagina and vulva and that she was not the only woman to have undergone what Burt called "surgery of love."

Creepy Surgery Performed on New Moms

James Burt began performing what he called surgery of love in the mid-1950s on women after they gave birth; it was, he initially claimed, a modification of episiotomy repair. An episiotomy is an incision made by physicians from the opening of the vagina toward the rectum done on women during childbirth with the intention of preventing undue tearing as the baby's head emerges from the vagina; physicians then repaired this cut by stitching it up following the birth. By around 1975, Burt began calling his modification of episiotomy repair love surgery and offering it as an elective to women of whom he was not delivering a child, although he also continued to perform it routinely on his obstetric patients. Burt performed love surgery until 1987. In October 1988, a group of women upon whom he had performed love surgery, who were suing him for malpractice, accused him on CBS's prime-time news magazine show *West 57th* of operating on them without their informed consent. After this negative national exposure, Burt was pressured to give up his medical license; in January 1989, he voluntarily surrendered his medical license and stopped practicing medicine.[1]

The popular press, including local and also national newspapers, followed this story as it developed after Burt's appearance on the fall 1988 television show. Additionally, once exposed, the Burt story was covered in national magazines directed at female readers. In these magazines, the stories were almost always framed as Burt having performed an experimental operation on trusting women without their consent and that other doctors in the community knew about it but did nothing. This was the angle in, for example, the *Savvy Woman* article with the headline "A Crime against Nature" and in the *Woman's Day* article with the headline "The Gynecologist from Hell!"[2] Burt has also been used as an example of the "good doctor gone bad," as when Atul Gawande wrote about him in his 2002 book, *Complications*.[3] In all of these accounts, Burt has been framed as a rogue doctor, a framing that has remained within the more recent stories about him found online.[4]

This narrative played well in 1989 and continues to do so today because it sounds right, for it frames Burt as a freakish physician practicing outside the norms of medical practice. It further frames the Burt story as a horror any woman could experience, per the 1989 *Mademoiselle* article on Burt that began, "This is a story about a group of women and the doctor they trusted, but it could be about any of us," or the more recent *Jezebel* blog post with the headline "Creepy 'Love Surgery' Performed on New Moms' Unwitting Vaginas."[5] The Burt narrative has quite often been reduced to that of a rare Frankenstein physician whom we (especially women) should all be frightened of, not least because his peers will abdicate their responsibility to protect us by not stopping him.

The popular narrative of what Burt did is meant to be read as a horror story because what occurred evokes powerful fears many of us have: fears about not being in control of our own bodies, fears that those in power will abuse us, fears that our trust in a scientist or in our own physician are misplaced and that they will exploit us for their own gains at our expense. Indeed, some of the earliest horror stories concerned physicians with unchecked power and madness harming the innocent. As historian Susan Reverby noted, "The monster doctors-are-infecting-the-vulnerable story is a powerful tale where our horror deepens as we expect to see the hapless victims and the evil scientist." As Reverby also wrote, it is difficult when, as historians, we write about historical events that draw forth such strong fears and emotions to "escape from the moral outrage and stock assumptions about what happened."[6]

The stock assumption regarding the Burt story has been that this was a case of a lone clinician practicing outside the norms of medicine by experimenting on unsuspecting women who did not give consent while other doctors looked on—this is what the Burt story is *supposed to be* about.[7] But this assumption leads to a dead end, for it fails to acknowledge that doctors in the community did intervene and were successful at regulating Burt's practice, although because of a variety of factors—including restraint of trade concerns, fears of lawsuits, and the time-consuming manner in which knowledge of medical problems often arises—Burt's peers did not stop him from practicing medicine completely. Moreover, limiting this story to what it is supposed to be about fails to place the story within what historian Robert Aronwitz has noted are the "the social and structural realities in which routine innovation, training, and practice have occurred."[8] By considering the Burt story within the "social and structural realities" of medical practice, research, and regulation, one can use the specifics of this case to consider larger questions about how medicine regulates itself, including: Why wasn't Burt stopped sooner? How was it that his peers managed to limit Burt's practice but failed to stop him from performing love surgery? How was it that he was able to perform a surgery he developed that no one else apparently performed? How was it that he was able to do so initially without the explicit consent of the women and later with a very noninformative consent? And how was Burt ultimately stopped from practicing both love surgery as well as medicine?

These questions, while specific to the Burt case, are also more broadly about contemporary medical practice and remain relevant to the regulation of medicine today, for they call attention to the strengths and weaknesses of medicine as a self-regulating profession. As Gawande wrote in his book *Complications*, when it comes to regulating unethical physicians, the expectation is that medical "colleagues are expected to join forces promptly to remove them from practice and report them to the medical-licensing authorities, who, in turn, are supposed to discipline them or expel them from the profession." But, as Gawande stressed, "it hardly ever happens that way. For no tight-knit community can function that way." The Burt story illustrates Gawande's point that medical regulation is neither as direct nor as simple as what he called the "official line about how the medical profession is supposed to deal with these physicians."[9]

To consider the story of James Caird Burt as a means of exploring the regulation of medicine, the book unfolds in a (mostly) chronological manner, interweaving an account of Burt's career with considerations of the wider context and implications of what happened. Starting with Burt's early career, I place his development of love surgery within a larger context of how surgeries in general are developed and how surgical development is regulated. Following this pause, I return to the Burt story to consider how the Dayton medical community responded to Burt in the 1970s before pausing again to pull away from the specifics of the Burt story to consider the larger context of problematic medical practices uncovered by journalists and legislators in the early 1980s. After that, I consider the Burt story as it progressed during the early 1980s before again pulling back to consider the stories of the many women who publicly told of their own experiences with love surgery. Reentering the Burt story with the broadcasting of the CBS show in the fall of 1988, I subsequently explore its aftermath, including not just more stories within the popular press but also actions by state legislators and lawsuits by numerous former patients, all of which ultimately ended not just the career of James Burt.

Although I am considering the Burt story within its historical context as an example of "the social and structural realities" where the practice and regulation of medicine have occurred, by doing so, I am not excusing what Burt did. My goal, rather, is to undertake what historian Susan Reverby termed "responsible history," that is, to undertake a historical analysis that attempts to "understand, but not support," the actions of James Burt.[10] I do so by unpacking the dominant narrative of, and stock assumptions regarding, the Burt story and use it instead to consider how multiple actors play a part in the regulation of American medicine—how physicians, nurses, patients, health activists, lawyers, the courts, legislators, and the media all play a role. The roles of each of these actors are interwoven throughout this book. I begin, though, by first explaining how Burt developed love surgery from the mid-1950s through the 1970s as part of his medical practice.

Chapter 1

The One in the White Coat, 1921–1978

James Caird Burt Jr. was born on August 29, 1921, in Dayton, Ohio, at Miami Valley Hospital. He was one of two children born to Benjamin, a superintendent at Dayton Manufacturing Company, and Stella Burt, who stayed home to raise their two children. James Burt attended Auburn University in 1939 where he met Lucretia Perry, his future wife.[1] Although he went to Auburn initially, James Burt received his undergraduate degree from Alabama Polytechnic Institute in 1942 and then attended medical school at the University of Rochester in New York. Before beginning medical school, James and Lucretia married.[2] James Burt finished medical school in 1945 and interned at Baylor College of Medicine's Hermann Hospital in Houston.[3] He then spent time in the U.S. Air Force Medical Corps before his residency at Chicago Lying-in Hospital. He left Chicago for residency at Columbia Presbyterian Medical Center in New York City.[4]

On June 21, 1951, Burt received his medical license from the State of Ohio and set up his gynecology and obstetrics practice in Dayton.[5] Burt was never board certified in obstetrics and gynecology (although this certification is not necessary for practice).[6] By late 1952, James and Lucretia Burt, now with two sons and a daughter, separated and he filed for divorce, saying Lucretia was unhappy with his economic situation. In 1953, with his divorce from Lucretia still pending in Ohio, James Burt obtained a divorce in Mexico and shortly thereafter married his second wife, Gerre, across the border of Ohio in Lawrenceburg, Indiana.[7]

Gerre and James Burt lived in a modern, one-story house on a hill with a swimming pool in one of Dayton's well-off suburban neighborhoods. After one child and a decade together, however, she filed for divorce, reporting that her husband had "struck and physically abused her from time to time." In Gerre

Figure 1 James Burt, c. 1970. Reprinted with permission from the *Dayton Daily News*.

Burt's divorce filings, she asked that her husband be kept away from her and that their mutually held assets be protected from him. The divorce was, given these charges, unsurprisingly not amicable—he countered her claims for alimony, saying that his divorce from his first wife was not legal and thus he had never been married to her. The judge rejected his motion and awarded Gerre Burt alimony and child support. The Burts divorced in July 1966.[8]

In 1967, James Burt obtained a divorce in the United States from his first wife and married his third wife, Linda. His practice now flourishing, Linda and James Burt lived a reportedly lavish lifestyle, buying properties in El Salvador, the Dominican Republic, and a condominium in Vail, Colorado. They hosted pool parties in their Dayton home—rumored sometimes to be without swimsuits—and the couple became known for their lavish and extravagant lifestyle. But by 1973, Linda Burt had left her husband for a ski instructor in Vail, and her soon-to-be ex-husband was living with a woman twenty-five years younger than him, Joan Woodward. Joan and James married shortly after his divorce from Linda.[9]

The couple continued the expensive lifestyle. James Burt reportedly wore gold chains to accompany his long fur coats, and some recalled him wearing a pink safari suit. He was considered flamboyant and eccentric.[10] One Dayton doctor remembered Burt as caring little for golf; rather, for Burt it "was all indoor games."[11] Similar to her husband, Joan Burt also displayed signs of the couple's wealth by frequently wearing diamonds.[12] James Burt's solid medical practice enabled the couple's lifestyle, which included a yacht on Lake Erie.[13]

As the quotation above from one of his medical peers implies, James Burt was not embraced by the local medical community. Walter Reiling Jr., a physician in Dayton who began his practice in the 1970s, spoke out publicly regarding Burt when the story made national headlines in the late 1980s. Reiling recalled how other physicians and their wives avoided the Burts at social gatherings in the 1970s and how no one wanted to sit at a table with them at medical society dinners. Partly this was because of the manner in which the Burts behaved at such dinners; both Walter Reiling and his wife Susie Reiling recollected how Joan Burt, decked out in furs, would be physically all over her husband during medical society dinners, talking a lot, and bragging about how many orgasms she enjoyed. James Burt apparently did not seek out friendships with other physicians, and Walter Reiling could not recall a physician who sought out Burt's friendship.[14]

In the mid-1950s, Burt began altering the standard repair of an episiotomy.[15] In the United States, from the 1950s through the 1980s, episiotomies were quite common, even routine following a vaginal birth; the standard obstetrics text-book, *Williams Obstetrics*, noted in its 1956 edition, "Except for cutting and tying the umbilical cord, episiotomy is the most common operation in obstet-rics."[16] Some hospitals reported episiotomy rates as high as 85 percent during the 1950s, with national rates generally exceeding 70 percent in the 1960s and 1970s.[17] Because it was considered so routine, physicians often did not even discuss it as an option with their pregnant patients; physicians just assumed they would make the cut and the subsequently necessary repair.[18] Although many women did not like the procedure—the incision made with scissors cut deeply into their musculature, it was painful, and some women believed it made vaginal sexual activity after childbirth more difficult and often painful—many physicians thought it beneficial.[19] As the 1961 *Williams Obstetrics* noted, episi-otomies were popular with physicians because physicians considered a straight, clean surgical cut to be easier to repair than a tear and because it "spared the baby's head the necessity of serving as a battering ram against perineal obstruction."[20]

But because the cut made went into the vagina, an episiotomy repair stitched both the outer tissue on the woman's perineum as well as the immediate inter-nal part of the vaginal tissue. Some obstetric and gynecology texts in the 1950s and 1960s noted that, when performed on patients with "lax" vaginas, episiot-omy repair would "eliminate the source of trouble" in marital sex.[21] In other words, an episiotomy repair could tighten the vagina. One woman recalled hav-ing a "huge episiotomy," and while the physician was sewing her back up, he turned to her husband and said, "'Well, I put in an extra stitch for you.'" The woman took this to mean that the doctor had made her "tighter than I probably was before" and that this extra stitch resulting in a tighter vagina was for her husband's sexual "benefit."[22]

Between 1954 and 1966, Burt experimented with variations on episiotomy repair, mostly by adding a few extra stitches, thus making the entrance to the vagina smaller and tighter. But in 1966, Burt claimed to have discovered two things: the important role played by the clitoris in female sexual response, thanks to the recently published research by William Masters and Virginia John-son, and that the women on whom he had been performing his modification of standard episiotomy repair told him their sex lives had improved after childbirth.[23]

Central to Burt's ideas about female sexuality and the surgery he was devel-oping were his ideas about the role of the clitoris in female orgasm. "Prior to very recently," Burt wrote, the medical consensus had been that a vaginal orgasm was mature "and orgasm from manipulation of the clitoris was immature," and thus the "ultimate return of the vagina to 'normal' by repair after childbirthing was completed seemed adequate." But this, he noted, did not consider the role of the clitoris. Burt later wrote that he based his surgery and philosophy on female orgasm on the research published by Masters and Johnson in the 1960s that argued for the central role of the clitoris to female sexual response.[24]

Working from the belief that their research would benefit people directly and be useful in sex therapy, Masters and Johnson measured their male and female volunteers' physical reactions during vaginal intercourse, as well as directly observed individuals engaging in masturbation.[25] To best measure female sexual response and the sensitivity of the clitoris, radiologists created artificial penises made of plastic containing optics allowing for observation, enabling Masters and Johnson to see the response of both the vagina and the clitoris during orgasm.[26] Much of their evidence on the orgasmic response of the clitoris was done through watching women masturbate. No two women masturbated in the same fashion, although nearly all did so without directly stimulating the clitoris. Observing women while they were using, as Masters and Johnson described, "mechanical and manual masturbatory techniques," answered their question of how and how much the clitoris needed to be stimulated.[27] Masters and Johnson found that the clitoris acted differently during sex than the penis and responded best not to direct stimulation, like the penis, but to stimulation of the general area. In 1966, Masters and Johnson published their research in their book *Human Sexual Response*, spending an entire chapter on the external genitalia of women and another specifically on the clitoris. They labeled the clitoris a "unique organ in the total of human anatomy," with its only purpose sexual. Women, they wrote, have "an organ system which is totally limited in physiologic function to initiating or elevating levels of sexual tension." No such organ, they noted, existed for men. The clitoris, they argued, played a "definitive role" in women's sexual response.[28] Writing about this work in the mid-1970s, Paul Robinson argued Masters and Johnson's assertion of the uniqueness of the clitoris was one of the most impressive aspects of their work, one that allowed them to argue female sexuality was not simply a replica of male sexuality.[29]

But this new research on the clitoris as the organ of erotic sensitivity for women was not all that Burt took from the work of Masters and Johnson. Like Masters, Burt was a physician, and both understood the body and its problems in a strictly physiological sense, devoid of social, cultural, or gender influences. By locating sexual desire and response within the body, Masters and Johnson, as well as the sexologists who followed their lead, made both research and therapy of sexual problems simpler: social contributors—such as stress at work, power relations within a relationship, or the unequal place of women in society—would have both complicated treatment and made treatment much harder to sell as an enterprise.[30] But also like Masters, Burt was both an obstetrician and a gynecologist—the former a specialty that medicalized birth, the latter a specialty that looked for pathology in the body as an indicator for something to surgically fix.[31]

In addition to his discovery of the importance of the clitoris through the work of Masters and Johnson, Burt later stated he learned from his patients that their sexual response was easier and better following birth. According to Burt, he had not informed any of these women that he had done anything other than a standard episiotomy repair. The combination of realizing the importance of the clitoris in sex for women and that the modification he had made to episiotomy repair was improving the sex lives of his patients led Burt to conclude that women's bodies were not anatomically ideal for heterosexual sex.[32] For Burt, female bodies were pathological when it came to heterosexual intercourse.[33]

Based on the research of Masters and Johnson and the information about the improved sex lives he stated he heard from his patients, Burt decided the clitoris was too far from the opening of the vagina for women to receive adequate stimulation from the penis during heterosexual missionary position sex. Burt had been adding a few more stitches to women during episiotomy repair, thereby making the vaginal opening smaller and tighter, but beginning in the mid-1960s, he began building up the skin tissue and, by doing so, found he had moved the vaginal opening closer to the clitoris. In addition to moving the vagina closer to the clitoris, this added tissue also changed the angle of the vagina's opening.[34] As Burt stated in a 1977 talk about love surgery, "The clitoris is not moved. The vagina is moved to the clitoris."[35] During missionary position sex, the changed angle of the vagina forced the penis to hit the clitoris upon penetration.[36] The vagina's direction, when the woman was on her back, was no longer horizontal but almost vertical. In addition, a significant portion of the labia minora was also pulled into the vagina, which Burt believed provided greater stimulation for the woman from the penis during vaginal sex.[37] Burt did not ask or tell any of the women during this initial stage that he had done anything more than the usual episiotomy repair, and yet he claimed they told him their sexual responsiveness was better than before childbirth.[38]

According to Burt, while many of his patients told him their sex lives were better, some complained of pain; to solve this problem, by the mid-1970s, Burt added another component to love surgery: he cut the pubococcygeus muscle.[39] This constrictor muscle at the rear wall of the vagina is shaped like a sling and supports the uterus, ovaries, fallopian tubes, lower bowel, bladder, and vagina. Women can squeeze the muscle, thus constricting the rectum, vagina, and urethra, enabling control over defecation, vaginal feeling, and urination—it is the organ controlled through Kegel exercises.[40] But, according to Burt, after love surgery, this muscle was being hit during penetrative intercourse, causing discomfort for some women. To solve this problem, Burt, as he put it, "cut the damn muscle," thus lengthening the muscle and, according to Burt, preventing it from pushing the penis away from the clitoris by raising the underwall of the vagina. As a final touch to his love surgery and to further increase stimulation of the clitoris, Burt also began circumcising the clitoris, removing the foreskin of that organ. By 1975, Burt claimed to have performed love surgery, in one of its various stages, on more than 4,000 women.[41]

This is a large number of women, and there is only Burt's word for its veracity. Indeed, Walter Reiling Jr., the retired Dayton surgeon who recalled Burt not being socially popular among local physicians, felt it was an inflated number, one meant to show his experience and expertise at performing the surgery.[42] Bradley Busacco, a Cincinnati obstetrician and gynecologist who in the 1980s and early 1990s saw perhaps around 150 of Burt's former patients, felt similarly that Burt exaggerated when he claimed to have performed love surgery on 4,000 women.[43]

One would be right, then, to question the number Burt gave of how many women he had performed love surgery upon. He apparently was, however, quite a popular obstetrician and gynecologist in Dayton who attended many women. Working mostly as a solo practitioner and operating mostly at one hospital, St. Elizabeth Medical Center, Burt's medical practice reportedly thrived in the 1970s.[44] His office in the 1970s was on the top floor of one of downtown Dayton's tallest buildings.[45] These plush offices illustrated Burt's prosperity as well as his taste for the extravagant: they included eight examination rooms, a patient waiting room—where one of the couches was shaped like a woman's mouth—a large room for patient files, a consulting room, two bathrooms, a kitchen, and offices for both himself and his wife Joan.[46]

James Burt was recalled by his patients as an amiable physician. A stocky man with a short beard, he was soft-spoken, he listened to his patients, and his bedside manner was reassuring. Linda Cook, a former patient of Burt's, recalled

Burt being a calming presence, portraying "a peaceful inner self," leaving a patient feeling that he was a "refuge." Burt was considered by many to be one of the best obstetrician gynecologists in Dayton.[47] His crowded office testified to his popularity. Donna Oblinger, whose son Burt delivered in 1970, recalled planning on staying all day at his office when she went in for an appointment "because he'd get called away to deliver babies so often."[48]

At least some of his popularity probably came from his assurance of a pain-free childbirth, accomplished—as was fairly common for hospital deliveries during this time—with the use of strong drug combinations, rendering his patients largely unconscious during the birth.[49] Burt delivered three children of one former patient, and she recalled Burt guaranteeing no pain: "If you had one little cramp, you went to the hospital and woke up the next day or perhaps two days later with your baby." Another former patient, Coney Mitchell, who went to Burt in 1967 pregnant with her third child, also recalled Burt promising her pain-free childbirth.[50]

Probably an important reason for Burt's popularity was his capacity to reassure and to listen to patients as they expressed their concerns and fears regarding childbirth—this during a time when it was quite common for physicians, perhaps particularly obstetrician gynecologists, not to listen to their female patients. Indeed, Nancy Goodman, a nurse who often worked in labor and delivery at St. Elizabeth's hospital in the 1970s, recalled that Burt "communicated with women when a lot of doctors wouldn't." In the 1970s, Goodman said, "There were a lot of physicians who were patting women on the head and saying 'Now, sweetie, don't worry, I'll take care of it.'"[51] Burt was aware of this, for even he noted that many of his fellow physicians failed to listen to women, saying other doctors labeled women as "neurotic and emotionally unstable" when they told physicians of their pain upon intercourse, frequent need to urinate, or other problems after childbirth. Burt recalled hearing about doctors who told women when they expressed fears or concerns that the women should "get along better with their husbands; get a hobby; see a psychiatrist." In contrast, Burt seemed to sympathize with his patients.[52]

Burt's sympathetic ear perhaps appealed to many women as he listened to their worries and fears about their upcoming labors or hysterectomies. And he seems to have believed that he was acting sympathetically toward them by performing love surgery in addition to delivering their child or performing a hysterectomy. In his view, Burt surgically altered their bodies to alleviate their concerns and problems, all of which—regardless of what the women may have been telling (or not telling) him—he felt were essentially about sex. Burt maintained that love surgery was "conducted with great concern for the welfare of women," to help the many women "with problems involving vaginal intercourse that are either not being adequately addressed or not being addressed at all" by other doctors.[53] He performed the surgery even on women who gave him no indication that they were experiencing problems with sexual intercourse. By the mid-1970s, Burt had been performing love surgery, in one of its variations, on nearly all women for whom he delivered a child; according to Burt, love surgery was "carried out in the delivery room at the time of episiotomy repair" although it was "actually far more extensive than merely closing the episiotomy repair." He also performed love surgery when he performed vaginal hysterectomies and often during surgeries for abdominal uterus suspension.[54] In short, whenever Burt anesthetized a woman for delivery or surgery, he claimed to have also performed love surgery, believing it was for her benefit.

Surgical practice and surgical development are based on ideas of how the body works—and on how the body can be fixed.[55] For Burt, female bodies—all female bodies—needed fixing as they were all pathologically designed for heterosexual missionary position sex—the only "normal" sex, according to Burt. Because of this belief, he felt no need to be particular about who he operated on. Burt stated that women were structurally inadequate for missionary position intercourse, and he developed love surgery to correct this "pathological anatomy of the female coital area."[56] In his view, all women needed love surgery.

By the mid-1970s, love surgery to correct what Burt had come to regard as women's pathological anatomy essentially consisted of tightening the vagina, circumcising the clitoris, decreasing the distance between the vaginal opening and the clitoris, and cutting the pubococcygeus muscle. Burt incorporated all of these procedures with the intention of enabling women to enjoy sex—presumably vaginal, heterosexual sex—more. Although novel when used together, with the exception of the latter, none of these were new procedures. And, as with Burt's intention for love surgery, these other procedures were performed for similar reasons: to better enable women—or their male partners—to have an orgasm during penetrative sex.

Burt claimed he developed love surgery from standard episiotomy repair. Episiotomies were rarely performed or advocated outside of difficult births until early in the twentieth century, when obstetricians R. H. Pomeroy and Joseph DeLee started to advocate for the routine use of forceps and thus, by necessity, episiotomy. "Freely" admitting his method of treating labor was a "revolutionary departure from time-honored custom," DeLee stressed the "sound scientific basis" for his recommendation because it would, in part, preserve the "integrity of the pelvic floor."[57] Many obstetricians picked up on the use of episiotomy, believing the procedure shortened childbirth and reduced the chance that a woman may tear during childbirth—in particular, tear down to the rectum.[58]

But, in addition to these reasons, DeLee also believed episiotomy repair often "restored" women to "virginal conditions," implying the repair created a tighter vagina.[59] In her critique of the medicalization of childbirth in the United States published in the 1970s—half a century after DeLee made his comments—Suzanne Arms argued that this "restoration and preservation" of the vagina was really based on a more "insidious" reason: physicians advanced episiotomies on their patients because otherwise, "after birth husbands will be unable to enjoy intercourse with their wives if an episiotomy has not been performed, because the vagina will be permanently enlarged and misshapen."[60]

Although not all practitioners regarded the reason to perform an episiotomy as based in a need to restore the vagina to "virginal conditions," there did exist a surgery specifically meant to restructure the vagina. Never performed as commonly as episiotomies, perineoplasty was used to treat a variety of conditions, including looseness at the entrance of the vagina.[61] Physician Wallace Shute, writing in 1959, claimed he had "for many years" performed a "plastic restoration of the perineum" in order to tighten the "vulval orifice." This "corrective treatment" performed on patients "who have lost much of their libido from previous thoughtless obstetrics," according to Shute, "cannot be recommended too highly, for patients so treated are most grateful."[62] Chicago gynecologist J. P. Greenhill similarly performed perineoplasty when the "vagina is actually too large or the muscles are too lax for a woman to perceive and feel the penis properly in the vagina," although this was seen only in "rare cases."[63]

Greenhill's perspective—that it was rare for a vagina to be "too large"—was not universally shared. Writing about surgical interventions to treat sexual disorders in 1976, James Ryan described the problem of "penile-vaginal disparity" arising from "excessive capaciousness of the vagina, particularly the entrance of the vagina or introitus to the vagina." This state, Ryan wrote, was most commonly found following "multiple vaginal deliveries," and the increased "capaciousness may contribute to a significant diminution of pleasure with intercourse." Moreover, this "condition of vaginal enlargement" was frequently also seen with "anterior and posterior vaginal wall laxities with urological or rectal dysfunction." When such was seen clinically, physicians could treat the woman by reinforcing the front and back walls of the vagina, thus "significantly" reducing the "volume of the vagina," according to Ryan.[64]

This surgery, called anterior and posterior repair (or A and P repair), was (and is) used to correct dropped pelvic organs, as can happen when the ligaments that hold these organs up fail due to reasons that can be related to the age of the woman or childbirth. Anterior repair tightens the front wall of the vagina and is performed when the bladder drops and then protrudes into the front of the vagina, resulting in the front wall of the vagina to drop. Posterior repair tightens the back wall of the vagina and is performed when the rectum drops and then protrudes into the back of the vagina, causing the back wall of the vagina to drop and resulting in possible bowel dysfunction.[65]

Although such repairs could help alleviate a number of problems, including incontinence, some clinicians used A and P repair to tighten the vagina for its purported sexual benefits. This was the reason why psychiatrist David Reuben recommended the procedure in his 1974 book *How to Get More Out of Sex*. Calling it a "simple procedure" that took less than an hour but that could "make a woman of forty almost the same sexually as a girl of eighteen," Reuben then provided a "man's point of view" on the benefits of the surgery:

> I never believe in miracles, Doctor. All my life I told myself that a person just has to learn to accept things as they happen. Well, now I know that isn't true. My wife and I have been married for twenty-five years and I was beginning to take sex for granted—just like most husbands, I guess. After three kids she was pretty stretched out; I don't know if that had anything to do with it, but I just didn't get the same kind of erections anymore. You know, half-hearted and half-hard—and sometimes half-hardly. So Tina, my wife, must have sensed that something was wrong—I guess she wasn't feeling much herself—and she started reading all those articles in the ladies magazines. She heard about this operation that they do on women's sexual organs and went to her doctor and asked him. Boy, he didn't want to have anything to do with it! He said as long as she wasn't sick, he wasn't going to operate. What he didn't know was that she *was* sick—half the time she couldn't reach climax anymore and she was getting a real complex about being so big down there.
>
> Would you believe that she had to go to six doctors before she found *one* that would do the job? But it was worth it. . . . Would you believe that at fifty-five I can go twice almost every night? When I paid the doctor I sent him a box of cigars along with the check. Believe me, he earned it.

Reuben compared the surgery to "turning back the clock," a procedure that would restore "the penis's little grotto of pleasure" from the "Carlsbad Caverns" by pulling together excess tissue, thus reinforcing the muscles and supporting tissue, ensuring that "man and woman can really get *close* again."[66]

As proposed by Ryan and Reuben, surgery could reduce the size of the vagina and thus improve women's—or perhaps more their male partners'—sexual lives. Writing in *Cosmopolitan* in 1976, Seymour Isenberg and L. Melvin Elting noted that it had become something of a "popular myth" that how to keep a marriage together "is to tighten up the woman's vagina to enhance the pleasure of intercourse." While, they noted, it was "true that in older women, or those who have had many children, the vagina becomes stretched, loses its 'tone,' and is no longer as responsive to the penis as it once was," no "vagina can be made tight enough to catch the husband completely." But despite this rather striking caveat, Isenberg and Elting stressed that sometimes the organ could be toned, and it could be necessary for some women—those women with, as they described, vaginal openings that seem to be "gaping, if there is flaccidity of the area between the bottom of the vagina and rectum, if the inner and outer lips fall to the sides, and if the muscles of the vaginal floor appear separated in the midline" when a woman ran her finger "down that section." These were indications for a vaginal tightening surgery, a surgery they called vaginoplasty. Although also noting that Kegel exercises could help, they ended their article by telling women, "You wouldn't hesitate to go to a doctor for surgery on a faulty appendix, so why hesitate when the happiness of your sexual life may be at stake?"[67]

Their article was not the only one that addressed vaginal tightening to a popular, female audience—the consumers of such surgeries. Victoria Andrews, perhaps a pseudonym, wrote about her experience in a 1974 *Ladies Home Journal* article. Learning about vaginal tightening from skimming an article at the beauty parlor, she decided to discuss it as an option with her husband. Andrews told readers of her concern regarding her sexual life with her husband after twenty years of marriage, the vaginal delivery of five "eight-and-nine-pound babies," and the comments of the ex-husband of a friend who left his wife of twenty-one years because he "had to have that firm flesh." At first nervous, she broached the topic with her gynecologist, who told her, "My dear young woman, I've done this kind of vaginal tightening for several of my patients who have had a lot of children." Andrews decided to go forth with the operation, which she told readers cost $875.75, although most was covered by her health insurance, and stressed that it worked: "The old marvelous sensation is back." While ending her article by noting, "The operation I underwent may not be right for every woman, or even for most women," it was "right for me. I'm glad I did it. And so is Bill" (Andrews's husband).[68]

In addition to tightening the vagina, Burt added female circumcision to his innovation on episiotomy. And, like the variety of vaginal tightening surgeries, he was not the first to use it as a sexual enhancement surgery. While there is no indication that it was performed as often as an episiotomy, female circumcision had been used as an aid to female orgasm for several decades before Burt added it to love surgery. The first published use of female circumcision—the removal of the hood around the clitoris (but not the clitoris itself)—as a sexual enhancement surgery to better enable a woman to experience orgasm during (marital) heterosexual sex occurred in the late nineteenth century. Doctors understood the sexual nature of the clitoris and its importance to female sexual pleasure, and thus some blamed the clitoris for a woman's failure to orgasm with her husband. The removal of the clitoral hood was an attempt to fix this concern. Beginning in the late nineteenth century, at a time when the espousal of female orgasm during marital sex was increasingly seen as an important component of a healthy marriage, physicians performed female circumcision to help married women who wanted—or whose husbands wanted their wives to have—orgasms during vaginal sex.[69]

To illustrate, in 1900, A. S. Waiss, a Chicago gynecologist, removed the clitoral hood of Mrs. R., a twenty-seven-year-old woman who had been married for seven years and who was "absolutely passionless." Her unresponsiveness troubled either her or her husband enough for her to seek a medical treatment. The doctor found Mrs. R.'s clitoris "entirely covered" by its hood. Waiss circumcised the clitoris and the patient "became a different woman"—she was, the doctor wrote, "lively, contented" and "happy."[70] By removing the clitoral foreskin, some doctors and laypeople, such as Mrs. R., thought the clitoris would be more exposed to the penis during penetrative sex and would thus receive direct stimulation from the penis, thereby increasing female orgasmic potential.[71]

This surgical correction of the clitoris continued throughout the twentieth century.[72] In his 1940 *Sex Satisfaction and Happy Marriage*, Alfred Henry Tyrer noted that for some women, "intercourse terminates" in a "partial orgasm." Women experienced this, Tyrer believed, because of "a hooded clitoris," which he noted could be "corrected by a trifling operation in a few minutes by a surgeon."[73] This therapeutic use of female circumcision to treat a lack of orgasm occurred even during the height of the popularity of the Freudian vaginal orgasm theory, a theory that stressed the normality of the vagina rather than the clitoris as the principal organ of female sexual sensation and which was most popular from the 1940s through the early 1970s.[74] In the 1970s, physicians began to speak directly to women in popular magazines and books about the benefits of female circumcision. Doctors Elting and Isenberg, in their 1976 *The Consumer's Guide to Successful Surgery*, wrote about the positive sexual effects of female circumcision for making orgasms easier for women with "clitoral inadequacy" and thought the procedure could probably be beneficial to 10 percent of women. Although they do not say how they came to this percentage, they did note that there was "a lot of debate by surgeons over the necessity of this surgery."[75]

Finally, Burt was not the first to think that the distance between the clitoris and the vaginal opening contributed to female sexual response during vaginal sex. Robert Taylor wrote in 1905 that in "some women the clitoris was placed well above the opening of the vagina" and in "coitus wholly escapes friction from the penis, and as a result there is no orgasm."[76] In the 1930s, marriage counselors and physicians Hannah and Abraham Stone measured "the span between the clitoris and the vagina" and found that the distance varied "from one-half to two and a half inches, with an average of one and a half inches." While the Stones did not feel their evidence was conclusive, they saw a direct correlation between the distance of the clitoris from the vaginal opening and an ability to reach orgasm—women who had shorter distances more likely belonged to the "group who reach a satisfactory climax."[77] In the 1940s, in answer to a question regarding female circumcision posed by a physician from New Mexico to the "Queries and Minor Notes" section of the *Journal of the American Medical Association* (*JAMA*), the editor noted the possibility that "the increased distance of the clitoris from the vaginal canal may account for some cases of unsatisfactory reaction at intercourse" for women.[78] In his 1949 book, *Human Sex Anatomy*, gynecologist Robert Dickinson referred to a French study that made a correlation between the location of the clitoris to the opening of the vagina and the ability of a woman to orgasm: the closer the two, the greater the likelihood of an orgasm. (Dickinson, however, disagreed with these findings.)[79] As a final example, in their 1950 textbook on gynecology, Arthur Curtis and William Huffman wrote that for women who had problems reaching orgasm, "The question arises as to whether the increased distance of the clitoris from the vaginal canal may account for some cases of unsatisfactory reactions at intercourse." Women with a distance longer than normal were more likely to be frigid, they theorized.[80]

Burt developed love surgery from, he claimed, episiotomy repair, but he also incorporated ideas regarding the distance of the vaginal entrance to the clitoris and the existing procedures of female circumcision and vaginal tightening into his development of love surgery. Although Burt maintained that his obstetric practice was thriving, his interest seemed to focus more narrowly on the surgery he was developing. By the mid-1970s, he decided it had evolved to the point where he could share it with the public.[81] So in 1975, he and Joan Burt coauthored *Surgery of Love*, a nontechnical book James Burt published by paying for it himself.[82] Burt gave copies of the book to his patients, sold it through bookstores, and sent complimentary copies to some physicians.[83]

Surgery of Love included chapters with titles like "There Is No 'Foreplay' in Ecstasy of Living and Loving: Only Orgasmic Loving," "Optimal Sexual Functioning Is Sexual Ecstasy Beyond the Wildest Imagination of Most People, but Within Reach of All!" and "Love As Most People Have Been Living It with Their Mates Will Ultimately Destroy Their Sexual Ecstasy." Burt outlined his beliefs on marriage and sexuality, as well as the details of love surgery, but, as these chapter titles tellingly reveal, the book also concerned Burt's vision of himself as an authority on sexuality. In the authors' biography at the beginning of *Surgery of Love*, the Burts wrote that they "manage the children still at home, two small boys, and their homes in Dayton and Vail" and that their "lives are totally dedicated to each other with their hobbies of travel and skiing and writing secondary always to just being together and pleasuring each other."[84] This sentence seems to encapsulate the two core concepts that pervaded his conception for love surgery: first, that sex should dominate everything in a couple's life and, second, implied here, that a woman should be submissive to her male partner.

For Burt, sex should be the center of a couple's life. Throughout *Surgery of Love*, Burt decried the "current definition of love as defined by the daily living habits of most people." He believed couples should structure their daily living around sex, to have sex be the central purpose to reach "the ecstasy of living and loving that is potentially possible for all persons." Burt frequently stated in *Surgery of Love* that couples must "disregard previous definitions of the word love" and instead concentrate on his definition to achieve "the ecstasy of living and loving that is potentially possible for all persons." To achieve this, Burt wrote that couples needed to engage in every opportunity for "caressing and intimate manipulation." As one example of taking every opportunity, if the woman was cooking bacon, the man could "through her clothing" manipulate "her clitoris to the point of climax." Following love surgery, which would enable "optimal sexual functioning" for the woman, this climax would take mere seconds. According to Burt, "every aspect of daily living" should be focused on "love, physical loving and being loved."[85]

As described in *Surgery of Love*, sex should be the center of a couple's life, but this life regarded men as active and women as submissive. Although he stressed the importance of a woman's ability to orgasm as central to a couple's sexual relationship, Burt never wavered in *Surgery of Love* from his belief that men gave women orgasms. And although sex and the resulting orgasm could occur in any position, for Burt, missionary was the most normal. Burt's opinions concerning women's submissive sexual role were tied to his ideas concerning women's submissive social roles, and both were in keeping with the idea of the passive woman that dominated American culture after World War II. In postwar culture, many idealized the home in an effort to find security during the Cold War, an idealization that domesticated and subordinated women—or at least those women seeking to live up to the white middle-class "ideal."[86] While acknowledging the diversity of women's actual lives during this time, there existed a cultural insistence that a healthy and normal woman was sexually passive and happily devoted to her husband, children, and home.[87]

All of which were traits Burt very much believed necessary in a wife. Although Joan Burt was, according to the author biographies on the flap of *Surgery of Love*, an "accomplished actress and musician and a sought-after professional in real estate" with great "artistic abilities," in James Burt's view, a wife must give "exclusive attention in her private life to her husband in every and all ways and focuses attention on his wants, needs, goals and face her children and the world at large as a member of a loving couple; not as an individual." A good wife, according to Burt, "will never at any time in any way in public or private be *critical or demanding* of her husband" (Burt's emphasis). If the husband wanted his wife to gain or lose weight, dress a certain way, or wear makeup, she should do so.[88] Burt believed that in both their social and sexual roles, women were to be supine.

But although women were to be sexually responsive to their husbands, Burt continually emphasized the importance of female orgasm in *Surgery of Love*. "The image of the female that has been pounded into the members of our society," Burt wrote, "is that she properly is an erotic receptacle for the discharge of the sexual tensions biologically accumulated in the male." Burt asserted that women should also experience orgasm. And while for Burt, a woman's orgasm could occur through intercourse or oral or manual stimulation of the clitoris, it was love surgery that enabled a women's capacity for orgasm to reach new heights, because his surgery, he believed, made it easier for the clitoris to be stimulated by the penis during intercourse. Burt maintained that, following his procedure enabling "optimal sexual functioning," women could achieve orgasm "almost instantaneously upon manipulation in any manner of the clitoral area." Indeed, following love surgery, "with his eyelash on the clitoris," a husband could bring his wife to orgasm "with a blink or two." As an illustration, Burt told of one patient who had had few orgasms before undergoing love surgery, but following it, the increase in her orgasmic ability and her desire for sex grew substantially—to such an extent, Burt claimed, that her husband told him he had "created a monster!"[89]

While Burt espoused better enabling women's ability to have an orgasm as the basis for love surgery, female orgasms were principally for male benefit, as the capital-letter heavy chapter title "How Any Man Can Make His Woman Into A Seething Mass of Perpetual Passion for Himself; Your Own Private Sex Pot In Your Own Private World!" explicitly attests. Although Burt wrote it took "much more than even the new redesign operation" for couples to achieve better orgasms, love surgery was the beginning. Burt believed women who most benefited from love surgery were women for whom childbirth had made their vaginas too loose—"large enough to drive a truck through sideways," he wrote. These were women he described as "real clappers," meaning Burt could clap his hands in their vagina. Burt altered the female body to conform to an idea of the sexual desirability by men for a tight vagina: he considered the "reconstructive operation on the female to provide optimal coital area structure" as alleviating male complaints following childbirth that vaginal sex was like "taking it out in a warm room."[90]

Love surgery, according to Burt, made a woman "tight enough to offer her husband adequate physical stimulation during intercourse." And with her husband's increased "physical stimulation during intercourse" came her own, for the "knowledge that she is a more adequate partner for her man" increased a woman's sexual satisfaction.[91] Burt's belief that a man's sexual satisfaction meant a woman's sexual satisfaction mirrored those of others in the 1970s, such as Lois Bird. In her *How to Be a Happily Married Mistress*, Bird asserted a happy wife's world revolved around her husband and that, if need be, a woman should fake orgasms, so her husband would believe he was a good lover.[92] For Bird, and more importantly here for Burt, men were the active ones in sex, and love surgery enabled male virility.

Men were the ones responsible in the relationship for sexual response. In *Surgery of Love*, Burt said men, "with their superior physical strength," should ensure women had multiple climaxes—for when a man "lovingly physically forces" a woman to have repeated orgasms, "the intensity becomes so great that the woman 'just can't stand it' or screams 'let me breathe, let me breathe,'" he knew he was a truly loving partner. In several places in *Surgery of Love*, Burt wrote how men should force women to have repeated orgasms and for men to not take no for an answer; "using physical strength if necessary," a man should "force her to submit to more loving caressing" for "further and further and further repeats of climaxing" even if she no longer wanted to be having sex. Burt asserted that "SALESMANSHIP" marked the difference between rape and rapture. In addition to describing sex in such terms, he also asserted that with love surgery, no "salesmanship" would be needed, for love surgery turned a woman into a "horny little house mouse who couldn't contain her joy and anticipation at the prospect of being loved all over by the greatest Lothario in the world, the only man worthy of her attentions, her husband." Burt stated that following love surgery, "any man at any age" could "love his woman to exhaustion," because following the operation, "every man can be a stud!"[93]

Surgery of Love frequently described sex using pornographic suggestions and portrayed men as the dominant, physically forceful participant. In the chapter titled "Any Man Can Make His Woman A Seething Mass of Perpetual Passion for Himself," Burt gave as an example of the effect of love surgery by describing a couple who were having sex loudly and whose neighbors thought her screams of passion were screams of pain and so called the police. And although Burt wrote about female orgasm as important, often the importance centered on its effects on the male ego. Frequently in *Surgery of Love*, he provided ideas for women to play to the male ego, including that they develop attitudes of "complete eroticism" involving a "total lack of inhibition in deportment, dress, and undress." Burt suggested a woman open the door naked when her husband arrived home, hang mirrors on the walls of their bedroom or cover their bed with a fur bedspread, or perhaps make dinner wearing only high-heels and an apron. He also suggested that "as the husband walks into the house," he is told "by the children doing the dishes that momma wants to see daddy in the bedroom," and when daddy enters the bedroom, he sees his "loved and loving wife groomed in some different and erotic manner lying on the bed or the floor," murmuring that she loves him. This would, of course, prompt the man to "throw himself upon her," resulting in sex for "two hours until she has screamed so loudly and longly for so many countless climaxes that both are at the point of exhaustion."[94] (Burt does not indicate what the children were doing during these two hours.)

Men forcing supine women to have repeated orgasms for hours; such scripted sex was vividly displayed in pornography, and in *Surgery of Love*, Burt sometimes seemed to conflate sex with pornography. Burt's book blurring actual and produced sex was published during an era when many Americans' ideas about sex were being challenged and perhaps changed—in part because of an increased exposure and acceptance of produced sex. Pornography became more accessible after World War II with magazines such as *Playboy* circulating in the millions by the 1960s.[95] *Playboy* and similar magazines did not explicitly show sex or female genitals, although *Playboy* changed when *Penthouse* began in the early 1970s showing female genitals.[96] During that decade, sexually explicit movies—in particular *Deep Throat* and *The Devil in Miss Jones*—attracted large audiences. Newsstands and adult bookstores sold magazines that, a decade earlier, would have been removed by police. Further encouraging and enabling this trend, the invention and popular embrace of video-cassette recorders by the late 1970s meant people could view pornographic movies privately at home or in a hotel room.[97]

This rise in the availability and the acceptability of pornography was part of the growing acceptance of sexuality's place in the cultural marketplace that occurred in the 1960s and 1970s. *Surgery of Love* was written and sold when sexuality was increasingly woven throughout mainstream American culture in books, films, and television shows.[98] These decades proved to be watershed years for changes in social ideas concerning sex, but those changes were not isolated or set by the fringes of American society. While a visible portion of the nation's young people fought for a revolution in sexual ideas and behavior in the late 1960s and early 1970s, Americans outside this demographic lived out the sexual opportunities.[99] During these decades, sex became part of the public realm and consumer culture, and sexual pleasure came to be seen by many Americans as a legitimate and necessary part of life.[100] The revolution, however, was not an instant one or the same for everyone everywhere in the United States. As historian Beth Bailey outlined in her book on the history of the sexual revolution in the Midwest, the agenda "was not created by a set of radicals on the fringe of American society and then imposed on the rest of the nation." The national events that occurred and were publicized through the mass media affected people on a local level, and their responses to them were very much intertwined with their local situations.[101]

These changes regarding sexuality on a social level produced changes about the place of sexuality on an individual relationship level, including and in particular here within marriage. Couples were implicitly and explicitly encouraged to explore sex, and while men were still most often the ones to initiate sex with women, surveys conducted in the 1970s revealed other aspects of marital sex differed dramatically from the 1950s: in the 1970s, it was twice as likely couples had sex in nonmissionary positions, couples more frequently engaged in oral sex, couples had intercourse more often, and the number of women who were uninterested in sex declined. Couples were encouraged to find new ways to have sex with the help of the growing number of sex handbooks, and surveys conducted during the 1970s reported that men and women enjoyed their marital sex lives. Although many married couples reported being pleased with the sorts and frequency of sex they were having, this could also be attributed to individuals in an unhappy marriage in the 1970s being more likely to divorce than individuals in an unhappy marriage in the 1950s.[102]

James Burt regarded love surgery as a surgical route to achieve these higher sexual standards. Like Masters and Johnson, he believed the cause of a woman's inability to orgasm was based in a physiological problem—for him, the clitoris and its proximity to the vagina and the "tightness" of the vagina—not in any social or familial pressures. Surgery was a simple way, Burt stressed, to alleviate the problem of sexual relations between couples. As Barbara Demick, a journalist who interviewed Burt in 1978 wrote, "Love surgery has frightening commercial potential, especially if it is packaged without Burt's cloying sexual and social biases." Indeed, Demick quoted an early critic of Burt who worried that America was "ready, willing and able" to embrace love surgery, meaning Burt could be "successful, even more successful than [the popular and popularizing evangelical minister] Billy Graham" based on Burt's promise of an easy female orgasm—an orgasm enabled by (and largely for) the male.[103]

Burt envisioned love surgery as a surgical means to sexual nirvana of which most people had only fantasied. But it was not just sexual fantasy Burt sold; it was also the ability for a woman to keep her husband. Burt more than once hinted in *Surgery of Love* that women who submitted to their husbands' forceful sex and desire that they dress a certain way stayed married. According to Burt, "For the woman to be beautiful to the man, she must have his interests and needs and desires as her goal and focus attention thereon rather than making any demands or criticisms of her man." Women who did this, as well as who underwent love surgery, achieved "ecstasy in their living and loving permanently until death do us part."[104] As Burt conceived it, love surgery contained an added allure: it reduced a couple's chances of becoming one of the 50 percent who divorced.[105]

Chapter 2

Dayton Doctor Develops Corrective Surgery, 1975–1978

Dayton, Ohio, is located along the Miami River in the Miami Valley, about an hour north and slightly east of Cincinnati. Famous as the birthplace of the poet Paul L. Dunbar and of the inventors of the airplane, Orville and Wilbur Wright, Dayton has been called by some the "Cradle of Aviation." In the early twentieth century, it was a prosperous factory town, manufacturing cash registers, sewing machines, computing scales, bicycles, and, of course, airplanes.[1] A racially segregated city, its majority white population for the most part economically thrived during and after World War II and through the 1950s.[2] During the 1960s, however, like many midwestern cities of its size, Dayton saw many residents— in particular white residents—leave the city for surrounding suburban communities that began developing, causing a decline in the central downtown business district.[3] Dayton's population peaked in 1960 at a little over 262,000; a decade later, it had fallen by nearly 20,000 residents, and by 1980, it was only a little over 200,000.[4] The loss in population paralleled an increase in unemployment beginning in the 1970s with a huge reduction in manufacturing jobs; by 1981, the unemployment rate in Dayton was 8 percent, with unemployment in the state hitting 14 percent the following year.[5] Dayton's economic downturn was far from uncommon for urban centers during the 1970s.[6]

Despite the economic difficulties that started to hurt his native city and state during the 1970s, Burt's private medical practice thrived.[7] Seeking to expand his practice and promote his surgery, Burt used *Surgery of Love* to bring him both local and national attention. In September 1975, a month after the publication of *Surgery of Love*, the local newspaper, the *Dayton Daily News*, published a glowing description of the doctor and Joan Burt, as well as an uncritical look at love surgery. In the article, "Local Doctor Develops Corrective Surgery," James Burt claimed there were few side effects from love surgery, and nearly every woman who had undergone it was "ecstatic" with the results. Joan Burt agreed and was quoted as saying her husband had "given women the opportunity to enjoy sex," adding she had never had an orgasm before love surgery.[8]

Surgery of Love garnered Burt attention, but he wanted more, so he hired a New York City public relations firm to help him publicize love surgery, which he was now offering as an elective for $1,500 plus hospitalization costs.[9] Publicizing specific practices was new in medicine; in 1975, the Federal Trade Commission (FTC) filed a complaint against the American Medical Association (AMA) charging it with restricting its members' ability to advertise to patients. Following two years of hearings, an administrative law judge agreed with the FTC complaint, and in 1982, so did the U.S. Supreme Court. Burt, then, appears to have been advertising his surgery a bit before the Supreme Court ruling.[10] By publicizing his surgery, Burt was, in effect, challenging the long-held ethical tradition of physicians to not advertise, since to do so was seen as negating the professionalism of medicine; not advertising was regarded as one of the things that made the practice of medicine distinct from the practice of a trade.[11] Despite the ethical prohibition, Burt and his surgery were featured in both print and broadcast media, including favorable articles in the magazines *Playboy* and *Playgirl*. He made an appearance on the popular, nationally syndicated *The Phil Donahue Show* television program, a program that originated in Dayton.[12] And he made an appearance on the *Midday L.A.* television show. Seeking to capitalize on what they claimed was a growing interest in love surgery, the Burts reportedly planned to open a love surgery institute in Dayton to further the study and teaching of love surgery to other doctors. Although the details were vague, the Burts said in 1978 that they were working with private investors to finance the building, for which architectural plans were, they stated, in progress.[13]

The *Playgirl* article appeared in 1977, nearly two years after Burt began offering love surgery as an elective. In addition to speaking with Burt, in her article for *Playgirl*, Linda Murray also interviewed several women who chose to undergo love surgery. The women, whose names Murray received from Burt, all raved about love surgery: one woman told Murray that "sex was so natural" now she and her husband no longer had "to work at it," a sentiment expressed nearly verbatim by another woman. A third woman told Murray she easily enjoyed multiple orgasms, sometimes so strong she nearly passed out. Murray interviewed ten women for her story, including Joan Burt, who told Murray that since having love surgery she could now "count on climaxing" during sex.

Murray, impressed with what these women told her, considered at two points in the article putting herself on James Burt's operating table.[14]

According to Burt, 200 women had requested the surgery during the first two years of his offering it as an elective. The two-hour-long surgery required five days in the hospital, at least a week sitting on an inner tube, and six to eight weeks without vaginal sex.[15] Burt claimed that "more and more" women were electing to have love surgery to improve their sexual response after delivering a child, stating that "the number of patients seeking coital area reconstruction by virtue of patient referral as their presenting request when first seen in the office is on the increase."[16] Burt, as journalist Barbara Demick wrote in 1978, was a capable surgeon with excellent bedside manners. But to the women who sought him out and who went to him for love surgery, he was more than that: he was an "emotional and sexual cult figure," Demick wrote.[17] And, with his national publicity, the women who sought out James Burt were now not just from around Dayton but across the country.[18]

Burt maintained a heterosexual woman who climaxed easily through clitoral manipulation and who wanted but seldom experienced orgasm during vaginal sex was the ideal candidate for love surgery.[19] This, according to national polls conducted in the 1970s, would have been a lot of women. Only 30 percent of the women who answered Shere Hite's survey said they regularly had an orgasm from vaginal intercourse without additional direct clitoral stimulation. Forty-four percent regularly reached orgasm when manually stimulated and 42 percent when orally stimulated, although many women were hampered from even trying the latter for what one woman called feeling "dirty down there."[20]

For many women, reaching orgasm during missionary position sex was not easy. Hite's survey found that women felt pressured to have an orgasm during intercourse to make their male partners feel good.[21] According to a 1975 *Redbook* survey of married women, most women did not have an orgasm during missionary position sex. One woman who participated in the survey wrote that she conducted a survey of her friends and found that none of them had ever had a "'real' orgasm through intercourse—only through clitoral stimulation." She reported that men found this hard to believe: "try convincing a *man* you don't have orgasms his way. He won't believe you." Another woman who participated in the survey said she felt many women "are faking orgasm during intercourse because they are too embarrassed to tell their husbands or lovers that no matter how long they keep their erection, they just can't make her have an orgasm." This woman begged *Redbook* to print her response to "ease a lot of tensions and make sex a lot better for thousands of women like me."[22]

Burt considered the inability of a woman to orgasm during missionary position intercourse without, as he described it, "gymnastics"—the man or woman touching the clitoris during the act—a sexual dysfunction.[23] Burt agreed with Masters and Johnson both regarding their argument for the unique importance of the clitoris to female orgasm and that women who could not achieve "hands-free" missionary position orgasm were suffering from a sexual problem.[24] In Burt's view, by enabling a woman to achieve orgasm "hands-free" during sex, his surgery was treating her for what he considered a sexual dysfunction.

Burt presented his ideas regarding love surgery as a treatment for sexual dysfunction during the 1970s to at least one professional conference, the International Academy of Sex Research. Following his presentation on love surgery, Ira Reiss, a professor of sociology who later served as president of the academy, suggested to Burt a less expensive and a less invasive method to help enable women to reach orgasm during missionary position sex: a small, soft cushion that could be attached to the base of man's erect penis. The cushion during sex pressed upon the clitoris. Reiss suggested to Burt the cushion was a "far easier solution than surgery for those women who insisted on hands-off coital orgasm." As Reiss recalled, Burt seemed surprised and said to Reiss it "might work, but you and I both know that most men would never bother to wear such a contraption."[25]

Reiss found Burt's response a "most revealing commentary on our culture"; women "will undergo major surgery but men will not wear a simple sex gadget." Reiss further found Burt's reason for love surgery—to cure women of what Masters and Johnson labeled a dysfunction—problematic. Because the term *sexual dysfunction* was lifted from physiology (since many of the early sex therapists were physicians, like Masters) and referred to the disruptive operations of bodily organs, it implied that there was something wrong with the way women functioned sexually. Masters and Johnson, according to Reiss, defined sexual dysfunction as "conditions in which the ordinary physical responses of sexual function are impaired." But what exactly were ordinary sexual functions, wondered Reiss. Since the majority of women responded mostly to direct clitoral stimulation, Reiss considered that to be a woman's "ordinary physical response."[26]

Not long after *Surgery of Love* was published, Joan Burt began to distance herself and her husband from what she described as an unprofessionally written and openly sexist book, saying that while it was "good for the caliber of patients we had at the time, we need something better now."[27] The Burts sought to dissociate themselves from the sexist overtones of the book to attract a larger audience. But James Burt also wanted to convince sex therapists such as Reiss, as well as his medical peers, of the efficacy of his surgery. And to do so, he began seeking evidence. As part of this effort, he commissioned psychiatrist Arthur Schramm to study love surgery's effects on the female psyche. After learning about the surgery, Schramm decided first to listen to what Burt's patients had to say, so Burt identified four women upon whom he had recently operated, and Schramm met with them. The women were "remarkably positive," Schramm recalled.[28] Taking the information he learned from these four women, Schramm started a preliminary study of thirty women. By the summer of 1978, Schramm had developed a word association questionnaire in order to pick up subtle attitude changes among the women before and after the surgery.[29] A typical question was: "Since your surgery, has there been an increase or decrease in your overall ability to be a nicer, better person in any and all dealings in general with other people?" According to Burt, none of the women who answered that question felt there had been any degree of decrease, while 53.3 percent "felt there had been an improvement."[30]

In addition to working with Schramm, Burt also began conducting his own research on the effects of love surgery by developing a postsurgery questionnaire. He sent the twenty-seven-page form to his love surgery patients. In 1977, Burt claimed that the first 100 women who responded to his questionnaire were overwhelmingly pleased with the sexual benefits of love surgery.[31] He tried to present this information at the Eastern Association for Sex Therapists but was denied.[32] Burt also sought to publish the results from this survey in the *American Journal of Obstetrics and Gynecology* and wrote frequently to the editor, Frederick Zuspan, a professor of obstetrics and gynecology at Ohio State University, but the journal rejected his articles.[33] As Burt told a reporter in 1978, his files overflowed with letters rejecting his love surgery articles.[34]

During this time when he actively sought peer-reviewed publication of his findings, Burt also sought the support and endorsement of his fellow physicians individually. Burt wrote to Mary Calderone, a prominent physician, sex educator, and a founder of the Sex Information and Education Center of the United States, presumably seeking her endorsement of his surgery.[35] He also wrote several letters to another prominent peer, Luigi Mastroianni Jr., an obstetrics and gynecology professor at the University of Pennsylvania School of Medicine.[36] While a few physicians and sex therapists who learned about love surgery said that for certain women it possibly held some benefit, they also said the surgery needed more study. Lawrence S. Jackman, the director of the division of human sexuality at Albert Einstein College of Medicine in the Bronx, New York, stated he had performed an older version of the surgery on two patients with good outcomes. But, he said, love surgery's value was still unproven. At best, he thought a woman with a low perineum (the tissue between the vaginal opening and the anus) may find the surgery of benefit. But few women had a low perineum.[37]

Burt, however, believed his surgery was beneficial to many (if not all) women and that it was in fact a surgery that should be an option for all women. Advocating for it, Burt continued to solicit the acceptance of his medical peers around the country, in particular two of the biggest names in sexual medicine, Masters and Johnson. Burt, who possibly spoke with Masters at a conference in 1977, received an invitation from Masters to speak in St. Louis at his Reproductive Biology Research Foundation. Burt eagerly accepted; in an August 23, 1977, letter to Masters, Burt stated how much he was looking forward "to the stimulation of having a scientifically-open minded group participate in a dialogue regarding female surgical therapy of coital dysfunction." Burt ended his letter by stating that he wished Masters to know "I consider it a great honor to visit your foundation and have the opportunity to speak to your staff."[38]

On September 21, 1977, Burt presented, with slides, to the staff at the foundation during a two-hour lunch. His presentation, "Surgical Improvement of Vaginal Response by Female Coital Area Reconstruction: A New Modality of Treatment," began with noting that the "pioneering work of Masters and Johnson" proved that "'normal' female coital area anatomy results normally in indirect clitoral penile manipulation." In order to more directly stimulate the clitoris during penetrative sex, Burt proposed a "new concept of that which 'normal' female coital area anatomy should be from the standpoint of adequate vaginal function." The new anatomy "differs from 'normal' anatomy," Burt told his audience, and "it has been termed 'optimal coital area anatomy.'" Burt described the woman who would most benefit from his anatomical redesign: a heterosexual woman "dissatisfied with physical response restricted to masturbatory and/or female homosexual clitoral manipulatory technique by their partner before, during, and/or after coitus," or a woman who wanted sex without "extended foreplay." Using such criteria, Burt believed that "millions of women" were ideal candidates for the surgery.[39]

But just as in *Surgery of Love*, in his talk before the staff of Masters and Johnson's Reproductive Biology Research Foundation, Burt focused not only on what love surgery would do for female sexual response but also on what he felt the surgery did for women's nonsexual behaviors. Women were, Burt stressed, nicer, less irritable, and more attractive after love surgery. The surgery resulted, too, in the man liking his female partner better and an increase in the male partner's self-esteem. "It is of importance to the male psyche that the penile 'magic

wand' is truly 'magic,'" Burt stated during his talk.[40] To illustrate the importance of the "magic wand," Burt used as an example a young woman whose male
partner adamantly and vehemently refused to change his technique—to stimulate his partner's clitoris—and so she underwent love surgery to enable orgasm
without such manual stimulation. The couple now, Burt enthused, both focus
on "pleasure, rather than technique and performance."[41]

While it is unclear if either Masters or Johnson was present during Burt's
talk, that Masters knew and was at best lukewarm about love surgery can be seen
in his response to a letter from another physician asking about it. Three months
after Burt's presentation in St. Louis, Masters received a letter from an obstetrician gynecologist in Colorado who had a patient bring him a copy of Murray's
Playgirl article; the Colorado physician wanted Masters's opinion on both the
article and the surgery it detailed.[42] Masters replied to the Colorado physician
later that month, writing that Burt's method "has been demonstrated to us,"
although currently "the only theoretical value that we can ascribe to it is that
there may be some indication for women who have had loss of integrity of the
vaginal barrel, presumably due to obstetrical trauma." He continued, noting that
Burt "has done a few cases" but without clinical controls "and has not established criteria of selectivity as of two months ago." Masters continued, "From
our point of view, we would only make this suggestion as an ultimate last resort,
after all other possibilities for effective therapy had been exhausted." He concluded his letter by stating that he hoped "the above is of some value."[43]

It is doubtful that Burt knew of Masters's hesitation regarding love surgery,
or perhaps Burt did know but felt Masters's support was important and that he
could win Masters over to the efficacy of love surgery as applicable to more than
a few women. Regardless of his understanding of Masters's belief regarding love
surgery, Burt continued to seek him out. In March 1978, Burt asked Masters to
be a referee of the paper he was submitting for publication consideration to the
American Journal of Obstetrics and Gynecology. Masters, however, declined,
telling Burt he did not have enough information to do so.[44] Burt followed up
and asked whether Masters's offer to "review hard date when available" was
still good, an offer the secretary who handled Burt's call that March day assured
him it was, "assuming he [Burt] didn't expect instant turn-around."[45] Burt then
sent a letter to Masters, asking him if his staff would be available to help with
"conducting an independent pre- and whatever post-operative follow-ups at
whatever intervals would seem indicated study of patients upon whom I would
operate." He then reminded Masters that he had no grants or other funding "and
am supporting any data accumulation at my own expense," so he presumed
"that financial support for such a study would have to come from candidates

for Female Coital Area Reconstruction," another of Burt's terms for love surgery. Burt ended his letter with praise and thanks: even though Masters had declined to be a referee for his paper submission to the *American Journal of Obstetrics and Gynecology*, "I want you to know how much emotional support your listening to me in September was and the fact that I am totally appreciative of having a person of your scientific and personal stature just listen with an open mind." He concluded, "Your inability to be a referee for my paper in no way lessens my great appreciation for the emotional support you have already given me personally and your offer to review protocols and perhaps at some time in the future give consideration of some possible actual research collaboration."[46]

Although Masters appears to have been cordial with Burt, his letter to the Colorado physician in late 1977 indicates his apparent hesitancy about fully endorsing Burt's surgery. But Masters soon backed entirely away from Burt, possibly because of an unflattering article that appeared in April 1978 in the national medical news journal, *Medical World News*. For this story, the journal interviewed Burt, described his surgery, and explained his various attempts to convince sex therapists of its legitimacy. In the article, "Furor over Vaginal Surgery for Anorgasmy," Burt acknowledged that most sex therapists were not impressed by the surgery. But, Burt claimed, this was because "pelvic surgeons rarely think about sexual function, and sex therapists don't think of surgery for women at all."[47]

Burt's patients were not interviewed, but several sex therapists and physicians were, and they all expressed the same thoughts on love surgery. Sex therapist and associate professor of obstetrics at the State University of New York at Stony Brook, Diane Fordney, said that while Burt was a "nice person," he was "a zealot, and that makes him dangerous." Fordney described love surgery's rearrangement of female genitals as seeking to meet a "male-induced and -desired goal" and was a "sexist, woman-reducing process." Selig Neubardt, an assistant clinical professor of obstetrics and gynecology at Albert Einstein College of Medicine, added that "Dr. Burt wants to build everyone a vagina to please himself." Although the journal contacted the Montgomery County Medical Society for a comment, the president of the society declined.[48]

Unlike the local physician who declined comment, physicians outside of Dayton were not hesitant. Asked by the *Medical World News* whether they thought the surgery could work, Fordney thought there was a chance love surgery had a placebo effect but said further studies in the form of an independent clinical trial needed to be done. Leon Zussman, a physician and director of the Human Sexuality Center of the Long Island Jewish-Hillside Medical Center, said "it might work only on a placebo basis on some women" because the operation "violates everything we know about the production of orgasm and the modern concept of human sexual response." The operation, Neubardt concluded, was "lousy," but if it or any other surgery was presented honestly and openly and "a woman chooses it anyway, then it is okay."[49]

Shortly after this article appeared, William Masters received a letter from a physician in Massachusetts asking about the surgery in the *Medical World News* article. "The technique," this doctor noted in his letter, "you are probably familiar with, but essentially consists of reconstruction of the posterior wall of the vagina to ensure that there will be direct penile stimulation of the clitoris during intercourse. He also performs clitoral circumcision to prevent the glans from retracting under the hood at the plateau phase of excitement." The physician asked for Masters's opinion on the surgery, adding, "I know no-one who will give a more objective opinion than you, and would very much appreciate your comments."[50] Masters responded, writing, "I do regret that I cannot provide you with a definite opinion about the surgical technique for anorgasmia proposed by Dr. James C. Burt." Although noting he had "seen Dr. Burt's work, talked to him personally," Masters had not "to date have had the opportunity to see his control research data. Without this review, I am unable to evaluate his work." Masters ended his letter saying he was "sorry" he couldn't "help this matter."[51]

Presumably still stinging from the April 1978 *Medical World News* article, later that year, Burt agreed to be interviewed by a reporter from a small weekly publication out of Cambridge, Massachusetts, although he was at first hesitant because, Burt said, of "the distortionist drivel that's come out from people who haven't talked to the patients and who have refused my research paper."[52] It was the first story Barbara Demick, who went on to work for the *LA Times*, wrote for publication.[53]

Although a novice reporter, Demick was not hesitant to ask Burt some direct questions concerning his surgery, including if he felt discouraged by the poor reception love surgery had received from sex therapists and other physicians. Burt said he was not discouraged; he was "disgusted." He told Demick he "expected scientifically minded people to be scientifically and intellectually honest," accusing sex therapists of demanding more "proof of my surgery than for any of their own work because they are afraid I'll take their $100-an-hour counseling fees away." Burt stated that the real reason other clinicians rejected love surgery was because they feared they would lose clients. Few couples, Burt told Demick, "could afford the expense" of "direct personal consultation with

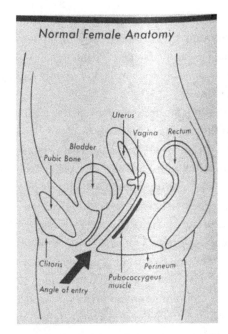
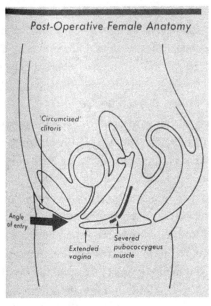

Figures 2 and 3 Drawings that appeared in Barbara Demick's article on Burt to illustrate female anatomy before and after love surgery. The original caption read: "The complete reconstruction involves three separate procedures: 1) constructing from the perineum a significant additional length of vagina opening near the clitoris, 2) severing (lengthening) the pubococcygeus muscle, 3) 'circumcising' the clitoris by cutting back the clitoral hood to further increase stimulation by the penis. The result: the entire axis of the vagina is tilted so that the penis enters in direct contact with the clitoris. And, according to Dr. Burt, the lengthened muscle will not push the penis away from the clitoris by elevating the under wall of the vagina." Source: Demick, "Love Surgery: Sexual Panacea or Mutilation for Profit?" *The Real Paper*, August 26, 1978, 18–19. Courtesy of the Northeastern University Archives and Special Collections.

professional therapists."[54] Since Burt regarded sex as the basis for all marriage problems, he believed love surgery to be the more effective—and less expensive—approach.

During his interview with Demick, Burt informed her that he and Masters were friends and that Masters actually used a procedure similar to his. Probably in order to verify this, Demick called Masters. In a memo dated July 25, 1978, the staff member who took Demick's call at the Reproductive Biology Research Foundation wrote that "Ms. Barbara Demick called today—she is preparing to go to Dayton to interview Dr. James Burt who indicated Dr. Masters is a friend of his and that Dr. Masters used similar procedures as those used by Dr. Burt. (Keep in mind that this girl is inexperienced, naïve, etc.—interesting, eh?)." The memo continued, noting that Demick wanted to interview Masters "before next Tuesday." The staff member quoted Demick as saying, "I would hate to print that Dr. Burt has your approval without verifying it." At the end of the memo, the staff member wrote, "Suggestions for handling, please!"[55]

Instead of Masters, however, Virginia Johnson answered the plea for assistance on how to handle Demick's request by calling Demick back herself that day. During their conversation, Johnson recorded she told Demick they had no connection with Burt other than visits, that they had "no interest" in his surgery, and that they did not use his technique. In her note to the staff member who asked for help fielding the call from Demick, Johnson also added that she spoke negatively of Burt "off record" to "discourage" any connection between Burt and the foundation since Johnson felt sure Demick "will use negative in her interview with Burt."[56] Johnson did not want, it would appear, to have Masters connected with Burt; in her article, Demick wrote that while Burt claimed Masters as a "close personal friend," Demick noted Johnson "vehemently" denied such a relationship.[57]

In her article, Demick took a decidedly skeptical, although not outright negative, stance regarding Burt. Burt, she wrote, considered himself more than a good surgeon: there was "a Grand Concept behind all this—and it is no less presumptuous than the surgery itself." According to Demick, Burt saw the surgery as treating sexual malfunction by fixing what he regarded as anatomical problems. Not that Burt considered the mental aspect unimportant, but as he told Demick, "It's like trying to win a race with a lousy car no matter how good a driver you are." As Burt explained, the process of treating sexual problems was physical and psychological; love surgery corrected both. According to Burt, after the surgery, the women had a "dramatic attitude change." The women were more positive and "nicer to their husbands," Burt told Demick. He claimed to see the surgery's benefits "when the women come back into the office after their surgery—in their faces, in their dress, in their posture and bearing, in their lack of bitchiness. . . . They have a much greater ability to look at the roses instead of the thorns."[58]

To illustrate the marital relations and sexual response benefits of his surgery, Burt's secretary arranged for Demick to interview in his office eight women who elected to have love surgery and who were happy with the results. One of the women was Judy, who was twenty-seven and had been married for eight years. Demick, who did not use the women's last names, wrote that Judy had not had problems with sex until she had children. Judy heard about Burt and love surgery from her niece; needing a hysterectomy and repair of her bladder, Judy decided in 1977 to also undergo love surgery. Bruce, her husband, went with Judy when she met with Burt, and Burt showed Bruce, Judy told Demick, "exactly what he was going to do." Judy and Bruce were impressed Burt explained the procedure; they were equally impressed with the results of the surgery. Judy said to Demick, sex was "a whole new thing now," saying "Bruce hits me exactly where he has to." Judy, who said she seldom had an orgasm before undergoing love surgery, continued, "Now I can have as many as I want." Love surgery "actually changed my life," Judy said. "Even though I am not the greatest person in the world, to him [Bruce] I am. I feel the pleasure that he does and I feel that I am good for my husband, that I am really extraordinary. I feel more confident in bed, more confident socially." Judy continued, informing Demick about her disappointing early sexual experiences and how she thought this was typical for all women. Judy insisted on the benefits of the surgery: "Other women should know they don't have to live the rest of their lives like that. I feel that women just are not made right, seeing how much better I'm made now."[59]

Pat, another patient, echoed Judy's enthusiasm for love surgery and for Burt, saying, "I've never had a doctor as kind." Sex had been painful for Pat, but other doctors told her the pain was only in her head. Then she saw Burt. Her appointment was at two in the afternoon; by four, she was in surgery. Pat told Demick that before love surgery, "all I was good for was pleasing my husband, I felt like I wasn't a woman. But since, my life has just gotten better. If another woman can do it [climax] once in five minutes, I can do it twice."[60]

Demick noted that, like Judy and Pat, twenty-year-old Kathy was also self-conscious during her interview with Demick. Demick spoke with Kathy and Jim, Kathy's forty-one-year-old boyfriend; the couple lived together and had a one-year-old child. While "sex felt good," Kathy told Demick, she rarely reached orgasm, making her feel insecure; often she faked it. They learned of Burt from Jim's mother, and after meeting Burt and hearing him speak about love surgery, Jim paid for Kathy to undergo it. "It cost me 1,500 dollars," Jim told Demick. "I could have bought me a car for that, but why shouldn't I spend it on her cause I enjoy her a lot more." Jim also told Demick that after love surgery, Kathy was "much firmer and our bodies are much closer together during sex." Jim said that now, after the surgery, foreplay was no longer a concern for him; he didn't have to "try for her to enjoy herself." A man, he said, "feels like he ain't much of a man, like she might be seeing other men. Now, why would she when she's getting satisfied at home?" Love surgery was, he said, "one of the greatest things I've ever seen for saving a relationship."[61]

Demick interviewed four more women. Dolores told Demick she stopped her daily intake of Valium, and her boyfriend said her "vagina feels like a velvet glove." Minnie said love surgery probably saved her marriage. Beverly, a nurse in her mid-thirties, decided to have love surgery because she wanted to have an orgasm "without a whole lot of fooling around." But Demick was most impressed by Ernestine. In her early sixties and a retired grade school teacher from a suburb of Dayton with black hair and dressed in a "chic pale green silk," Ernestine was, according to Demick, "a striking figure." Moreover, Demick wrote, her "self-assured comments" lacked the "traumatic overtones" of the other women. Ernestine had been married for forty years and had last experienced an orgasm in 1942, before the birth of her first child. She read about love surgery in the local newspaper and decided to undergo it. She told Demick that she and her husband "are as happy as two bugs in a rug. We enjoy our sex life more than when we were newlyweds." Ernestine echoed Burt, stating how following love surgery, a woman "feels like a better person, she's nicer to people. . . . And my husband's much nicer to me." Since the surgery, Ernestine said her husband had given her three fur coats and a new Monte Carlo, despite not having a driver's license.[62]

All eight of the women Demick interviewed provided enthusiastic praise for Burt and love surgery. None of the women said they consulted another doctor about love surgery before having it; indeed, Demick wrote the women saw Burt as the first doctor to take them seriously. None of the women or their partners had sought sex counseling before deciding on love surgery, and not one of the women even implied to Demick if there was indeed a sexual problem in the relationship, the one with the problem was the man. Demick further observed how nearly all of the women had married when they were young; they had little knowledge or experience before marriage about sex, and except for Ernestine, all the women had experienced either marital or sexual trauma. Finally, all of the women were convinced love surgery saved their relationships, and all believed it necessary, regardless of its price. This was especially compelling to Demick, who noted that none of the women she interviewed were rich. "Whether or not Burt's love surgery has physiological merit, there is more than enough to indicate a potent placebo effect," she concluded.[63]

According to Demick, before the surgery, Burt told the women and their male partners who came to him requesting the surgery what he was going to do, showing them before-and-after love surgery diagrams and photographs. He gave many of the women, as well as their partners, their first and perhaps only sex counseling, taking time to show them how female orgasm was achieved and how love surgery would better facilitate that orgasm.[64] But what Burt did not tell his patients was that it essentially limited sexual positions to just one: missionary. He also downplayed possible complications from love surgery, describing them as "no more than the standard perineorrhaphy [episiotomy repair] carried out as described in the surgical textbooks."[65]

The year Demick's article in *The Real Paper* appeared, Burt claimed that his combined obstetrics and gynecological practice grossed $400,000 annually. (For comparison, in 1978, the average obstetrician gynecologist earned nearly $64,000 annually, and the average salary for a white married man that same year was a little over $22,000.)[66] But by 1978, Burt began focusing on promoting and performing love surgery, essentially halting his obstetrics practice.[67] The poor reaction to love surgery by his medical peers disappointed him and made him even more driven about proving the validity of his surgery, going so far as to compare his rejected work to the initially rejected work of Sigmund Freud and William Masters. Determined with proving to others the effectiveness of love surgery, he was also becoming perhaps, as Demick described, a touch paranoid in his perception of how others saw him.[68]

To help market the positive effects of love surgery to a diversity of women, Joan Burt joined the local chapter of the National Organization for Women (NOW), calling love surgery a feminist choice. "If women can indeed be made the sexual equals of men, why shouldn't they have that choice?" she was quoted as saying in her interview with Demick in *The Real Paper*. "They [insurance companies] pay in full for impotent men to get silicone implants," argued Joan Burt, "so why not do the same for women?" As she told Demick, "We have to stop treating the penis as a special sex symbol."[69]

Using this reasoning, Joan Burt and her lawyers went to the Ohio Civil Rights Commission to attempt to force insurance companies to pay for love surgery. Insurance companies, such as Blue Cross Blue Shield, paid for the hospital portion of the bill for love surgery but were less consistent in their payment of Burt.[70] Moreover, in January 1978, the insurance company Ohio Medical ceased paying Burt for "vaginal reconstructive surgery," and Metropolitan Life followed a few months later.[71] A representative for one of the insurance companies told Burt that love surgery was no longer covered because it was not a generally accepted procedure and, per the policies of the insurer, thus not applicable for reimbursement.[72] Given the reason was, apparently, that love surgery was no longer a "generally accepted procedure," the decisions were perhaps tied to a recent decision about paying for female circumcision, a component of love surgery. On May 19, 1977, the *New York Times* reported that Blue Shield Association recommended its individual plans stop routine payments for twenty-eight surgical and diagnostic procedures considered outmoded or unnecessary by groups such as the American College of Physicians, the American College of Surgeons, and the American Hospital Association. Of the twenty-eight, one of the procedures deemed no longer medically necessary was "the removal of the clitoral hood."[73]

Although Joan Burt argued for love surgery as a woman's sexual right and for women to have a choice in obtaining the surgery, many feminist health activists disagreed. The feminist critique of the health care system in general, and of doctors in particular, charged that men dominated medical care and knowledge, thus controlling women's bodies. Women within the movement expressed frustration that male doctors were condescending and that routine passages of women's lives—birth control, pregnancy, childbirth, menstruation, menopause—were overmedicalized.[74] The Boston Women's Health Book Collective, the authors of the formative feminist health text *Our Bodies, Ourselves*, sent in June 1978 copies of the Burt article that appeared in the *Medical World News* as part of their monthly mailing. The mailing, which was sent to 250 women's health organizations, included a letter stating members of the collective were "appalled by the vaginal and clitoral mutilation recommended by Dr. James C. Burt" as described in the *Medical World News* article. The letter continued, saying to suggest "women need vaginal surgery because they do not have orgasm with each penile-vaginal intercourse is to inflict upon women male fantasies and assumptions about female sexuality." They urged "all medical professionals and their organizations to take a stand condemning this practice and to bring pressure on Dr. Burt to stop performing this surgery." Similarly, the Women's Community Health Center in Cambridge, Massachusetts, sent their own letter speaking out against love surgery to women's health organizations in the United States.[75]

As illustrated by the Boston-area women's health groups, activists and lay organizations during the 1970s more actively and publicly voiced concerns regarding the practice of medicine—and the regulation of those practices.[76] Several feminist publications followed the lead of the Boston women's health groups and criticized Burt and his surgery for its assumptions about the female body and female sexuality.[77] The July 31, 1978, *off our backs* ran an article called "Vaginal Mutilation American Style" in which author Tacie Dejanikus called love surgery "one of the latest and grossest practices in a long line of tampering with women's bodies." Dejanikus wrote that, according to Burt, love surgery "made the clitoris more accessible to direct penile stimulation so that a woman can have more frequent and intense orgasms in intercourse." According to Dejanikus, it was not known "if the surgery is effective even if it weren't unnecessary mutilation."[78] The *National NOW Times* in October 1978 carried a brief story on love surgery, similarly questioning Burt's belief that it enabled women to have more and better orgasms.[79] The San Francisco–based *HerSay: A Woman's News Service* also reported on Burt, and this story was picked up by a few other feminist publications, such as *Big Mama Rag*, which criticized Burt in its July/August 1978 issue. With the title, "More Genital Mutilation," the brief story in *Big Mama Rag* quoted Burt saying the surgery could benefit "millions of American women" by enabling "more frequent and more intense orgasms" because the surgery made "the clitoris more accessible to direct penile stimulation." The brief noted that Burt used his wife, Joan Burt, as "'demonstrable proof that the operation works.'"[80]

Interestingly, the feminist publications that carried stories on Burt were not based in Ohio; *off our backs*, for example, was out of Washington, D.C., and *Big Mama Rag* was out of Denver. *What She Wants*, which billed itself as Cleveland's only women's paper, did not carry any story on Burt from January 1975 through January 1980.[81] The other Cleveland feminist paper, *The Cleveland Feminist*, ceased publication in 1974 and did not carry a story on Burt before it folded. Nor did Dayton's feminist newsletter, the *Dayton Women's Liberation Newsletter*, before it folded in 1975.[82] That neither organization ran a story about Burt before they folded is not surprising, however, since coverage of Burt in the popular press did not appear until the late 1970s.[83]

The *Medical World News* published its article on Burt in April 1978, and the Boston Women's Health Book Collective mailed a copy of it out in June; articles that appeared in feminist publications following this mailing used information provided in the *Medical World News* article. They did not, apparently, use the August 1978 *Real Paper* article written by Demick or, it would seem, Murray's 1977 *Playgirl* article. Murray and Demick, however, quoted women pleased with love surgery in their articles, and they also included women who sought love surgery—something some feminists at the time would have regarded as heavily influenced by the culturally prevalent patriarchal ideas of the female body and female sexuality.[84] This critique held a firm place within the growing feminist antipornography movement.

Although feminists challenged the limited social and political roles of women during the late 1960s and early 1970s, by the mid-1970s, some feminists also began to question the restricted roles of women within the media, particularly images that conflated women, sex, and violence. As Carolyn Bronstein noted in her analysis, antipornography activists "connected their insights about real-world media effects to a new body of radical feminist theory that revealed heterosexuality as an institution and ideology that created and maintained male supremacy."[85] In her history of feminism, Christine Stansell argued that although the more radical women's liberation movement slowed during the 1970s, feminism spread. The women's liberation movement, however, narrowed its focus to body politics and, with this more narrow focus, grew larger and spread across generations of women. Starting with the publication of Susan Brownmiller's 1975 *Against Our Will*—in which Brownmiller argued normal male behavior was entangled with rape—some women started rallying for rape laws to be changed and for society as a whole to change ideas about rape. The antipornography movement arose from these actions, and the movement was summarized when feminist legal scholar Catherine MacKinnon stated, "Pornography is the theory, rape is the practice." During the latter part of the 1970s, antifeminism grew, and in response, it became more culturally and politically acceptable for women to start a rape crisis center or a hotline—which, while important, sustained the idea of women as vulnerable to male violence—rather than confront structures of inequality as had been the focus of the earlier women's liberation movement.[86]

Furthermore, as historian Jane Gerhard noted, many women became frustrated with the sexual revolution, one that seemed to confine women to sexual passivity and submissiveness.[87] These women saw the so-called sexual revolution as having everything to do with heterosexual men's needs and desires and little to nothing to do with women's sexual needs and desires. This reaction, combined with a growing concern about male violence against women in the media and society, the recent dramatic expansion during the 1970s of the commercial sex industry, and a larger critique about heterosexuality as normative, centered for some women upon pornography as a problem.[88] Antipornography activist Beverly LaBelle in the late 1970s recalled that while some women started organizing against pornography previously, it was the 1976 film *Snuff* that created a larger feminist antipornography movement.[89] The film, which became notorious for showing a woman's violent murder as part of the culmination of a man's orgasm, galvanized women; two years after its release, more than 5,000 women traveled to San Francisco to attend a "Feminist Perspectives on Pornography" conference organized by Women against Violence in Pornography and Media.[90] After 1978, Women against Pornography chapters appeared across the country.[91] As Laura Lederer, an antipornography activist, wrote in 1980, "Pornography is the ideology of a culture which promotes and condones rape, woman-battering, and other crimes of violence against women."[92] But although the original antipornography movement was concerned with a spectrum of media depictions of sexual violence against women, by the late 1970s, much of the movement became focused upon such images just within pornography.[93]

The idea of sexual violence, however, was extended publicly at least three times to love surgery. In late 1978, the Boston Feminists Working against

Violence against Women wrote a letter to *Science for the People* critical of Burt, calling love surgery "mutilating." Saying the surgery happened "under the guise of bringing about sexual 'pleasure' for her," they stressed the surgery "clearly has men's interests at heart, and men's alone," a clear example, they argued, of "remaking women to fit men's image of what they should be."[94] Janice Raymond, an antipornography activist, spoke out against Burt at the 1979 Women against Pornography conference in New York City during her speech on "The Medical Creation of the Pornographic Woman."[95] And that same year in Denver, in a speech delivered to the National Conference on Violence against Women, activist Robin Morgan similarly criticized Burt (although she placed him in the wrong state):

> Anyone here hear of love surgery? Well, moving right along in the category of "If-the-shoe-doesn't-fit-then-change-the-foot" category: Rather than change male attitudes toward women . . . a California gynecologist—male—has come up with a wonderful solution. Noting that 70 to 80 percent of American women are pre-orgasmic, as we would call them, or as they would call them, frigid; because American men seem to refuse to understand the basic clitoral anatomy, this particular doctor has decided that rather than going to the trouble of teaching men how to be halfway, decent, courteous lovers—which might begin with even locating the clitoris—that what you do is simply move the clitoris. I'm quite serious. Since most men are, according to his research into sexual practices, interested in penile insertion into the vagina, then what you do is simply move the clitoris down nearer to the vagina. Then there might actually be some clitoral stimulation. Now this goes so much into the atrocity area, beyond even plastic surgery, enforced beauty standards, silicone breast transplants.[96]

Morgan, the Boston feminist health and antipornography activists, and the feminist periodicals that reported on Burt all regarded love surgery as a means by which a male doctor transformed the female body into an instrument for male sexual pleasure.[97]

But while in the late 1970s, feminist health activists in Boston were disavowing the merits of love surgery, and feminists in the antipornography movement criticized him, the Dayton-area NOW Chapter and the Dayton Women's Center expressed concern yet were not active in opposing Burt or his love surgery. During the 1970s, Dayton had a fairly robust and active feminist network, one that began with the formation of consciousness-raising groups in the late 1960s.[98] After the local paper made patronizing remarks about their activism at a 1970 rally to make abortion legal in Ohio, several consciousness groups came together and formed Dayton Women's Liberation.[99] Dayton Women's Liberation remained active until 1975, but feminist organization and activism continued with the opening in the fall of 1974 of the Women's Center, in 1975 with the formation of a local chapter of NOW, and in 1977 by the formation of Dayton Women Working, a group interested in women's employment status in the city. But although some women were quite active in these groups, they were all beset by small membership numbers, declining activism by the late 1970s, and personal and ideological conflicts; by 1980, the Women's Center, the local chapter of NOW, and Dayton Women Working had all folded.[100] Thus, these groups were perhaps unable to do much more in the second half of the 1970s than monitor Burt, who, despite whispers and rumors around the city about his numerous ex-wives, his flamboyant lifestyle, his sex life, and his controversial surgery, continued to enjoy a thriving medical practice.[101]

Janet Phillips, 1981

Janet Phillips was born at Miami Valley Hospital in Dayton on January 4, 1946. Her mother died giving birth to her, and her grandparents in Wilmington, Ohio, raised her. Phillips left high school in the tenth grade to marry.[1] She had her first child, a son, in 1963 when she was eighteen, and her second child, also a son, two years later.[2] This marriage ended.[3] Janet met her second husband, Edmund Phillips, when he was the reporting officer following her call to the police to report kids fighting in her neighborhood. The couple married in 1974 and four years later had a daughter.[4]

Phillips first went to James Burt in early 1981 for relief of painful cramps, excessive bleeding, occasional spotting between periods, and back pain when she menstruated.[5] There was also pain at times during intercourse, but this was usually only before the start of her period. All of this concerned her enough to seek medical attention, and she chose Burt because she worked outside the home and needed a doctor with late hours and whose office was close to where she lived.[6] Phillips also apparently went to Burt for another opinion, as two doctors had recommended she have a hysterectomy.[7]

In Burt's August 1981 case notes for Phillips, he wrote that she told him she responded easily and quickly to sex and that she enjoyed sex. Burt's dictated notes said he discussed with Phillips performing both a hysterectomy and that the "patient is interested also in vaginal reconstruction." According to his notes, Burt informed Phillips of the latter surgery's "uniqueness and that it is not the standard practice vaginal reconstruction and would change the design of the vagina from normal."[8] Burt recommended a hysterectomy, including removing the ovaries, as well as "vaginal redirection and extension by FCAR," the abbreviation for female coital area reconstruction, another of Burt's terms for love surgery. He transcribed in his medical notes that Phillips knew about, perhaps even requested, love surgery: "Also, the patient describes awareness of marked increase in adequacy of vaginal function in a good friend of hers operated upon by the undersigned and has expressed strong desire to have the same type of surgery as her vaginal reconstruction," according to Burt's medical notes for Phillips on October 23, 1981.[9]

Phillips later disputed the accuracy of these notes. She recalled that in his office, Burt informed her she had cancer in her ovaries and that it could "spread rapidly" if they "let it go," so he recommended a total hysterectomy. Phillips remembered she discussed having the surgery with Burt and decided to go forward after she received Burt's assurance there would be minimal stitches in her abdominal area. Phillips remembered being "very scared" upon hearing she had cancer since she had "children to raise" and her grandparents had raised her after her mother's death.[10] "He scared me," she later recalled, "I didn't want my children growing up in anybody's house but mine. If there was cancer, I wanted it out."[11] So on November 4, 1981, Janet Phillips went to St. Elizabeth Medical Center for a total hysterectomy.[12]

Chapter 3

Surgical Development and Regulation

In the April 1978 *Medical World News* article regarding James Burt, physician Diane S. Fordney stated she doubted the efficacy of love surgery but stressed the real answer would have to wait until an independent research study confirmed or disproved whether the surgery had more than possibly a placebo effect, as she contended.[1] Although Fordney called for an independent trial, that is, a research study not conducted by Burt, Burt was, it would appear by the time of the publication of the *Medical World News* article, conducting research on the efficacy of love surgery: recall both his work with Schramm and Masters's hesitation to either review his research for publication in the *American Journal of Obstetrics and Gynecology* or assist Burt with his research on love surgery. Burt, then, once he had begun offering love surgery as an elective sometime around 1976, began also to study its effects.

According to the 1978 *Medical World News* article, although Burt had not obtained consent while he was developing love surgery from episiotomy repair, once love surgery evolved from a variation to a new procedure, Burt told the journal he had begun to obtain consent. From the article, it would appear Burt began to get consent perhaps as early as 1976—although what that consent entailed he did not say—nor was it clear if the consent was only for those women electing for the surgery or for women who went to him to deliver a baby, upon whom he apparently was still performing love surgery. Finally, Burt, the *Medical World News* reported, had hired a public relations firm to help him "spread the word" about his surgery, now offered as an elective, because "he needs patients to raise money for a clinical trial that will impress his peers."[2] What all of this suggests is that by the mid-1970s, Burt apparently regarded his use of love surgery as both clinical care—he believed love surgery to be beneficial for his patients, so he was offering it as an elective while continuing to perform it on his obstetrics and surgery patients—and clinical research—he was also seeking to gather information about its effectiveness.

As historian Andrew Warwick observed, we know "relatively little about how new surgical procedures are developed," and we also know little about how "the credibility of new surgical procedures" are established and "maintained in the face of criticism and alternative procedures." We know little historically about how and why certain surgeries are embraced while others are not.[3] How does a surgery move from innovation by one physician to accepted practice by others? As historian and physician Christopher Crenner put it, "We may tend to think of surgical innovation as occurring in a single, defining leap, or, more comfortingly, as a product taken ready-made into effective use," but this is hardly (if ever) the case.[4]

To understand what Burt was doing at this point and, just as important, to place what he was doing within normative surgical development, we need to pause to consider how surgeries usually develop, why the space between routine medical care and innovation was (and continues to be) sometimes gray, and how the development of a surgery by one physician is regulated by other physicians. But because Burt claimed to have developed love surgery from changes he made to routine episiotomy repair, I will begin by first looking at the routine use of episiotomy and the practice of informed consent to routine medical care such as episiotomy.

As noted earlier, Burt claimed to have performed his variation of episiotomy repair on at least 4,000 women before he began to market it as an elective surgery around 1976. Regardless of the veracity of this claim, the women upon whom he performed love surgery before 1976 apparently did not know they were going to undergo it. During the time when Burt was still developing love surgery, that is, before the mid-1970s, he stated he did not ask or tell his patients he was doing anything different than a variation of episiotomy repair.[5] But that Burt did not inform or ask his patients was also rather normative behavior within routine medical practice during this time.

Take episiotomy repair, the procedure from which Burt claimed to have developed love surgery. Episiotomy repair occurred in the hospital following birth, and both episiotomy and its repair were considered such a normative part of giving birth, few physicians saw it as necessary to inform or ask; it was regarded as part of the routine of childbirth in a hospital. Indeed, because of its routine nature and because it was so incorporated into childbirth that happened in hospitals, this was probably true of episiotomy and episiotomy repair not just in the 1950s, the 1960s, or even the early 1970s, the time when Burt was developing love surgery: it was probably the case until the end of the twentieth century. To illustrate, Judith Parsley wrote in a publication for fellow nurses in 1990 that episiotomy was "the only surgical procedure that is done routinely without the knowledge or informed consent of the patient," and a 1999 article in *Obstetrics and Gynecology Clinics* stated this surgical procedure was rarely done with a patient's specific consent.[6] Moreover, this standard practice of not obtaining the consent of women to have an episiotomy extended into the twenty-first century: a 2005 article in *JAMA* noted that "clinicians have been the primary agents to exercise choice to conduct or not to conduct an episiotomy, rather than the patients," and a 2006 survey of women who had given birth revealed that of the 25 percent who had undergone an episiotomy, 73 percent said they did not have a choice to have one.[7] Women were rarely explicitly asked to consent to have, or given the opportunity to decline, an episiotomy during the time Burt practiced medicine—or indeed well after.[8]

Although episiotomy was a routine practice that was regarded by physicians as a usual part of childbirth, it was far from the only procedure physicians performed under a general blanket of consent during the 1960s and 1970s. Other forms of routine care conducted in hospitals were often done without the explicit consent of the patient because medical professionals expected that once patients were in the hospital, they would simply go along with routine care.[9] And not obtaining consent for routine practices such as episiotomy was upheld legally. In the late 1970s, if it was standard medical practice to not disclose the risks of a particular surgery to patients—such as episiotomies and episiotomy repair—courts rarely obligated physicians to make such disclosures. Courts found that, for example, neither the risk of a head injury to a child when a practitioner used forceps at birth nor the risk of a vesicovaginal fistula following a hysterectomy needed to be disclosed. Most courts through the late 1970s upheld that no disclosure was necessary if the procedure was simple and the risk was commonly believed to be low.[10]

Sometimes, as in the case of episiotomy, consent for a specific medical intervention was assumed under a larger consent for treatment. Consent to treatment at its most basic level began when people began seeking out professional medical care—physicians or other attendants typically at least stated to the person seeking care how they intended to intervene; most patients could then agree or decline the proposed intervention (or just not return). A more formal understanding began in the nineteenth century when courts started to regard the relationship between a doctor and a patient as quasi-contractual, based on fiduciary obligations requiring a patient to consent as part of the agreement.[11] In the early twentieth century, as the number of surgeons who were sued by their patients over an unauthorized surgery increased, some surgeons and hospitals began to obtain written consent from patients prior to surgery. But patients continued to complain that their physician had acted against their wishes, and by the early twentieth century, some took their complaint to the courts, in particular the 1914 suit *Schloendorff v. Society of New York Hospital*.[12] This lawsuit upheld an individual's right to prevent unauthorized medical treatment upon his or her body, and judge Benjamin Cardozo famously wrote in the decision that "every human being of adult years and sound mind has a right to determine what shall be done with his own body."[13]

But prior to the late 1950s, the issue was whether consent had been given, not whether it was informed, the latter meaning the patient had been provided information about the risks of treatment and alternative treatment options from the one being proposed and were, at least in theory, able to agree to or decline the proposed treatment based on this information.[14] While consenting to medical procedures was not novel, this idea of an "informed consent" originated in a 1957 malpractice case. In the years following this ruling, informed consent evolved into a more explicit duty on the part of the physician to disclose certain types of information prior to obtaining consent.[15] But what to disclose was at the discretion of physicians. This discretion was based on a long tradition within medical practice that physicians need only reveal particular information to patients, a tradition supported by both medical ethical codes and by the legal doctrine of therapeutic privilege.[16] The premise for this traditional paternalistic model of medical practice was one built upon trusting both the technical competence and moral sensitivity of the physician as well as one that placed the patient as dependent upon the physician's authority.[17] Physicians, though, according to Harvard law professor Charles Fried in 1974, still had to justify why withholding information was of interest to the particular patient—and not because, for example, that the patient would decline the recommended course of treatment: "If the information is withheld just in order to subvert what the patient would choose if he had the information," wrote Fried, "then the privilege itself is abused."[18]

In the 1950s through the 1970s, when Burt was making modifications to episiotomy repair and not disclosing or asking his patients for their permission to do so, his not doing so was far from uncommon among his peers. As historian Nancy Tomes noted, through the late 1960s, "the procedures for obtaining consent and sharing information with patients remained highly variable across

institutions and specialties." Physicians maintained "great discretion in deciding what information to share and what to withhold," Tomes wrote, "confident
that they knew best what patients needed to know."[19] Moreover, physicians also
regularly assessed not just what the patient should know regarding the medical
aspects of the intervention or procedure but also weighed the personal appropriateness of the patient having it. Physician Atul Gawande recalled his physician father telling him that, during the 1970s and indeed through much of the
1980s, his father decided not only if it was medically appropriate for the man
seeking a vasectomy but also if he deemed it personally appropriate for the man.
According to Gawande, his father would routinely refuse to perform the operation if the man asking was not married, or married but without children, or if
his father thought the man too young.[20] And up until the early 1970s, neither
this withholding of information nor the physician making judgment calls
regarding a therapy based on medical and personal information were, by in large,
controversial issues, either among physicians or among the general public.

But this complacency regarding informed consent became a national, public concern in the 1970s for a variety of reasons, beginning with the highly publicized revelations of the failure of obtaining informed consent in medical
experimentation. Most infamous of these ethical failures was the Tuskegee Syphilis Study, but during the late 1960s and early 1970s, additional examples of
humans as the subjects of medical research for which they did not (or could
not) consent also came to the fore, as well as more examples of physicians not
having had the best intentions of their patients in mind. And although these
cases regarded medical research and not medical care, concerns regarding the
lack of consent found within these research scandals prompted a similar concern regarding consent in clinical care.[21]

Concerns regarding consent in clinical care paralleled, and were propelled
by, calls for greater respect for human autonomy and dignity as an outgrowth of
the civil rights, women's rights, and patients' rights movements.[22] Cultural challenges to what constituted informed consent came from women active within
the women's health movement, like those in the Boston Women's Health Book
Collective, who pushed for female patients to make decisions about their health
care.[23] For example, feminists involved in the women's health movement pressed
the issue of consent in the doctor's office, encouraging women to be assertive.
Francis Hornstein, writing in 1975 in the *Feminist Women's Health Center
Report*, provided women with a thirteen-point list of how to be effectively assertive when speaking with their physician, including reminding women that as
patients, they had "a right to full and complete explanation of all examinations,
treatments and medications," including any of the risks or side effects.

Moreover, she encouraged women to shake their physician's hand when they first meet to indicate "that you intend to be an ACTIVE participant in the visit" to break the "tradition of the patient as a passive object."[24] Such concerns also arose from those who advocated for patients' greater knowledge about health care as the consumers of health care, such as Ralph Nader and Sidney Wolfe's Health Research Group.[25] Further, concerns also arose as part of a larger distrust in postwar orthodoxy, including medical authority, and this "crises of competence," as one historian noted, came to define the decade.[26]

In addition, the concept of patients' rights arose out of concerns expressed by low-income women, who, organized within the National Welfare Rights Organization (NWRO), pressed the American Hospital Association (AHA) for a Patients' Bill of Rights in the early 1970s.[27] And while not nearly as expansive or inclusive as what the NWRO members pressed for, in 1973, the AHA introduced a Patients' Bill of Rights, which included statements that a patient had the right to learn of their diagnosis and recommended treatment as well as prognosis "in terms the patient can be reasonably expected to understand" and that the patient "has the right to receive from his physician information necessary to give informed consent prior to the start of any procedure and/or treatment."[28] In a 1978 article published in the *Journal of the American Hospital Association*, Norma Shaw Hogan, director of the patient representative program at Northwestern Memorial Hospital in Chicago, wrote that such a statement was necessary because "the public is angry with health care providers for what they perceive as indifference to patients as human beings and individuals."[29] As historian Tomes argued, "of all the protections included" in the AHA's Patients' Bill of Rights, "the demand for informed consent had perhaps the most far-reaching implications."[30] For many, such as Hogan, it was also the "most controversial aspect" of the bill because it invited governmental and judicial oversight into what constituted consent.[31] Although that may have been the most controversial aspect of the bill, the entire bill was only ambivalently embraced even by hospitals that adopted it quickly, and indeed, other hospitals were slow to adopt it, with some refusing to do so at all.[32] To illustrate, nearly two years after its creation, only about a third of America's 7,000 hospitals had adopted any part of the Patients' Bill of Rights.[33]

Furthering the concept of individual autonomy in making health care decisions, several major legal cases regarding informed consent were decided in 1972, including *Canterbury* and *Cobbs*. Both of these cases concerned physicians who had not disclosed the risks to the patient prior to surgery. In the *Canterbury* decision, the court moved to having a reasonable patient be the standard for informed consent, replacing a physician-oriented standard. In *Cobbs*, the court ruled that physicians needed to disclose the risks and benefits of the proposed therapy, as well as alternative treatment options, including no treatment, that a hypothetical reasonable patient would find relevant to making a decision.[34] These decisions pushed the concept of what should be disclosed during the informed consent process to the view of what the patient would *want to* know, rather than what the physician thought the patient *should* know.

By the mid-1970s, state legislatures also began considering informed consent; indeed, between 1975 and 1977, nearly half the states passed legislation regarding informed consent, moved to do so in part out of concern for the mid-1970s crisis in medical malpractice. This crisis manifested itself in a sharp rise of malpractice insurance for many physicians, and in some parts of the country, even expensive medical malpractice insurance was unavailable.[35] I will return to this crisis later, but for now I want to concentrate on the legislative response to informed consent. Although not every state legislature was explicit, the intent of legislation at this time regarding informed consent was to make it more difficult for a patient to recover damages from their physician in a malpractice lawsuit, with the expectation this would lower rates of malpractice lawsuits. During the 1970s, in all but two states, either through the courts or by legislation or both, physicians became legally bound to disclose the risks of treatment as a core aspect of disclosure.[36] Looking at Ohio, in 1976, the state initially adopted an informed consent law that required physicians to disclose only certain types of risks to patients to garner their consent, namely, if a risk included death, brain damage, quadriplegia, losing the function of an organ or limb, or disfiguring scars. But, in the revised 1977 law, the list of specific risks was deleted. Instead, the revised law necessitated the disclosure of all risks that were "reasonably known."[37] An increasing number of courts had moved from a professional standard to a patient standard of disclosure beginning in the early 1970s, and the Ohio legislature adopted such a standard of disclosure. This disclosure standard obligated physicians to make known information a reasonable patient would desire to know before consenting or declining to undergo a therapy. The Ohio statute only applied to written consent; consent was only regarded as valid if it was in writing.[38]

Alongside these court cases and state laws, and occurring against a backdrop of a rise in social interest in informed consent arising from patients and activists, more commentary on informed consent written by physicians began to appear in the medical literature, with much of it hostile toward the practice. Some physicians believed obtaining informed consent from their patients was both impossible as well as incompatible with their providing good care to their patients.[39] Physician Ralph Alfidi, for example, writing in *JAMA* in 1971, stated that upon asking his peers about whether they thoroughly explained to their patient their proposed diagnostic and therapeutic procedures, including possible complications, the majority said if they were to do so, they believed their patients would refuse to undergo the procedure.[40] This idea—that informed consent served to undermine the authority of the physician and created distrust among patients in physicians—was evoked by physicians, who felt that the most important part of the patient–physician relationship was patients' trust in their provider, not in understanding the information in the consent document.[41]

Reflecting upon this changing environment when it came to what informed consent entailed and how it was obtained, attorney James Vaccarino, writing in a 1978 editorial for the *New England Journal of Medicine*, argued that his profession had enabled physicians to misunderstand the meaning of informed consent by confusing the patient signing a consent form with a patient understanding the proposed therapy. As Vaccarino stressed, a signature was not enough: physicians also needed to view informed consent "in terms of the direct discussion between the doctor and the patient."[42] That the signing of a consent form did not mean a patient understood what was going to occur was borne out in studies. Although about clinical research and not clinical care, Bradford Gray found in his early 1970s sociological study on the conduct of two clinical research studies that a "subject's signature on a consent form is no assurance that the subject has given informed consent." As his study found, nearly 40 percent of those who consented to one of the studies he examined did not know they were part of a research study—even though they had signed the consent form.[43]

Although some physicians exhibited an initial ambivalence to these cultural and legal changes regarding informed consent, the results of a 1982 survey of physicians showed what at first glance appeared to be a shift toward more acceptance. This survey found that over 80% of physicians obtained either written or written and oral consent from their patients prior to inpatient surgery. Such a large percentage of physicians saying they obtained consent prior to surgery suggests clinical practice changed between Alfidi's 1971 article and the 1982 survey. However, as ethicists Ruth Faden and Tom Beauchamp noted in their examination of changes regarding informed consent, although physicians widely reported that they sought patient consent, the doctors who answered this survey still had a very narrow view of what informed consent entailed. According to Faden and Beauchamp, this was most tellingly revealed by physicians' responses to the survey question, "What does the term informed consent mean to you?" Only slightly more than a fourth of physicians—26 percent—indicated "informed consent had anything to do with a patient's giving permission, consenting, or agreeing to treatment," and only 9 percent indicated informed consent "involved the patient's making a choice or stating a preference about his or her treatment."[44]

Physicians' ideas of informed consent, it appears, remained firmly within the idea that physicians knew what was best for their patients and that physicians would act in the best interest of their patients. In his 1984 critique of medical consent, *The Silent World of Doctor and Patient*, psychiatrist and law professor Jay Katz charged that "what passes today for disclosure and consent in physician-patient interactions is largely an unwitting attempt by physicians to shape the disclosure process so that patients will comply with their recommendations."[45] Informed consent—or lack thereof—had long been a concern for Katz, as seen in his 1977 statement that it existed only as a "fairy tale" within medical practice.[46]

James Burt, then, when he was making what he saw as variations on episiotomy repair through the mid-1970s, would not have been out of line with normative practice by not asking or telling his patients: episiotomy and its repair were routine parts of childbirth in hospitals, which few of his peers would have sought consent to perform. Does it matter though that, around the mid-1970s, Burt began to see love surgery as not routine but rather as a new surgery? To answer this question, we need to first briefly look at variations in the procedure of episiotomy in the United States, the use of variations in surgery, how innovations in surgical practice occur, and what some have called a gray area that exists between clinical medicine and clinical research, particularly when it comes to surgical development.

Burt went to medical school and began to practice when there was a switch in the standard method of performing episiotomies in the United States. Although episiotomies began to be used more commonly beginning in the 1920s and 1930s, the cut used was mediolateral: thinking about the female perineum as a clock face, the cut began in the lower opening of the vagina and went at an angle, toward the 7-o'clock position. This technique was considered the safest. But by the 1930s and 1940s, the median cut—a cut made straight down toward the anus from the vaginal opening—began to be advocated in the United States, based on reports from physicians of it being safer and more satisfactory to patients. Such reports continued into the 1960s and led to a change to median episiotomies becoming more common in the United States. During this time of transition, physicians were also altering how they performed episiotomy, with some physicians using multiple cuts, performing bilateral incisions, and also making a cut known as the "J-incision" (a cut begun as a median and then, with curved scissors, directed outward rather than downward) in an effort to discover the best approach.[47] Indeed, in his 1959 article, physician Wallace Shute noted that a "wide variety of episiotomy incisions have been advocated." Shute further provided his own "new technique in episiotomy repair," one he had used in 416 consecutive cases.[48] When Burt in the mid-1950s began making variations on episiotomy repair, he was doing so at a time when other physicians were also varying their approach to performing the cut that would be in need of repair.

Variations on a standard surgery, not just episiotomy, were not uncommon during this time and indeed remain part of surgical purview. Physicians routinely made and make individual variations on the surgeries they perform.[49] Even on a single day, a surgeon may perform the "same" surgery somewhat differently on each patient.[50] This is because a specific technique may need to be modified for each patient to address the unique problem that is the reason for the surgery. Surgeons may tailor a procedure, adapting it for the body of a specific patient or for their specific condition.[51] This modification was, according to Myron Freund, a surgeon at Cornell University Medical College writing on surgical ethics in 1982, "a necessary and appropriate action for a surgeon to take."[52]

An innovation occurs when a surgeon varies an accepted procedure but with the understanding the benefits are the same as the accepted, nonaltered procedure. Innovations are an accepted and expected part of surgery. As the Society of University Surgeons' position statement on surgical innovations, issued in 2008, noted, "Surgeons are trained to perform continuous situational assessment, decision analysis, and improvisation, in preparation for the challenges and creativity required by nearly every clinical case." The practice of surgery, they asserted, "is steeped in innovation."[53] Indeed, many consider much of standard surgical practice to be innovative.[54] Surgeons, then, regard a certain amount of innovation as necessary, expected, and inevitable in clinical practice as unexpected findings are encountered.[55]

Clinicians make these innovations for the clinical benefit of their patient. Making innovations to standard surgeries was and remains an important method of improving surgeries.[56] This is because many physicians consider, as Francis Moore did in his 1970 article examining innovation in medical therapies and drugs, that "every operation of any type contains certain aspects of experimental work."[57] This has been a common theme within surgery: in 1985, Keith Reemtsma, the chair of Columbia University's College of Physicians and Surgeons surgical department, wrote that "all treatments have an element of experimentation."[58] Moore and Reemtsma's contentions were reiterated more recently by physician Angelique Reitsma and ethicist Jonathan Moreno when they wrote that "all medical and surgical practice is, in a sense, 'experimental' insofar as every patient presents unique circumstances; the very term *practice* embodies this point."[59] Others, however, have critiqued this point, arguing that the implication of this belief blurs the boundary between clinical care and clinical research, as well as confuses uncertainty with experimentation. As ethicist Ruth Macklin argued, although "uncertainty pervades all of our life," we do not think of ourselves as living in an experiment. Rather, we in our daily lives, as well as clinicians in their daily practice, "are guided by past experiences and general knowledge of the consequences of our actions."[60]

But just because a surgery is an innovation does not mean it is experimental. I will return to the consideration of experimental surgery later, but for now note that an innovation in surgery can still be regarded as nonexperimental so long as the outcome is considered as predictable and as beneficial as the standard surgery from which it was derived.[61]

Some surgical innovations, then, are changes made to an accepted procedure or technique with an expected similar outcome as the accepted procedure or technique. If one patient, however, has a better result following an innovation, the surgeon may attempt to replicate what was done on that patient in other patients. Surgeons may then track the outcomes of these patients to evaluate the innovative method.[62] This collection of information is part of the gathering of clinical information, although the information gathered could later be published as evidence of the safety and efficacy of the innovation.[63]

But an innovation on a standard surgery is also how a new surgery develops—and, because it is new, this means that the outcomes are unknown. Surgical development has largely been experiential, arising from a need to solve a problem or because repeated failures have stimulated a surgeon to find a new, better way.[64] And this new, better way, as Freund wrote in 1982, "may progress, and in a given setting they may ultimately lead to something that may be different from their 'classical' point of origin."[65] That is, as Reemtsma wrote in 1985, "new surgical procedures are based on extrapolations from prior work," or, simply, the innovation has led to a new surgery.[66]

Deciding, however, when something has progressed to being a new surgery is often difficult, and there is no agreement among surgeons about when an innovation has moved from within the realm of standard and accepted to new and unique. More than one commentator on surgical innovation has described a gray zone between what should be considered within the scope of clinical practice to what should be considered a surgical innovation that no longer falls under the area of clinical practice but has instead moved to something novel.[67] As

Reitsma and Moreno pointed out in their 2005 critique of innovative surgery, there are "uncertainties and disagreements among surgeons as to what an acceptable variation on an existing surgical technique is versus what is a new or innovative technique."[68] In part this may be because, as an article in the medical journal *Lancet* outlined in 2009, "the most common process for innovation in surgery is related to the intrinsically iterative nature of the surgical practice itself" as surgeons may "routinely experiment with an established operation in such a way that it might ultimately change unrecognizably."[69] In part this may be because, as Reitsma and Moreno observed in 2002, "there appears to be a tradition in surgery that significant changes" regarding a procedure "are regarded as mere modification" and not a new surgery—and, thus, not a surgery that should now be regarded as experimental.[70] There is a difference, Reitsma and Moreno argued, "between innovations that fall under acceptable everyday routine variation" and are still within the scope of the existing, standard surgery, "and innovations that are, in fact, experimental."[71] These "acceptable everyday routine variations" are done for the benefit of the individual patient, and they are done with an understanding that the benefit will be similar. They are, then, still considered clinical care for that one patient.

When, then, in this process does the gray zone become clear, and the innovation necessitate an assessment in the form of a research study?[72] Although surgeons often are hesitant to make a distinction between everyday routine variations with those that are experimental innovations, the distinction is important, for when a surgery is both innovative and the outcomes are not known, or not known to be as safe and effective as the surgery from which it arose—that is, the outcomes are no longer predictable—the new surgery should then be seen as an experimental surgery.[73] As Reitsma and Moreno contended, "When outcomes of the procedure are largely unpredictable because they have not been previously described, innovations become essentially experimental and should be conducted, at some point, as a research project."[74]

This division is important, because there is a difference between clinical care and clinical research. In clinical care, "the welfare of the patient" is the "prime objective," while in research, "the discovery of new knowledge" is the "primary objective."[75] This definition of clinical care compared to clinical research, made in 1969, acquired legal standing a decade later. According to the 1979 Belmont Report, which came to be the basis for legal oversight of all federally funded human subject research, clinical practice—even practice with an experimental aspect to it—is done for the individual patient, while clinical research is conducted with the idea that it will produce generalizable knowledge—that is, information to benefit others.[76] According to the Belmont

Report, the "term 'research' designates an activity designed to test an hypothesis, permit conclusions to be drawn, and thereby to develop or contribute to generalizable knowledge (expressed, for example, in theories, principles, and statements of relationships)." When, though, "a clinician departs in a significant way from standard or accepted practice," that does not mean that the departure should now be considered research; even when something is new or experimental, it "does not automatically place it in the category of research." However, the authors of the Belmont Report felt that "radically new procedures" should "be made the object of formal research at an early stage in order to determine whether they are safe and effective."[77]

The Belmont Report was meant to provide guidance for those engaged in research. But what divides routine and accepted surgical innovation from novel innovation remained unclear within the report. As commentators noted in 2003, the Belmont Report acknowledged a spectrum of innovation within clinical practice, but it remained unclear about just what it meant that an innovation had to be a "radically new procedure" to fall outside the spectrum.[78] Moreover, as many observers have stressed over the years, the boundary between surgical research and clinical care was and remains murky.[79] And it is a murky area some have no doubt abused. Florida ophthalmologist and pathologist Curtis Margo stressed this when he noted in 2001 that some practitioners, as well as institutions, tacitly used this deviation—that it is research when a set of questions are asked, a set of protocols established—to allow new surgeries to be used on (uninformed) patients by not having either in place when the new procedure was introduced clinically. Some regarded this as research, albeit not official research, while others considered it within the gray area of medical practice. Margo noted that there was a "contentious and threatening" debate regarding this gray area, since the distinction between the two can be "ill-defined." However, Margo contended, "if a surgical procedure is described by the surgeon at meetings or to the public as 'new,' 'innovative,' or 'a major breakthrough,' it can only be interpreted as a departure from normal procedure."[80]

Given, then, that there was confusion about when a surgery was a variation, an innovation with predictable outcomes, or an innovation with unknown outcomes, how was it decided where a certain change in surgery fell, and who would oversee such a decision and, more widely, oversee the development of surgery? In the 1970s, there were calls for federal oversight of surgeries akin to the oversight of drug development. Boston physician David Spodick, who in 1975 called for a Food and Drug Administration (FDA)–like entity to assess and regulate the development of surgeries, argued that surgical development should

stop being considered as having "the status of a Sacred Cow" but should instead
be subjected to research oversight.[81] Arguing along similar lines, a 1978 article
in *Science* stressed that new procedures should "be subjected to testing and controls that are as timely and no less rigorous than those required for drugs."[82]
Others, however, argued that part of the reason it was so difficult to subject new
surgeries to formal research oversight was because surgical development was
not the same as drug development. Responding to Spodick, Jack Love, who was
on the editorial board of *JAMA*, argued that while it was a "worthy goal" to have
surgeries "tested without bias" to ensure the surgeries are safe and effective,
because surgeries required manual skills, a new procedure was "rarely introduced as fully defined." Because details "typically" changed and evolved with
experience, surgery was not so easily subjected to the same sort of study as a
drug. Instead, Love argued that the "American College of Surgeons, surgical
societies, surgical boards, and hospital credential and tissue committees function to protect the public from unsafe and ineffective surgery."[83]

In the 1970s, as today, there is no federal regulatory oversight regarding this
gray area or even regarding surgical innovation more generally.[84] Moreover, federal oversight on research only exists on federally funded research—clinical
research conducted with private funds within private practice is not federally
regulated.[85] As Spodick famously stated in the mid-1970s, there is no FDA for
surgery.[86] And in the 1970s, as in the decades after, "in many cases, between
innovation and harm to the patient lies little more than a surgeon's sense of
responsibility, dedication, and fear of medico-legal consequences," as the
authors of a 2009 article in the *Lancet* stressed.[87]

Spodick was not the only one in the 1970s to raise the question about oversight, and others took up the discussion. But not many; indeed, in a study that
compared the surgical literature in 1992 with that of the medical literature for
the same year, researchers found that compared to the medical literature, the
surgical literature discussed ethical issues significantly less often.[88] And those
that did continued to see the gray area regarding when surgeries were variations,
innovations, or innovations with unexpected outcomes. In the mid-1980s, for
example, the Hastings Center held, as part of its ongoing work looking into the
ethics of medical research, a conference on ethics and surgical research. Ethicist Ruth Macklin, on attending the conference, wrote that it seemed surgery,
"compared with other areas of medical practice, subjects fewer innovative procedures to prior review and sustained clinical investigation." This needed to
change, she argued, for "if surgeons fail to develop research protocols for their
experimental or innovative procedures, then those procedures will not receive
the sort of detailed scrutiny that drugs and devices must get before being

approved by the FDA." She told surgeons it was incumbent upon them to "develop such research protocols and adhere to the canons of clinical investigation practiced by researchers in other areas of medical science" to "protect patients from ethically unacceptable interventions."[89]

Within the decade following this conference, some surgeons, ethicists, and surgical associations began calling for such guidelines regarding innovation in surgery and for defining when an innovation in surgery needed to be considered an experimental surgery and thus be tested in a research study.[90] During the 1990s, the American College of Surgeons adopted guidelines for innovative surgeries, although these guidelines were self-imposed—meaning it was up to each surgeon to take them up.[91] And although doubtless some saw this as major improvement, others were not convinced voluntary guidelines were enough. In 2002, Reitsma and Moreno argued that the "current system" of "voluntary professional guidelines to protect patients from unwittingly becoming subjects of research appears to be inadequate to meet the challenges of surgical innovation."[92]

Although a push began in the 1990s for more guidelines and protocols regarding surgical innovations and surgical research, nearly two decades later, this had yet to be formalized and remained up to the individual practitioner to follow. As the authors of the position statement of the Society of University Surgeons noted in 2008, "The absence of any organized oversight or mechanism to protect patients from becoming unwitting research subjects is, however, problematic."[93] Indeed, still today, patients may not be told that they will undergo or have undergone an innovative surgery.[94] It remains up to the discretion of the individual surgeon as to how much and what sort of information they provide to patients regarding an innovative surgery.[95]

What does this mean regarding consent? Just as in clinical therapy, what consent looked like—and how it occurred, if it occurred—was in flux during the time when Burt was developing his surgery. Although consent was seen as important when it came to clinical research, in an analysis on research with human participants published by the Russell Sage Foundation in 1973, the authors found that while most biomedical researchers were aware of the importance of voluntary informed consent, they found a "significant minority" who were unaware or unconcerned with the importance of obtaining informed consent from subjects prior to clinical research.[96] Although perhaps increasingly acknowledged as just as important to clinical research as to clinical care in the 1970s, when it came to consenting to an innovative surgery, the problem of adequately informing the person remained. As Freund observed in the early 1980s, "Any surgeon utilizing a new procedure is in essence conducting an

uncontrolled experiment, without adequate records, controls, or explicit consent from the patient."[97] The physician carrying out the in-progress procedure
would be unable to provide information essential to obtaining an informed
consent—such as the risks of the procedure—as the physician would not know
the risks.[98] The obligation, as Charles Fried, a Harvard law professor, wrote in
his 1974 book on medical experimentation, to advise a patient of alternative
therapies did not extend to untried or experimental procedures or therapies
that the practitioner was still developing. "Where, however," he continued, "the
therapy used is itself experimental, then this fact and the existence of either
alternatives or professional doubts become material facts, which like all material facts should be disclosed." Consent, asserted Fried, had to be obtained for
an experimental procedure.[99] Regarding the decision to undergo an innovative or experimental surgery, patients would first need to be provided with
enough information to make an informed choice, but that has not always happened, sometimes because that very information is what the surgeon seeks to
discover.[100]

This, then, led to charges that patients were seriously unprotected against
unwittingly undergoing an innovative or experimental surgery. Writing in 1999,
the law and medical ethics professor R. Alta Charo stated that, regarding human
subject research overall, "Americans shouldn't fear being treated like guinea pigs
in research"; they should, instead, "clamor to be treated as well."[101] Echoing this
sentiment two years later, physician Curtis Margo stated, "Currently there is
greater oversight protection in place for laboratory animals than there is for testing innovative surgeries in humans."[102] So despite the growth of oversight
regarding clinical research since the late 1970s, it continues to remain up to surgeons to regulate themselves when it comes to assessing surgical innovation.[103]
There were no federal or formal regulations that applied to or oversaw surgical
innovations in the 1970s, and there continues to be no such regulation or
oversight.[104]

Based on Burt's outline of what his surgery involved, how he spoke of it to the
Medical World News as a novel innovation, and how he marketed it as "love
surgery," it appears that the procedure was by 1976 beyond a variation or an
innovation with anticipated outcomes similar to those of standard episiotomy
repair despite Burt's claim that it arose out of a variation on standard episiotomy repair. It was a new surgery. Local doctors also saw love surgery as more
than a variation on episiotomy repair. Physicians who later examined some of
Burt's patients said the vulvas of the women looked entirely different: the vaginal opening was smaller, it had been moved about an inch closer to the clitoris,

and the urinary tract had been cut and moved inside the vagina on some of the women.[105] Until 1975, Burt's version of an episiotomy repair could have been considered a surgical innovation on a standard surgery. But by around this time, love surgery was seen by Burt as well as other physicians to not be a variation but rather an innovation on a standard surgery that became a new surgery altogether, one that only Burt seemingly performed. Moreover, it was around this time that Burt apparently wanted to test love surgery for its efficacy. Burt claims to have told the women who were electing for love surgery that it was not standard—although what this conversation included, let alone if it actually happened between 1975 and 1979—is not verifiable.

It is necessary to stress a few points here that the above history highlighted. First, when Burt was seeking to discover whether love surgery did what he claimed, he was doing so *two decades* before the American College of Surgeons put out voluntary guidelines on how to evaluate new and innovative surgeries. Second, the procedure from which love surgery arose, episiotomy repair, was a routine part of childbirth in hospitals, and physicians routinely did not obtain consent before they performed it. Finally, it would appear that when Burt decided the surgery was no longer a variation but rather a new surgery that needed to be studied, he claims to have told his patients that it was experimental, and, *if* he *did* consent them to an experimental surgery, Burt was acting in a manner physicians were increasingly expected to be acting.

A diffusion of an innovation within medical practice, including a surgical innovation, may or may not occur before clinical trials have demonstrated efficacy and safety of the innovation.[106] Indeed, some have argued that it is probably more common for an innovation to become a normal part of medical practice before being carefully evaluated than not.[107] This is particularly perhaps true regarding surgery, where the most commonly used means of evaluating a surgery is through an initial case report describing the use of the innovation, a case report followed by cases reported by other surgeons, all of whom have different skills and experience than those of the first surgeon.[108] This progression occurs because, historian David S. Jones wrote regarding the development of cardiac care, when new treatments become available, the initial reaction from clinicians "almost always arises from the anticipated benefits the treatment will provide."[109]

Novel innovative surgeries are taken up by physicians because of this belief in the "anticipated benefits" often based on the good outcomes of a small number of patients—meaning no formal study of the new procedure is conducted before the innovative or new therapy is used by other physicians as part of their clinical practice.[110] This trajectory, however—where one or two practitioners use a new or innovative surgery on a small number of patients before it is used more widely as a standard therapy option—can have multiple stages; medical sociologist John B. McKinlay, for example, laid out seven (possible) stages in the career of a medical innovation. According to McKinlay, medical innovations typically started with "the appearance of an enthusiastic report on some promising performance." This "promising performance," often based on a handful of observational reports, then moved to professional adoption of the innovation. Physicians, McKinlay noted, were moved to adopt the innovation into their practice for a variety of reasons, including peer pressure to follow what is regarded as an improvement in care, to be seen as current and scientific in their medical practice, and their desire to respond to their patients' needs. Once the profession adopted an innovation, McKinlay argued, it then entered a third stage, public acceptance, and with the acceptance of both the profession and the public, an innovative practice/procedure then moved to the "privileged status of a 'standard procedure,'" as McKinlay outlined.[111]

It was during the fourth stage, McKinlay argued, when calls for evidence of effectiveness began to be heard, and increasingly by the 1970s, this meant randomized control trials (RCTs). An RCT is a research study that compares outcomes in two groups of participants: an experimental group receiving the therapy being tested and a control group receiving either the currently used therapy or a placebo if no currently used therapy exists. In the 1970s, it was commonly regarded as the "gold standard" form of research.[112] McKinlay asserted that while observational reports appeared to settle the issue of whether or not an innovation was worthwhile, such reports "never really place the issue of the *effectiveness* of an innovation beyond dispute." Sometimes these data supported the innovative—and now standard—therapy. But when the RCT data questioned the safety or effectiveness of a standard procedure, McKinlay saw the beginning of the sixth stage, the stage of professional denunciation. The final stage, the stage of erosion and discrediting, followed, sometimes taking more than a decade, according to McKinlay, with the original "enthusiastic claims" modified, perhaps moving from a universal applicability to a more limited one. McKinlay's work provides a useful, although simplistic, heuristic device to outline the usual stages in a medical innovation. But, as McKinlay himself noted, not all innovations follow such a path—some do not do so in this order, and some stages are circumvented or telescoped. Regardless, McKinlay argued, "The career of an innovation has at least a beginning point (the promising report) and an ending (established procedure, or erosion and discreditation)."[113]

This typical, or expected, route of an uptake within the profession of a medical innovation in surgery brings forth a question this chapter will end upon: why didn't love surgery follow this outline? Love surgery, in some ways, started off following this course—but for Burt, and for his love surgery, the course diverged and ended at a crucial, early point: his peers did not pick up and advance his surgery.[114] They were not, per Jones, excited enough about the anticipated benefits of the surgery to pick it up based on Burt's enthusiastic reports of the procedure. And this brings up a significant factor within medical innovation, perhaps one of the most important influences on whether an innovation will be accepted. As scholars discussed in the 1970s, the interaction between professional colleagues, this personal and direct contact, was what contributed the most effectively on whether or not a physician decided to adopt an innovation.[115] This decision on whether or not to adopt an innovation is, in effect, a form of regulating a specific therapeutic practice and, to a lesser extent, the practitioner promoting it.

Historian John Pickstone noted that whether or not a clinician takes up an innovation is contextually dependent; the social contexts of the physician promoting and considering the innovation matter.[116] Contacts, and the context of those contacts (as in that Burt introduced love surgery in Dayton, Ohio, in the 1970s and not, say, Los Angeles, California), matter in the introduction and diffusion of an innovation within medicine. Moreover, the personality of the innovative surgeon has been seen as central, if not critical, to the adoption of a surgical innovation or of a new surgery by other surgeons.[117] As historian Thomas Schlich argued, "Innovation in medicine involves a process of persuasion."[118] Although it perhaps helps that the person with the innovation is seen as an opinion leader in the community, what apparently matters more in the uptake of an innovation is that the innovator is well situated within the community to communicate with, to persuade, many physicians about the innovation, a situation sociologist Ann Lennarson Greer likened to the spread of a contagious disease, with the medical, or surgical, innovation as the spreading virus. As Greer described it, talk was important, and the more physicians talked about the innovation, "the more there is opportunity for consensus, practical problem-solving, and social pressure to change." Although perhaps some physicians raised questions regarding the innovation, those questions were answered—or dispelled—"when physicians learn that a technique or finding is being implemented in the area by local colleagues (with known skills), in local hospitals (with known equipment and capabilities), and on local patients (with their biological and social quirks and life histories)." Moreover, Greer argued,

"frequent discussion" between and among physicians created "a sense of movement," meaning a sense that the innovation had been taken up by others, and to
keep up, physicians needed to adopt the innovation into their practice—applying
"the wisdom in the dictum to 'be neither first nor last,'" Greer wrote.[119]

Recall Burt was not regarded as social with his physician peers in Dayton.
Recall too that despite soliciting feedback from those nationally working in
human sexuality, including but not only William Masters, Burt and his attempts
to advocate for his innovative surgery were largely ignored or rejected. It does
not appear, then, that Burt was a physician working in a context in which he
could persuade his peers. For the majority of Burt's peers, both locally and
nationally, when it came to their adoption of love surgery, it would appear they
not only declined to be first or last in the uptake of love surgery, they declined
to be in the middle, too.

Chapter 4

The Dayton Medical Community Reacts, 1976–1980

The previous chapter looked at how Burt and his surgery fit within larger norms of accepting or rejecting surgical innovations. This acceptance, or rejection, of an innovation is a means of regulating the practice of medicine by regulating a particular therapy and, to a more limited effect, of the physician. This chapter focuses on the ways physicians regulate not just therapies but also the practitioners of those therapies by considering how physicians responded to the practice of James Burt in the late 1970s when Burt's practices were causing concern among his coworkers, colleagues, and the broader medical community. But although some in the medical community were concerned, they faced multiple obstacles in constraining him, illustrating the difficulties faced by efforts to enact effective professional regulation.

Although medicine is a self-regulating profession, physicians are not the only clinicians aware of what a physician is doing. Burt, after all, was not alone in the operating room. In addition to the woman whose child he delivered, whose uterus he removed, or whose genitalia he refashioned, there were other women present: nurses. Women largely dominated the nursing profession in the 1970s. But although nurses were a central component of hospital care in the 1970s and 1980s, medical authority essentially resided with physicians. Traditionally regarded as supportive of and to physicians, nurses were largely bound to the authority of the physician, a profession during the 1970s still dominated by men.[1] This was a role that physicians reinforced by mandating complete control over the nursing profession—their level and type of education, their licensure laws, their access to patients, their access to and use of medical knowledge and tools—throughout the twentieth century.[2] As one person critiquing the medical system in the 1970s wrote, the "most significant caste distinction in the hospital" was between doctors and nurses, with doctors rarely speaking directly with nurses and nurses rarely speaking directly with doctors.[3]

While some nurses in the 1970s began to challenge this power difference, on a daily, clinical level, many nurses were constrained in advocating for their patients by their limited influence with physicians and hospital administrators.[4] Moreover, while nurses were a constant presence in both the operating room and the hospital room, no one individual nurse was constantly with one patient. Nursing work was typically divided not by patient but by task, resulting in nurses knowing very little about a particular patient in their care. Indeed, a survey of nurses conducted in the 1970s found that fewer than half of registered nurses, one in three licensed nurses, and one in four nurse aids knew a patient's diagnosis and how the physician planned to treat that patient.[5] The power disparities between doctors and nurses meant that if a nurse offered criticism or reported a doctor for doing something the nurse knew to be wrong, the nurse risked losing a job.[6]

But at least a few nurses working at St. Elizabeth Medical Center—the hospital where Burt most often operated—in the 1970s were paying close attention to Burt's practices and tried to influence other doctors and hospital administrators that what Burt was doing concerned them. Some nurses did this by discussing Burt's actions with each other. They witnessed and discussed Burt's patients and how they suffered postsurgery complications such as difficulty urinating after love surgery because the urethra for some women was now in the vagina, which also resulted in yeast infections.[7] Beatrice Busse, a nurse-anesthetist at St. Elizabeth in the 1970s, later recalled Burt performed love surgery on all of his obstetrics patients during her time there. She further recalled nurses saying that unless Burt killed someone, the hospital would do nothing to stop him.[8] Carol Brewer, who worked as a nurse at St. Elizabeth from 1963 to 1974, similarly remembered another nurse saying, "If someone were left lying, dying in the gutter, they'd rather be allowed to die peacefully in the gutter than to be butchered to death by Burt or to be saved and rescued by him to live in agony." Although Brewer worked in pediatrics, she recollected nurses attending Burt's patients often asked for child-size catheters. The nurses seeking the small catheters did so while protesting how tightly Burt had stitched up his patients, necessitating use of the small catheters.[9]

Nurses, especially the ones who attended Burt's patients, were appalled.[10] Some voiced their concerns to the director of nursing. During at least one staff meeting in the 1970s when the subject of Burt arose, many of the nurses became visibly upset, but the nurses recalled the director's response to them was that so long as Burt was not killing any of his patients, they had to put up with him.[11] A few nurses, however, went beyond sharing their concerns with their peers. Nancy Goodman, who occasionally practiced as an obstetric nurse while working at St. Elizabeth in the early 1970s, expressed her concerns about Burt and his surgery to E. C. Kuhbander, the chief administrator at the hospital.[12] She, like other nurses, felt Burt overmedicated his patients during labor. Yvonne Curington, another labor and delivery nurse at St. Elizabeth in the 1970s, recalled that Burt's philosophy seemed to be that "if they fluttered an eyelid, they weren't medicated enough."[13]

Goodman was also concerned the surgery Burt did to repair episiotomies was not standard. But she was told that the hospital could do nothing to stop Burt. Kuhbander, Goodman recalled, informed her the hospital administration had "spent hours—hundreds of hours" discussing Burt and his unorthodox surgery with the hospital's attorneys. The attorneys, Goodman remembered Kuhbander telling her, had informed them that "because of the restraint of trade issue"—Burt did not have full privileges at any other local hospital, meaning if St. Elizabeth limited him, it would essentially erode his whole practice—"that he [Burt] could sue the hospital" if St. Elizabeth limited his privileges. Goodman later recalled that although Kuhbander had supported and understood her concern, "he wasn't sure anything could be done."[14] Curington, who assisted Burt in the delivery room in the 1970s, went even further. When she brought up to the director of nursing and the hospital's chief of staff that Burt's extensive episiotomy repair actually altered the vaginas of the women and the hospital administration still did nothing, Curington quit.[15]

Doctors—including James Burt—are not lone actors, for they rely upon other physicians for referrals and advice. But the peer relationship is also a means of assessing the work of other physicians. A 1975 state law required physicians to report to the State Medical Board of Ohio—the entity with licensing power over physicians—any colleagues who were practicing medicine below standard. More than a few physicians labeled the law the "snitch provision."[16] Goodman recalled Kuhbander telling her at the time that a physician needed to report Burt before the hospital could do something. Goodman remembered Kuhbander telling her, "I cannot get one physician in this town to stand up and say to me that what Jim Burt is doing is outside of current medical practice." If just one did, Goodman recollected Kuhbander telling her, then "we could do something."[17]

Despite having firsthand experience watching Burt perform his surgery or having the knowledge of the effects of love surgery because they cared for the women in the hospital after the surgery, it remained the purview of physicians, not nurses, to come forward to state that Burt's practice was outside standard medical care. And some physicians had seen his work firsthand. Stan Garber recalled when, as a first-year resident in the mid-1960s he watched Burt do an episiotomy repair, he thought it looked different enough he felt he should mention it to his chief resident. Garber questioned the "extra sutures" Burt put in, and he was "curious about this build-up of tissue" because it was "unusual." The chief resident mentioned Garber's concern to the head of obstetrics and gynecology at St. Elizabeth, who reportedly said there was a "movement underway" regarding what to do about Burt. But Garber recalled this "movement" never leaving the obstetrics and gynecology section.[18]

Walter Reiling Jr., who, recall, practiced medicine in Dayton in the 1970s, remembered Burt as no charlatan; indeed, according to Reiling, Burt "believed he was accomplishing some good with his surgery." But Reiling also later recalled that Burt, around the time he published *Surgery of Love*, "seemed to become obsessed with" love surgery. Radiologist Konrad Kircher, who in 1977 was chief of staff at St. Elizabeth, recalled "everybody" knowing that Burt "had this obsession with probing women's sex lives, but most people just smiled about it."[19]

Although there were physicians who were not smiling about it, they were also not talking about their concerns publicly. When Barbara Demick was writing her story for *The Real Paper* in 1978 and called several physicians in Dayton for comment, all refused to publicly make statements, fearing lawsuits (with justification for this fear) from Burt. One, however, agreed to speak on condition of anonymity, and this physician told Demick that several doctors were shocked that Burt had scheduled a nineteen-year-old woman, who weighed less than 100 pounds, for love surgery. "It's inconceivable," the doctor told Demick, "that this operation is recommended for women who plan to have babies." Burt, the doctor said, "has such a manipulative way with women," it was "almost like a seduction." The young woman scheduled for surgery had only been married a year, and the doctor recalled her as being "young, timid, and scared, and she thought—and he made her believe—she was sexually inadequate because she couldn't climax at the *exact* same time as her husband." The anonymous doctor told Demick that like this particular young woman, "women who think they're inadequate are very susceptible." Women who trusted Burt were "generally low- to-middle income people," and Burt in turn charged them $100 an hour for consultation, the doctor told Demick. "It's like selling a cancer patient Laetrile," the anonymous doctor complained.[20] That the physician compared Burt's work to Laetrile—an alternative, supposedly miraculous, cancer treatment drug that in 1977 the FDA commissioner stated was not just ineffective as cancer therapy but also highly likely to result in cyanide poisoning and so banned it—is both interesting and evocative of the time.[21]

Tied to these concerns about the surgery being promoted to women based on notions of sexual inadequacy, another doctor Demick interviewed also questioned the physiological basis of the surgery as having an impact on sexual response. Recall that part of love surgery involved shortening the distance between the clitoris and the entrance to the vagina. But as John Grover, a gynecologist at Massachusetts General Hospital, argued, believing this mattered to the capacity for female orgasm flew "in the face of broad and well-documented studies of female sexuality." No evidence existed, Grover asserted, to suggest the "anatomical position of the clitoris has anything to do with an orgasm."[22]

But perhaps the primary concern among clinicians was Burt's lack of selectivity for the surgery, with Burt admitting he had turned down only three women for it.[23] Some of those concerned physicians had seen Burt's work, as they had examined some of Burt's reconstructed patients, and according to what they saw, these women's vulvas looked entirely different. The opening of the vagina was smaller and was about an inch closer to the clitoris, and on some women, the urinary tract had been cut and moved into the vagina.[24] Following surgery, the labia minora were pulled inside the vagina during intercourse. The women's genitals "were completely disfigured," one doctor anonymously stated to Demick in her 1978 article, with "their vaginas looking like funnels."[25] Stan Garber recalled that all of Burt's former patients looked "the same" and that he always knew they had been patients of Burt.[26] Moreover, some of the women who had undergone love surgery had been so tightly sewn they had to be opened to have vaginal intercourse. An additional problem pointed out by these physicians, one that Burt reportedly only hinted at, was that women who had undergone love surgery had too small a vaginal opening for vaginal childbirth. In order for a baby to be delivered vaginally, the women had to undergo an extensive episiotomy.[27]

Physicians also heard stories from patients regarding what Burt discussed—or did not discuss—with them about their sex lives and sexual difficulties. Obstetrician gynecologist Stephen England, who was asked by Burt in 1976 for a second opinion regarding his recommendation for a hysterectomy, recalled that in the woman's chart were notes regarding sexual problems of the woman and that she was also scheduled for love surgery. England asked the woman whether she had any sexual problems, and she told him she and her husband had not had sex in five years. Moreover, according to England, she had not told Burt anything about her sex life, let alone any problems she was having.[28]

While Dayton physicians were not commenting publicly, a few gynecologists in the city were concerned about Burt's practices and, like the nurses, tried to work within the hospital system to stop, or at least limit, Burt's ability to practice surgery. One of those physicians was Donne Holden, who years later was remembered as leading the charge against Burt and who in 1989 spoke on record with a national medical journal regarding Burt.[29] Holden was one of only a few female obstetrician gynecologists in Dayton in the 1970s and the only one she could recall who was also married with children. She had moved to Dayton with her husband and completed her residency training at Miami Valley Hospital. She was in private practice in 1976 when she became aware of love surgery. Holden began noticing that Burt's patients, when they came to deliver at Miami Valley Hospital, could not have vaginal deliveries because their vaginas after love surgery were shaped like funnels. The women had to have their babies through cesarean section or after an extensive episiotomy. In an effort to understand more about this, Holden read Burt's *Surgery of Love*. Based on her experience seeing the patients at Miami Valley Hospital and reading *Surgery of Love*, Holden became very concerned about the surgery. Many of her fellow obstetrician gynecologists at Miami Valley Hospital agreed, deciding they did not want him to be allowed to operate at their hospital.[30]

But it was the nineteen-year-old woman Demick wrote about in her 1978 article that galvanized Holden into action. Holden learned that Burt had recommended love surgery to the woman whom she generically named "Maria" because the young woman told Holden's resident—who was piercing Maria's ears—that Burt could fix her inability to climax at the exact time as her husband by correcting what he told her was wrong with her anatomy. The resident advised Maria to speak with Holden, the young woman's primary obstetrician gynecologist, and Holden told Maria she did not recommend she have the surgery, that her anatomy was normal. Holden asked if she could use Maria's information to consult with other clinicians regarding the surgery. Several other physicians saw Maria, did a physical exam, and concurred that the surgery should not have been recommended. They wrote letters along with Holden to the county medical society and to St. Elizabeth in 1977.[31]

These actions were not easy for the physicians to take since, in the case of Maria, they were questioning the appropriateness of an elective surgical procedure. An elective surgery is different from an emergency surgery—which needs to be done immediately—and includes both cosmetic surgeries as well as surgeries that are medically indicated but not immediately required.[32] Part of the difficulty is that an elective surgery is often just that: a patient who wants a surgery that is not perhaps medically indicated elects to have it.[33] An additional reason for the difficulty physicians had regarding limiting Burt's use of love surgery was that there was disagreement on its medical necessity, with Burt thinking love surgery was indicated and some of his peers considering it medically unnecessary. By taking such a stance, Burt's peers who challenged him—in this instance and in instances to come—were essentially questioning the appropriateness of Burt's decisions on how to diagnose and treat his patients: they were questioning his professional judgment.

Decades later, Holden recalled their actions to limit Burt as "very brave" and she felt "very proud" about their efforts, that the actions they took was "everything they could do." Moreover, what they did—the evidence they gathered from Maria and the letter they wrote to the county medical society, keeping Burt from practicing surgery of love at Miami Valley Hospital—was about as much as they could have legally done regarding limiting the practice of an elective surgery.[34] Holden defended the actions she and her four peers took regarding Burt. "What were we supposed to do, tell the [state medical] board that Dr. Burt had suggested something to patients we disagreed with?" And this is essentially what, based on one patient, it amounted to: a second opinion in disagreement with the surgery recommended by another physician. Holden, during an interview in 1989, reflected that in the late 1970s, the State Medical Board of Ohio did not have much power—for reasons I will shortly describe— so she and the other doctors worked carefully to limit Burt's ability to do love surgery, keeping him, for example, from obtaining full privileges at other area hospitals. "That was very aggressive for the time," Holden stated.[35] Indeed, by the late 1970s, although there were four Dayton hospitals, Burt only had full operating privileges at St. Elizabeth. In the mid-1970s, the board of gynecologists at another Dayton hospital voted to suspend Burt's privileges entirely, but Burt threatened suit and the hospital backed down.[36]

Physicians realize mistakes are inevitable within medical practice and that many decisions regarding a diagnosis or therapy are based on a physician's own judgment, a judgment not to be second-guessed by other physicians; it is considered a break in the etiquette of medicine for a physician to criticize the work of a peer.[37] When a physician, however, does not act responsibly, his or her peers are expected to hold their peer accountable—this holding of peers accountable is self-regulation. As AMA President Milford Rouse put it in 1968, "The public has of necessity been forced to put its trust in physicians to insure that physicians practice competently and ethically," but only if physicians maintain "competence and ethical conduct will medicine be allowed to continue to govern itself."[38]

In his 1970 study of how medicine self-regulates, sociologist Eliot Freidson described a "profession" as an avowal or promise. As an occupation, a profession is one that has "assumed a dominant position in a division of labor, so that it gains control over the determination of the substance of its own work," meaning that unlike "most occupations, it is autonomous or self-directing." The test of such autonomy, Freidson argued, was its ability to self-regulate—a "special privilege of freedom from the control of outsiders." The granting of such freedom is based on three claims: first, the knowledge of the profession is such that one outside the profession could not evaluate it; second, that those in the profession are responsible and able to be trusted without supervision; and third, on the rare occasions when someone within the profession is not acting responsibly, the profession will regulate that person.[39]

In his observation of how the latter occurred, Freidson outlined a rather slow process, one in which individual physicians accumulated observations until they could no longer, in his words, "contain his [sic] indignation or until he discovered from others' hints that they too had doubts about the same individual." Given the need for accumulation before a physician may share his (or her) doubts, Freidson noted that "a considerable amount of time could elapse before any widespread opinion about the man [sic] emerged." According to Freidson, "Arriving at a certain critical mass of discontent with an individual seemed to be necessary before most physicians would begin complaining about him [sic] to each other and the administration" of the hospital.[40]

When Freidson asked physicians what they would do if they encountered an offending colleague, he was usually told "nothing." If, however, the offence happened more than once, the physicians then told Freidson they would talk to the offending physician. This "talking to" seemed to involve, Freidson found, a blend of "instruction, friendly persuasion, shaming, and threat." Such a talk was most likely to occur if the physicians were in the same department at a hospital or if the offending physician were younger than the one initiating the talk. If, however, the offending physician were older and/or more senior, once a physician became "angry enough he would complain instead to his peers or even to the administration" of the clinic or hospital, according to Freidson, not directly to the offending physician.[41]

In addition to this "talking to," concerned physicians also "attempted to bar a man from working with them individually or with their own patients." This meant in practice that offending physicians were not sought out for advice, not called in to look at an interesting case, or not consulted about a case relevant to his specialty. In sum, Freidson found, "the characteristic sanctions were never so strong as to reduce income and minimize or prevent work on the part of the offenders, and they were rarely organized." Most often, according to Freidson, the offending physicians were personally excluded, and as such, they *"punish him only insofar as he is sensitive to the good opinion of those particular individuals who exclude him."*[42]

This method of sanctioning—of regulating—an errant peer, though, as Freidson noted, only works when the physician who is errant cares about the opinion of his peers. Although Burt courted approval for love surgery from many nationally who worked within sexual medicine, including William Masters, evidence also suggests that when he failed to garner such approval, he considered it as a negative reflection of the other physicians. On a local level, evidence also suggests Burt did not seek the approval or the collaboration of his peers in Dayton; recall that Dayton physician Reiling stated Burt purposefully distanced himself from his colleagues at social events. As one doctor who complained to Demick in her 1978 article said of Burt, "He's always been a Johnny-out-of-step, so he attacks other professionals—he just says we're the ones who are wrong. He's just a menace here."[43] The regulation that Freidson found to be often used by physicians to rein in errant physicians, then, only works if, as he noted, the errant doctor is "sensitive of the good opinion" of his peers—something Burt perhaps was not.

Most physicians interviewed by Freidson believed that if a colleague did something "really serious," they would know and there would be a reaction by the offending colleague's peers. But Freidson found what was considered to be "really serious" "so extreme as to be removed from their everyday experience." In essence, what they were saying, Freidson wrote, "was that butchers and moral lepers would be spotted and controlled quickly." However, as he also pointed out, "almost all forms of deviance lie somewhere between the performance of a moral leper and that of the saint." And it was in this "somewhere" "that the observed controls are problematic," Freidson wrote.[44]

This initial regulation of Burt by his peers followed along some of the paths laid out by Freidson: physicians noted an irregularity within the practice of a peer and discussed it among themselves, deciding it was serious enough that they did not want Burt practicing with their patients. Instead, though, of "talking to" Burt, Holden and her colleagues voiced their concerns to the hospital where they practiced and the county medical society. In response to the letters from Holden and her colleagues, the Montgomery County Medical Society decided to look at Burt and his surgery, including a review of *Surgery of Love.*[45] Since the dean of the Wright State University School of Medicine in Dayton was, by virtue of being the dean of the local medical school, on the board of the county medical society, he was asked to review it.[46] The dean described the book as "poorly written" and "medically unfounded" and stated a "rebuttal to the author would only add dignity to its existence."[47]

Burt knew the society was investigating his surgery, and in an April 1978 letter, he threatened to sue the county medical society for slander if they issued a statement disavowing it.[48] Regardless, in July 1978, the society did issue a statement describing love surgery as "undocumented by ordinary standards of scientific reporting" and "not a generally gynecologically accepted procedure" with results not "duplicated by [other] physicians." Moreover, the society's statement noted love surgery had only been described in "nonscientific literature."[49] This statement was, in its careful manner, labeling love surgery as not an accepted—and perhaps not an acceptable—surgery. The society read their statement to any person who inquired of them about Burt and also sent it to the local hospitals, including St. Elizabeth.[50] Walter Reiling Jr. later said local doctors did as much as they could when they issued their statement regarding the surgery through the medical society. After the summer of 1978, anyone who called the society to inquire about love surgery was read the society's position statement, according to Reiling. Additionally, the society published its position in one of the local newspapers, *The Journal Herald*, on October 22, 1980.[51] "I can't believe someone would go through with that procedure" after learning of the society's position, Reiling said years later.[52]

State and county medical societies, such as the Montgomery County Medical Society, are elective membership groups made up of physicians. These societies had previously held a bit more power when it came to regulating a physician. In the 1950s and 1960s, medical societies established grievance committees to handle disputes between physicians and patients, giving patients a place for their complaint to be heard while also ensuring the profession could contain the dispute within private mediation and keep any disciplinary action similarly private. State medical boards, the ones with the legal authority over the practice of medicine because they were the ones with licensing power, followed the lead of the state and county medical societies when it came to disciplining errant physicians. Until the 1970s, nearly all conflicts went through the local or state medical society. Physicians, however, were often reluctant to take their concerns regarding their peers to medical societies, instead choosing to not refer patients to those they deemed to be poor practitioners—another, though less public, form of regulation.[53]

This, however, changed during the 1970s, when state medical licensing boards assumed, in addition to licensing physicians, the authority to hear and investigate complaints regarding physicians and to discipline unprofessional physicians.[54] State medical boards hesitatingly began making this shift in the 1960s.[55] By the 1970s, boards began to assume this role as part of a larger response to control costs from what was then called the malpractice crisis—a steep rise in malpractice insurance rates for many physicians some saw as resulting from a growth in the number and size of malpractice lawsuits—by seeking to discipline physicians practicing beneath the standard of care in an attempt to reduce the number of malpractice lawsuits.[56] Thus, by the time Burt came to the attention of the Montgomery County Medical Society, it no longer had the power to discipline an errant physician.

A local medical society could, however, report what it knew about an unprofessional local physician to the entity with the power to remove or limit a physician's ability to practice medicine, which was, by the time the county medical society issued its statement, the State Medical Board of Ohio. And, in addition to writing the statement regarding love surgery, it appears the county medical society also contacted the state medical board about Burt. Richard Tapia, then the Montgomery County Medical Society's executive director, later stated he had engaged in several discussions regarding Burt with an investigator from the state medical board in the early 1980s but received no response from the board.[57] The state board, however, later professed to have no record of any complaint.[58]

But even if it had heard of the complaint, would it have been enough for the state medical board to act? On February 1, 1976, as part of her larger exposé on the practice of medicine in the United States published in the *New York Times*, Jane Brody reported that, according to medical professional groups, about 5 percent of the physicians practicing nationally were unfit to do so. Moreover, medical professional groups also asserted the problem was more widespread than they had suspected. "Perhaps the greatest obstacle to improving the situation, many experts say, is the traditional reluctance of physicians to criticize and discipline their errant colleagues," Brody wrote. According to Brody, state licensing boards between 1963 and 1976 revoked only a combined average of 66 doctors' licenses annually in the United States, meaning each state revoked an average of 1.32 doctors' licenses each year, "even though incidents of careless and incompetent treatment are known to almost every physician and many patients," Brody wrote. Since doctors dominated membership on the state licensing boards, critics charged that medicine's regulatory bodies were weak and ineffective "because of the professional veil of silence that commonly shields serious incidents from outside attention, and because of the difficulty of getting patients to complain and testify against their doctors," Brody wrote.[59]

Brody's report challenged assertions such as those made in 1978 by John Budd, president of the AMA, that "only professionals can police their ranks competently and knowledgably. And this we have been doing."[60]

Even though the basic legal responsibility of state medical boards was to ensure physicians were competent to practice—indeed, they were (and are) the only body with the legal authority to grant, limit, or revoke a physician's ability to practice medicine—it was a very rare thing for a doctor to have his or her license suspended or revoked. Drug abuse was the most common reason for doing so in the 1970s, accounting for nearly half of the disciplinary actions medical boards took, followed by mental incompetence, although in most states, it was not grounds for limiting or revoking a medical license unless the doctor had been committed to an institution. Physicians could also lose their right to practice because of fraud, conviction of a felony, unprofessional conduct, moral depravity, fee splitting, or gross immorality. Malpractice because of incompetence arising from, for example, a physician's failing skill or intelligence, lack of attention, or overwork, however, were rarely reasons for disciplinary action from a medical board; indeed, between 1970 and 1975, only eight doctors in the entire United States received disciplinary action because of their incompetence. In 1973, professional incompetence was not even a basis for disciplining a physician in thirty-five states.[61] State medical boards, before the 1980s, rarely disciplined physicians, and if they did discipline a doctor, it was almost never for incompetence.[62]

Finally, in addition to noting how infrequently state medical boards disciplined physicians, in particular for incompetence, it should also be noted that it was even more rare for them to do because of sexual misconduct. Although in 1972 the first code of the American Psychiatric Association included a provision condemning sexual contact with patients, it was not until 1986 before the Council of Ethical and Judicial Affairs of the AMA provided a similar proscription against sexual misconduct for all physicians.[63] In 1991, the AMA Council defined as unethical for a physician to be engaged in a sexual or romantic relationship with a current patient, while such a relationship could be unethical if with a former patient.[64] State medical boards did, beginning in the late 1980s, increase their actions against physicians violating this prohibition; in a study conducted by the Public Citizen's Health Research Group, in 1989, 42 physicians were disciplined in the United States, a number that grew to 147 in 1996, with a total of 761 for the entire span of years.[65] Sexual misconduct by physicians did not become a salient public issue until the 1990s, when the sexual exploitation of patients became a greater regulatory issue for medical boards. Addressing this growing concern, in 1996, the Federation of State Medical Boards, the organization that represents all the state medical boards in the United States, made a distinction between "sexual violation" and "sexual impropriety," with the former including sexual intercourse or contact. The latter included sexually seductive, suggestive, or demeaning behaviors, gestures, or expressions made by a physician. It was in this second category of behavior—sexual impropriety—that Burt could have been accused for repeatedly asking his patients about their sex lives or for turning discussions to ones about his patients' sexual performance. That he was not is, within this historical context, unsurprising, given that few sued physicians for sexual misconduct before 1975 and that even if they had sued, sexual impropriety was not part of the definition for another two decades.[66]

In 1975, Ohio passed a law requiring doctors to report colleagues believed to be practicing substandard medicine to the State Medical Board of Ohio, a law doctors labeled the "snitch provision."[67] As this negative label suggests, although obligated to report an errant physician, many physicians found this onerous. In their 1978 book on medical malpractice, Sylvia Law and Steven Pollan wrote that physicians failed to report their peers' medical incompetence for a variety of reasons, but perhaps one of the largest reasons, they hypothesized, was that "doctors, like the rest of us, empathize with the problems of colleagues." Law and Pollan found "overwhelming evidence" that professional ethics did not "motivate physicians to take their peer-review responsibility seriously," and thus Law and Pollan argued for a change in the law "to make it absolutely clear to physicians that they have a responsibility to provide state medical boards with information about colleagues who cannot or do not practice within minimally acceptable professional standards." When Law and Pollan published this in 1978, only nine states—including Ohio—required doctors to report.[68]

Beyond empathizing with their peers, however, there are other understandable reasons for doctors not to report. Specifically regarding Burt, but by no means limited to him, doctors fear lawsuits if they are wrong—or even if they are right. Dayton doctors were perhaps hesitant to report Burt out of concern for legal retaliation from Burt, either directly through lawsuits or indirectly through patients. And their fears were real: recall he threatened to sue the Montgomery County Medical Society in 1978 for its criticism of love surgery.[69] Moreover, reportedly at Burt's urging, perhaps two women in the late 1970s sued other gynecologists for trying to reverse love surgeries.[70] One of these women, according to local gynecologists, had wanted the surgery undone, but her husband had not and, with encouragement from Burt, sued the doctor who tried to undo his wife's love surgery.[71]

There is an additional factor to consider regarding local physicians reporting to the state medical board about Burt and his surgery: the pacing or, perhaps better phrased, the lag time at which other Dayton physicians saw former Burt patients and noticed a trend in complications among them. Holden and her fellow obstetrician gynecologists responded to one particular patient whom they thought Burt had given, at best, a highly questionable recommendation for an elective surgery. But recall Freidson's findings regarding how physicians dealt with problematic peers, a process of observing and collecting information before sharing and comparing with other physicians, a process that worked rather slowly, for, as Freidson wrote, the "system of control can work only as rapidly as the information necessary for control can accumulate."[72]

When I spoke to Walter Reiling Jr. about Burt, he repeatedly stressed the importance of understanding how timing determined when other Dayton physicians became suspicious. According to Reiling, since many of the women who underwent love surgery did not seek another physician's care or did so only years after having undergone surgery, it was hard for physicians to spot a trend among Burt's former patients. Reiling recalled Burt as being very persuasive with his patients, so some of the problems these women ended up having were not seen by other physicians until years later. This delay, then, interrupted tracking of the women's problems back to Burt's surgery and recognizing commonalities linking the complications to the same cause. Given these limiting circumstances, Reiling still considered the county medical society's statement to have been the strongest statement they could have made; indeed, it was, he feels, a "brave statement."[73] Short of taking away Burt's membership in the county medical society—and, since it would have had no impact on his ability to practice, the only thing this would have possibly done would have been to make him angry—the statement was the only recourse the county medical society could take, Reiling argued.[74] At the time, the society did not know there was a pattern of problems originating from the surgery; instead, it had a questionable elective procedure.

Holden and other concerned physicians may have thought love surgery was of dubious merit and thus undergoing it not worth the risk. It was in their view an unnecessary surgery. But an unnecessary surgery another physician is recommending is distinct and different from a surgery known to have poor outcomes: the former concerns a *doubtful* effectiveness and/or safety while the latter concerns a *recognized* lack of effectiveness and/or safety. And documenting the latter, as Reiling stressed, takes both a knowledge of poor outcomes regarding a particular surgery and the demonstration of a pattern of poor outcomes tied to the particular surgery. In other words, recognizing a surgery as not being effective and/or as having poor outcomes takes time.

The granting of hospital privileges is another avenue to control the actions of a physician, and there were physicians at St. Elizabeth who were concerned about Burt. Hospital privileges are determined by each hospital; medical societies were not involved in determining them. And in the 1970s, St. Elizabeth was under national pressure to begin strengthening the review of what all physicians with hospital privileges, not just Burt, were doing in the operating room. A large reason for the increased vigor within all American hospitals for auditing surgeries and surgeons arose largely from a series of malpractice cases that underlined hospitals' responsibility to prevent gross negligence and incompetence within its walls. By 1976, nearly half of the hospitals in the United States had begun to systematically review surgeries performed under their auspices. These internal audits were meant to improve patient care, detect incompetence, and reduce the number of unnecessary surgeries. The reviews were part of a medical audit system that had recently become required for a hospital to receive accreditation from the Joint Commission on Accreditation of Hospitals (JCAH). Beginning in 1974, a hospital that failed to perform adequate audits lost its accreditation. Surgeries were one of the areas most looked at in the audits, with the goal of identifying doctors who were incompetent, careless, or ignorant, as well as to identify excessive numbers of medically unnecessary surgeries or postoperative complications. JCAH accreditation was vital to the financial well-being of a hospital; many doctors refused to practice at, and most major medical insurance providers refused claims from, unaccredited hospitals.[75] In the 1970s, to be accredited with the JCAH, a hospital had to meet certain criteria, including the requirement that the tissue committee compare a doctor's preoperative diagnosis with pathology reports on the tissues removed during an operation.[76]

In 1977, one year before the 100th anniversary of its founding by the Franciscan Sisters of the Poor, St. Elizabeth affiliated with the new Wright State University School of Medicine and with nursing programs at Sinclair Community College and the Dayton School of Practical Nursing. More than 1,700 people worked at St. Elizabeth, and it was a busy hospital: in 1977, 19,337 patients were admitted and 9,307 inpatient surgeries were performed.[77] A principal responsibility of a hospital's medical staff consisted of developing, enforcing, and adhering to medical staff bylaws, the structural framework of how a hospital and the independent physicians who treat patients within its walls operate.[78] The tissue committee at St. Elizabeth was responsible for auditing these operations and preventing gross negligence and incompetence at the hospital. According to the 1975 *Bylaws, Rules and Regulations of the Medical Staff* for St. Elizabeth, the tissue committee existed as part of the quality assurance program committee, whose purpose entailed the "evaluation of the quality of care"; if members of the committee found care that failed to meet the criteria of quality—defined as "having the characteristics of excellence"—the committee had the responsibility to "take corrective action." When the committee members found activities or conduct "of any staff member with clinical privileges" that were "lower than the standards or aims of the medical staff or to be disruptive to the operations of the hospital, corrective action against such staff member" was expected to be taken by either the committee or by any medical staff officer, by any clinical department chairman, or by the governing body within the hospital.[79]

The tissue committee at St. Elizabeth, like others at hospitals across the country, was made up of doctors who oversaw the quality of work done by their peers. This peer review consisted of evaluating physicians on the quality of their practice as well as their efficiency and effectiveness. Recall that peer review is a form of professional regulation. The American College of Surgeons in 1918 originated peer review as a method of assessing candidates for board certification in surgery. Thirty-four years later, in 1952, the JCAH added peer review as one of its standards for a hospital to receive its accreditation.[80] Recall, too, that physicians often regard serving upon such committees and reviewing the work of other physicians as onerous.[81] As Timothy Jost noted in his assessment of medical self-regulation, "It is never a comfortable task to sit in judgment of one's peers with whom one works on a day to day basis." This discomfort could lead, Jost recognized, to a "temptation to give the benefit of the doubt and gloss over a colleague's errors."[82] However, as one legal scholar put it in the early 1980s, because physicians are the only ones "with the professional expertise to do so," doctors "must take seriously their obligation to engage in sober and thorough criticism of one another." Criticism was not simply negative; indeed, a hospital's peer review committee was expected to consider both the negative and positive aspects of a physician's practice, and whatever the review found, the results were to be directed toward improving a physician's practice, not to chastise or punish.[83]

Burt's peers were not exclusively concerned about his questionable recommendations for love surgery; they were also troubled about other surgeries he recommended and performed. In April 1977, St. Elizabeth's tissue committee became concerned with three of Burt's cases. Late that month, the tissue committee sent Burt a letter, carbon copied to the hospital's credentials committee, asking him to detail why he treated three of his patients in the manner in which he did, including why he removed the healthy ovaries of twenty-five-year-old Harriet Niblick Williams. After two abnormal Pap smears, Burt advised Williams she should have her uterus and both ovaries removed, telling her while he found no cancer, he believed these organs could become cancerous. In addition, Burt also recommended love surgery, which Williams had never heard of before his suggestion. Burt showed Williams a slide show featuring women who had undergone the procedure, a presentation that included no mention of possible complications.[84]

Williams spent the next year recovering from various complications that ultimately resulted in Burt and two non-Dayton doctors recommending cosmetic plastic surgery on her genitals. "You change doctors and you change husbands and they say, 'what happened to you?'" Williams later stated. When informed years later that doctors at the time questioned the wisdom of removing a twenty-five-year-old woman's uterus and ovaries, not to mention performing love surgery, she expressed shock and bitterness that the surgeries had been allowed to take place.[85]

In the tissue committee's letter to Burt, they also questioned why he performed a dilation and curettage (D&C) on an eleven-year-old, a procedure that involved the insertion of a surgical instrument into the vagina in order to scrape a tissue sample from the uterus, tissue that was then tested for cancer. According to the committee's letter to Burt, "the committee felt that there are very few indications for such a procedure in a patient of this age." The mother of the child who underwent the procedure recalled that she took her daughter to Burt because of painful menstrual cramps. Burt apparently told the mother he suspected cancer and insisted that a D&C be performed. The tissue sample Burt removed revealed no cancer.[86]

Concern from the tissue committee about Burt's surgical practices was not limited to, or possibly even principally about, his performing love surgery. Perhaps not surprisingly, Burt responded testily to the tissue committee's questioning of his decisions, to which the committee responded tersely in July 1977, and the arguing by letters began.[87] Burt was not pleased that he was being called to task and questioned the "motivation of peer review when statements are made by physicians" on the committee such as "'we've been trying to get you for years' and 'how are we going to stop him?'"[88] Burt had reason to be concerned with being disciplined by the tissue committee, for an unfavorable decision from this committee meant not just the possibility of his privileges at St. Elizabeth being in jeopardy but also his ability to collect payments from public and private insurance.[89] In their response to Burt in a July 15, 1977, letter to him, the tissue committee wrote that "we as individuals make judgments and if we feel that there is a tremendous deviation from the standard of practice in the hospital do forward these results to the Executive Committee and chiefs of departments."[90]

As this letter indicates, the tissue committee took its concerns regarding Burt to the Executive Committee of the Medical Staff at St. Elizabeth, and in apparent response to Burt's lack of cooperation with the tissue committee, St. Elizabeth gave Burt a conditional reappointment, rather than a full reappointment, in December 1977.[91] The executive committee had the power to withdraw Burt's appointment entirely, but its members could not apparently reach an agreement on whether the case against Burt was strong enough to do so. Konrad Kircher, then chief of staff at St. Elizabeth, later recalled that they would have had an easier time dealing with Burt had the media not "made such a glory out of him."[92] Moreover, the hospital had just as much reason to fear a lawsuit from Burt as Burt did of receiving an adverse peer review from the tissue committee. Beginning in the mid-1970s, following a U.S. Supreme Court decision, physicians could sue a hospital in federal court under antitrust law for a restraint of trade if privileges were revoked. And although apparently few physicians won such lawsuits, the costs to a hospital of defending itself against one often meant the threatened hospital did not revoke privileges so long as the physician retained his or her medical license—in effect, deferring decisions on the capacity of a physician to practice to the state medical board.[93]

Walter Reiling Jr., who was chair of the tissue committee at St. Elizabeth for several years during the late 1970s, recollected the workings of the tissue committee.[94] The pathologist, William Abramson, would bring cases to the committee to review regarding all the physicians with surgical privileges at St. Elizabeth, but Abramson would bring a case involving one of Burt's surgical patients rather often, about every other month or so, Reiling recalled, which was in itself worrisome. Typically, Abramson brought the case because of something odd he saw in the tissues, typically tissues of a younger woman upon whom Burt had operated. In the hierarchy of the hospital, the tissue committee needed to refer their concerns to the executive committee and defer decisions to that committee. In turn, the executive committee reported to the hospital board, a group that, unlike the other two lower committees, was not made up of physicians; few physicians were on the hospital board. According to Reiling, the executive committee felt that Burt's privileges at the hospital should be terminated—apparently in agreement with those on the tissue committee. As Reiling recalled, however, the hospital board felt it could not afford to do so, for fear of a lawsuit from Burt.[95] Reiling remembered that, upon hearing the news regarding the decision of the executive committee, he told his committee to stop reviewing the surgical cases of Burt as "it wasn't worth the time."[96]

In July 1978, St. Elizabeth Medical Center celebrated its centennial anniversary.[97] As nurse Mary Ann Spearin told the reporter for the Dayton *Journal Herald* covering the celebration, the hospital didn't feel "institutional"; instead, she said, "there is a warm, caring family feeling."[98] That year, its accreditation—awarded, the medical staff bulletin noted, "after intensive onsite evaluation"—with the JCAH was again received.[99] Indeed, the medical staff bulletin reported that the JCAH evaluation team called St. Elizabeth "a well-organized, well-run hospital, where they would not hesitate to seek medical care themselves."[100] Walter Keyes, chairman of the Quality Assurance Program Committee at St. Elizabeth, called the reaccreditation a "compliment to the hard work of many people in diversified roles in this institution," an accreditation that occurred despite, Keyes wrote, recent criticism regarding their "quality control efforts." Moreover, Keyes further wrote, although there were two newer hospitals within five miles of St. Elizabeth and the Catholic "religious policy that lessens the attraction to OB-GYN practice," the maternity center practice—which included a recently added Lamaze room for giving birth—was growing.[101]

But while many were celebrating the centennial year of the hospital and in particular the growth of its obstetrics and gynecology practice, the hospital's tissue committee was still examining Burt's non–love surgery gynecological work. Around the same time as he was under scrutiny for these surgeries, in early 1979, Burt was appointed to the quality control committee, which oversaw the quality of care a patient received at St. Elizabeth, because all doctors with staff privileges had to serve on a committee. A few weeks after he received appointment to this committee, the tissue committee was back asking Burt more questions, this time centering on a young woman Burt had performed four D&Cs upon, the first when she was fourteen years old. On February 15, 1979, Burt replied to the committee, explaining that the girl had endometrial hyperplasia, a condition that caused her uterus lining to become overgrown, and while treating her with hormones, he also conducted periodic D&Cs to ensure that she was not developing cancer. The committee did not like his answer and replied in May that the pathology report of the young woman did not support his diagnosis and that "no disease was present and the surgery was not justified."[102] Burt tersely responded to the committee, accusing them of "harassment over this case and cases similar."[103]

Although the tissue committee was told (or itself decided) to stop reviewing Burt's postsurgical pathology reports, the executive committee continued to address Burt and in particular his practice of love surgery. Perhaps prodded by the Montgomery County Medical Society's labeling of love surgery as an undocumented and not generally accepted gynecological procedure in July 1978, or perhaps by this statement as well as concerns by other obstetrician gynecologists in Dayton, St. Elizabeth asked Burt to conduct a scientific study of love surgery to document that the surgery, as he claimed, benefited women. In a letter dated July 1, 1979, St. Elizabeth's chief of staff, E. J. Leschansky, informed Burt that the executive committee requested he "provide scientific statistical documentation of the results of your procedure, represented by a sequential listing of cases over a period of four years." The committee wanted to see the documentation by the end of the year.[104]

Family practice physician Walter Keyes was head of the newly created quality assurance committee, and Burt claimed Keyes told him he was considering having an external review of love surgery, something that did not occur, possibly because the hospital could not find a physician able (or willing) to evaluate it. Burt recalled being given "great latitude" in proving the value of love surgery "as opposed to bringing in somebody who might be termed an expert, for the simple reason that there's nobody in the world who's expert in the surgical treatment of vaginal hypofunction of the female."[105] Burt reportedly said he looked forward to conducting the study because he believed, based on his own initial research, the surgery was helping to reduce murder, domestic violence, and extramarital affairs.[106]

In early 1980, Burt delivered, per the request of St. Elizabeth, his documentation of the effectiveness of love surgery to the hospital in the form of a 159-page-long analysis of the information he had gathered with psychologist Arthur Schramm from their word association questionnaire.[107] Fifty-five women (out of 200 it was sent to) took both the before-and-after surgery questionnaires that asked the respondents to compare their sexual function before and after surgery, their level of pelvic pain, and if they had been beaten less by their partners postsurgery compared to before the surgery. Each survey also asked the women answering if they were nicer people since love surgery. Burt asserted that, according to the responses he received, the vast majority of the women responding expressed positive ideas regarding the effects of the surgery.[108] Among Burt's claims in the justification was that 91 percent of the women who responded to his questionnaire replied that their lives had improved postsurgery.[109]

In addition to the request for evidence supporting the effectiveness of love surgery, the July 1, 1979, letter from Leschansky also informed Burt he must use a special consent form to be signed by women before they underwent love surgery. The consent form appears largely derived from the county medical society's statement. It read:

Dear Patient:

The Executive Committee of the Medical Staff of St. Elizabeth Medical Center wishes to inform you that the "female coital area reconstruction" surgery you are about to undergo is:

1. Not documented by ordinary standards of scientific reporting and publication.
2. Not a generally accepted procedure.
3. As yet not duplicated by other investigators.
4. Detailed only in non-scientific literature.

You should be informed that the Executive Committee of the Medical Staff considers the aforementioned procedure an unproven, non-standard practice of gynecology.[110]

This consent form, unique to love surgery, was also unique compared to the standard consent form for medical or special procedures St. Elizabeth used around the same time. According to a form from 1976, the patient signing was told that they "had the legal right to determine the extent" of their medical care and were asked to read the form "carefully," and if they had any questions to "ask your physician before you sign this form." In addition, on this form was a statement directed at the physician, which read that it was their "legal responsibility it ensure that the patient is informed of and understands the nature of the procedure(s) to be performed as well as the inherent risks of all the procedure(s)."[111]

St. Elizabeth began requiring Burt to use this love surgery–specific consent form during a time when procedure-specific consent forms began to be used more often in the United States.[112] Meant to enable patients to exercise more autonomy in their decision making, there were still problems with such surgery-specific forms, problems illustrated by the one Burt was now required to use. According to a 1980 *New England Journal of Medicine* article by T. M. Grunder regarding the readability of surgical consent forms, the form more than likely would have failed the two requirements of a valid consent form: it did not contain necessary information regarding the surgery, such as the risks of the surgery, and it was not written in a manner that a patient could understand.[113] In this respect, though, this consent form was unremarkable; according to Grunder, most surgical consent forms at this time were unreadable, unless you were a physician.[114]

While Grunder perhaps would have seen the form as pretty standard in its relative uselessness in providing patients with information from which to make a decision regarding a surgery, the consent form also did not adhere to the law of Ohio regarding consent forms. In 1976, Ohio and a few other states began adopting laws that provided "that written consent to treatment will be presumed valid if it meets certain requirements," primarily that the consent form provided in general terms the nature and purpose of the proposed treatment, along with the risks, if any, of the proposed treatment. The law also necessitated that the form had to acknowledge that all questions about the treatment had been answered satisfactorily.[115] The specific consent form St. Elizabeth began requiring Burt to use in the summer of 1979 was meant to obtain an informed consent from women who were to undergo love surgery. The form, however, provided little information regarding the nature of the surgery, nor did it provide any information on possible risks or side effects or any information on alternative treatments. It is unclear not only what "female coital area reconstruction" surgery entails, but, just as if not more important, it is also unclear how a woman reading this form would know that an "unproven" and "non-standard" surgery meant its safety and efficacy were unknown—that the surgery was essentially novel or perhaps even experimental.

Finally, there is one more important thing to note about the hospital requiring Burt to use this special consent form: it was essentially a method of supervising his work, something seen as antithetical to a physician. As Freidson argued in his analysis of medical self-regulation, "to be granted freedom from supervision is a mark of being trusted, of being autonomous; in short of being professional."[116] The form, then, was a means to regulate Burt by essentially supervising him—and so it can also be seen as an additional indication that Burt was not seen as a trusted professional by his peers.

Burt began using the special consent form, printed on St. Elizabeth's letterhead, and also began to accumulate the information desired by the executive committee—the listing of cases.[117] In addition to this sequential listing of cases of women who had undergone love surgery over a period of four years, as demanded by the hospital, all women who were to undergo love surgery had to receive pre- and postoperative evaluations by a psychiatrist, something the executive committee at St. Elizabeth felt was another way of providing the women with information regarding the surgery before consenting to it. Burt, too, saw a benefit: recall that he had begun trying to accumulate evidence in support of the efficacy of his surgery as a therapy for female sexual dysfunction, seeking assistance from William Masters and working with Arthur Schramm. This insistence on the part of St. Elizabeth would provide him with further research to show the efficacy of his surgery, and he again asked Schramm, chief of psychiatry at St. Elizabeth, to help him with the pre- and postoperative evaluations.[118]

In 1979, Burt dropped his malpractice insurance and moved the majority of his assets into the name of his wife, Joan Burt. This left St. Elizabeth as the primary target for litigation if a woman sued James Burt. Although Burt, like many physicians, was not an employee of the hospital, this did not automatically mean St. Elizabeth was free from liability concerns regarding Burt's (or any other physicians') practice within their walls.[119] Presumably, attorneys for St. Elizabeth knew of his lack of malpractice insurance, and the desire to protect itself from a patient's malpractice lawsuit was possibly a further reason for insisting in July 1979 that Burt use a special consent form for love surgery.[120] Hospitals had recently become subjects of lawsuits, and the case that likely most alarmed hospitals was also the most notorious: John Nork, a physician practicing in Sacramento, California, admitted to performing, quite frequently poorly and while on drugs, unnecessary back surgeries on at least thirty-seven patients.[121] Mercy General Hospital, where Nork operated, had been held liable for his actions because it failed to implement a method of monitoring the quality of care provided by physicians operating within its walls. This decision, handed down in the mid-1970s, held the hospital liable for $1.7 million and worried American hospitals across the country.[122] *Nork* established a legal precedent for holding hospitals accountable for the actions of physicians who operated within their walls.

The available historical record ends with the tissue committee's work resulting in St. Elizabeth requiring the special consent form for love surgery and the request for follow-up data—both of which were and should be seen as a means to regulate Burt's practice. Because the available historical record ends here, however, it is not clear how the hospital monitored, and thus regulated, Burt after 1980. He remained a concern for the hospital, however, according to an unnamed former top official at St. Elizabeth, and he reportedly appeared repeatedly on the executive committee agenda during the 1980s. But the executive committee continued to feel that the case for reducing or revoking Burt's privileges was never strong enough, or at least not strong enough to outweigh the risks of revoking them. What the executive committee felt it needed to discipline Burt was for a patient to complain, and according to the unnamed official, Burt "had too many satisfied patients." St. Elizabeth, this anonymous hospital official told a journalist in 1989, "never got any complaints from patients."[123]

At least one patient, however, formally complained a few years prior to St. Elizabeth's decision to require Burt to use the special consent form. In September 1975, Nancy Houston gave birth to her first child, a girl, and Burt was her attending physician. Nancy and her husband Robert were elated when they learned they were pregnant, having tried for two years to conceive. They very much wanted to learn about natural childbirth, as Nancy Houston told Burt during their first visit with him. The Houstons were informed by one of Burt's nurses that Burt did not believe in natural childbirth, but Nancy Houston was "assured that it would be possible for me to have medication which would still allow me to be alert in the delivery room so that my husband and I could participate in the birth." The Houstons attended childbirth classes but became concerned over the medications Burt intended to give Nancy Houston, something they brought up with him. Burt "began quoting research regarding the dangers of natural childbirth," and the couple explained to him "that we wanted what was best for our baby and if medication was necessary, we would take it willingly," although they continued to emphasize their desire to participate in the birth and for Nancy Houston not to be heavily medicated. Burt gave them his assurance. However, when the time for the birth arrived, Burt prescribed a heavy dose of medication for Houston. In addition, she recalled having her legs strapped "in a wishbone position straight up in the air completely blocking my view of the mirror," meaning she could not see the birth. After learning she had a girl, the new mother fell asleep, and her husband later told her she snored through the seventy-minute repair done by Burt.[124]

Nancy Houston was so disturbed and angry, she wrote a letter to St. Elizabeth. In it, she noted how "after all the preparation and the anticipation at participating in the birth, [during] the best part—the delivery—I was rendered helpless." She described in her letter how she "felt like a chunk of meat being cut up not like a new mother giving birth to her first child." But while the birth was bad, she wrote, the "ultimate frustration" happened after the birth: Burt's "standard repair work." In her letter to St. Elizabeth, she wrote that while she realized the hospital

> is not able to control the techniques of an individual doctor, however, in our case where we were not informed such surgery would occur or told the consequences we feel the hospital has an obligation to make sure patients are not placed in such a position. When we discussed this with Dr. Burt, we got the impression he does not feel women need to be informed. Furthermore he feels he does not have the time to spend with patients explaining his procedures. For me ignorance of this surgery was the most

painful experience I have ever endured—emotionally and physically. My labor experience was beautiful, thanks to my supportive husband and the hospital staff but this so called routine repair was unbearable.[125]

Burt apparently told Houston she needed the surgery when she questioned him during her recovery in the hospital, but she later learned "from other medical sources" she had not needed it. "I am still not healed," she wrote, "and at times caring for myself and my baby has been painful and difficult." Houston's four-page letter to St. Elizabeth, written eight weeks after she gave birth to her daughter, was pointed in its praise for the nurses who took care of her, one of whom was Nancy Goodman. But the polite, well-worded letter made no effort to mask her anger at Burt's performing his "standard repair work": "It is my deepest hope," she wrote, "that no other couple have to endure what my husband and I experienced with Dr. Burt."[126]

Chapter 5

Investigating the Medical Profession in Ohio, 1980–1986

Because of their membership in a professional community, doctors are required to uphold community standards and stop transgressions of those standards. But physicians in the Burt case sometimes later complained they were unable to act because no patient complained. John H. Boyles Jr., who was president of the Montgomery County Medical Society in 1982, recalled receiving no patient complaints against Burt. As Boyles later told a journalist, a physician with a long history of bad surgical outcomes, malpractice suits, a felony conviction, or drug or alcohol abuse was easier to discipline. But it was "extremely difficult and dangerous from a legal point of view to police a doctor whose patients hold him in reverence and believe he has no history of bad results," Boyles said.[1]

There are two interesting points regarding medical regulation one can pull from Boyles's statement, a statement he made during the height of the Burt scandal in the late 1980s. First is his assertion that patients held Burt "in reverence"; Nancy Houston's letter to St. Elizabeth attests to the existence of at least one patient who did not revere Burt. What, how, or even whether Houston's letter was addressed by St. Elizabeth is not clear from the available historical record. But regardless of how the hospital administration did, or did not, respond to her letter concerning Burt, Boyles's comment further asserts that physicians were only able to regulate one of their own if patients initiated the process—if patients raised an objection to something done by the offending physician. Such a suggestion seems to move the responsibility of initiating action from the physician to the patient. But while patients are among the actors involved in the regulation of medicine, professionally physicians were (and are) required to regulate their own—and most important, the only entity with any legal power to regulate physicians was (and is) the state medical board, dominated by physicians.

Recall that Freidson noted in his examination of the manner in which physicians regulate themselves the assumption that when a really "difficult or dangerous" physician was in their midst—one with, as Boyles suggested, a "long history of bad surgical outcomes, malpractice suits, a felony conviction, or drug or alcohol abuse"—those physicians would be easier to stop. But even if Burt had a felony conviction or a history of drug or alcohol abuse, would the State Medical Board of Ohio—the only power with the authority to suspend, limit, or revoke a physician's license to practice—have acted? According to two exposés by the Cleveland *Plain Dealer* in the 1980s, the answer to that question is: probably not.

In an investigation into the state medical board published in 1980, the Cleveland *Plain Dealer* found that the state board "was doing very little in the way of public protection" by disciplining doctors because of a lack of funds and few laws with which to curb errant doctors from practicing.[2] In response to the *Plain Dealer* exposé, the legislature proposed a law to make the medical board investigate malpractice claims as a means of weeding out those doctors. The board, however, was not happy about it, concerned, as board president Henry Cramblett stated in May 1980, that there "were many malpractice lawsuits that are not legitimate" and that malpractice did not necessarily mean "bad medical practice."[3]

Before 1965, state boards lacked the legal ability to discipline physicians for incompetence. This, however, changed in the 1970s for several reasons. In part, the change resulted from a growth in malpractice lawsuits against physicians and the legal changes that occurred at the state level to address this crisis, changes that included empowering state medical boards with more disciplinary authority over medical practice. In part, the change occurred as a result of the increased role the federal government now played in health care funding with the advent of Medicare and Medicaid in the 1960s. And in part, the change was a result of consumers' dissatisfaction with the medical profession's neglect to discipline doctors in any formal way. During the 1970s through the 1990s, state medical boards grew; while previously they had been small in scale, they became large and bureaucratic, thus able to handle, in principle, more investigations of misconduct and malpractice by physicians. During the early 1980s, however, the disciplinary actions of state medical boards against physicians had hardly increased. Between 1969 and 1978, state medical boards averaged 1.21 actions a year per 1,000 physicians; in 1981, the average grew only slightly to

1.53 actions per 1,000 physicians and then fell slightly to 1.39 actions per 1,000 physicians in 1984.[4]

What happened in Ohio reflected this trend. Five years after its first exposé of the state medical society, the *Plain Dealer* followed up in April 1985 when the newspaper published another investigative report called "Doctoring the Truth." The series began above the fold of the Sunday April 7 paper, with the fear-inducing introduction sentence: "they sell drugs, they steal, they rape and they kill." Based on six months of investigation, the *Plain Dealer* labeled the doctors they uncovered as "virtually immune from prosecution" and the "dregs of Ohio's medical community." According to the article's author, reporter Gary Webb, the "only thing that stood between you and them is the State Medical Board," and that is "little comfort."[5]

According to Webb, the job of the medical board was to "protect the public from that minority of physicians who abuse their licenses and their positions of trust and from those too incompetent to treat patients." However, Webb wrote, the board "has compiled an appalling record of protecting the reputations and livelihoods of the state's medical outlaws." The investigation found board officials used secret hearings to hide many physicians' crimes from the public, hearings not even all board members knew about because "board members were advised by the board administrator and board lawyers not to attend and not to examine the records." Since 1975, the board had conducted almost 1,100 secret hearings but only 308 public ones, and the board refused to release information about the closed hearings.[6] Secret board meetings were hardly unique to Ohio; as sociologist Ruth Horowitz argued, "having assumed the right to define the proper doctor-patient" in the earlier part of the twentieth century, medical boards in the second half of the century largely "shunned publicity and kept their procedures closed to the public" to reinforce the idea that only physicians could regulate themselves.[7]

According to Webb, "hundreds of pages of secret board records show medical board officials have ignored crimes including drug abuse, illegal processing of drug documents and sexual abuse of patients." The board allowed doctors convicted of a felony—including drug trafficking, insurance fraud, theft, sexual assault, and drug abuse—to "remain in practice with little more than a lecture." As the *Plain Dealer* article noted, although state law required the board to suspend the license of a doctor under drug or alcohol treatment, the board rarely did so, allowing the physician to keep practicing—even performing surgery. The board made little effort to "police the profession for incompetent or negligent practitioners," and the board rarely looked into malpractice claims or complaints; even when a physician repeatedly violated the law, the board seemed "loath to pull a license" because board members worried the physician would be unable to earn a living, Webb wrote.[8] This concern of clinicians about the livelihood of their peers reiterated what Freidson found in his sociological study a decade and a half earlier: the suspension of a medical license was "an activity that, in their minds, ruins the man's [sic] life."[9]

Under a 1982 law, the medical board was mandated to publish quarterly a list of all closed investigative cases and a reason why the board closed the cases. But six months before the bill became law, the board met to decide how to work around the law, ultimately concluding they would not close cases but rather keep them open as "pending," thus circumventing disclosure. Before the law went into effect, the board had 94 pending cases, but after the law, that number jumped to 374, and nearly all of those cases had been pending for two to five years. Moreover, not even all members of the board had permission to see the pending cases or the evidence within them. A former attorney for the board told Webb, "For all intent, you've got two medical boards in the state of Ohio." There was the board with members who met a few hours a month and "then you've got the subterranean board" run by the top administrators of the board, the former board attorney informed Webb. Details of the secret meetings remained closed to many board members, and although in December 1984 the Plain Dealer filed suit to make the minutes of the hearings public, the board fought the newspaper's lawsuit.[10]

As sociologist Horowitz noted, the failure of medical boards to discipline physicians makes "great local headlines," for "popular media stories played up disciplinary failures" by medical boards, something Webb's series of articles certainly did.[11] Many of the examples Webb used concerned doctors not disciplined by the state medical board for abusing drugs. Physician Edward Seybold admitted to the board he had "excessively used controlled substances" and that he had also prescribed drugs not medically needed for his wife and family. In 1981, physician Robert Finch surrendered his medical license to keep the Dayton police from prosecuting him on drug charges. Finch stood accused of supplying amphetamines to drug addicts. However, the board returned his medical license to him three months after he surrendered it, and in May 1982, his federal drug license was reinstated. The Plain Dealer investigation also found that if one called and asked the state board for information about a doctor—say whether the physician had a drug or alcohol problem, was an ex-convict, or had a history of mental health problems—the information it received, if it received any information at all, would be false. When reporters—who did not identify themselves as such—called the medical board for information on physicians

Finch and Seybold, the journalists were told that Seybold was "ok" and that regarding Finch, "there was no derogatory information."[12]

According to Webb's *Plain Dealer* story, the medical board and the Ohio State Medical Association "collaborated to keep the public in the dark about physicians who are addicted to drugs or alcohol, in apparent violation of both the Controlled Substances Act and the Medical Practice Act." The newspaper gave examples of doctors slipping into the pharmacy of the hospital to take paregoric, an opium-based medicine; of physicians who took morphine and methadone while working; and, in one case, of a physician being addicted to Percodan and Demerol and also providing what turned out to be lethal amounts of the antidepressant Elavil to a girlfriend.[13] The board, according to the *Plain Dealer*, largely turned a blind eye to the drug abuses of physicians, placing the rehabilitation of physicians, as Webb wrote, "above the safety of the public." Board members, Webb continued, "have publicly said that removing such doctors from practice would jeopardize their 'recovery' by exposing their addiction to the public and interfering with their income and self-esteem." But months before the *Plain Dealer* stories broke, Carol Rolfes, one of two nondoctors on the board, recalled angrily reminding "her fellow board members that the board existed 'to protect the public, not to worry about a doctor's financial solvency.'"[14]

The police were also upset about the board's lack of cooperation with drug-abusing and drug-selling doctors. Philip Messer and Robert Clemmer, police detectives from Dayton and Mansfield, detailed to Webb their efforts to curb the flow of pharmaceutical drugs onto the streets. The two cities identified eight doctors responsible for a staggering 80 percent of the drugs sold on the streets of their cities and, after adding two more to the list, managed to convict half of them on drug felony charges. One of the doctors, a surgeon in Dayton, sold the powerful prescription drug Dilaudid to a prostitute he frequented. When Messer and Clemmer confronted this doctor, he denied the charge but then handed the detectives an envelope with $1,000 in it. In 1981, the doctor was indicted on one count of bribery and three counts of writing false prescriptions. The doctor pled guilty to bribery and then received a suspended jail sentence and had the drug charges dropped. The medical board put him on probation. Another doctor involved with the same prostitute "admitted to the board in a secret hearing that he had been giving the prostitute and her friends addictive drugs in exchange for sex," and the board allowed him to voluntarily give up his license. Things were little better with the other doctors on Messer's and Clemmer's list. The detectives gave their list to the state medical board, but the board allowed one Mansfield doctor to retire and two of the Dayton doctors to voluntarily surrender their licenses. Frustrated, Messer told Webb that the "state medical board is a big waste of the taxpayer's money," and Clemmer added, "they're worthless."[15]

But it was not just an illicit use of drugs, or the exchange of drugs for sex, for which a physician could be seen as practicing poor medical judgment; there was also the specter of poor surgical outcomes. Six fellow orthopedic surgeons observed Frederick Elder Jr., an orthopedic surgeon in Columbus, while he performed surgery and found that his spinal surgeries "posed a 'definite hazard of serious injury to patients.'" Others observed that Elder often became confused and disoriented during surgery, frequently lengthening the surgeries and thereby increasing the danger to the patient. Moreover, in just six months of 1979, more than half of his spinal surgery patients at one hospital suffered life-threatening complications from surgeries found to have been unwarranted, and another hospital, after conducting an internal audit, discovered that over the course of two years, 85 percent of Elder's patients suffered "abnormal or unusual complications." One woman, a fifty-eight-year-old waitress who sued Elder, said when she complained to Elder that following his operation on her hand it had become useless, he told her to stop acting like a crybaby. Following internal audits, Elder had his surgical privileges either revoked or suspended by three hospitals in Columbus, and he was sued for malpractice by former patients, all public information. Among the many faults of the board found by the *Plain Dealer* was the board's failure to record in a doctor's files if a hospital had revoked or suspended privilege or any information regarding malpractice claims against them.[16]

When asked, state medical board administrator William Lee told the *Plain Dealer* that a lack of resources was the reason the board failed to go after doctors like Elder, saying his staff of six investigators was inadequate. However, the board had received consistent budget increases over the previous decade, and it seemed to find the resources to "dig up evidence against nurse-midwives and physician's assistants, health food stores, chiropractors, acupuncturists, masseuses, manicurists, and others suspected of practicing medicine without a license," wrote Webb.[17] According to Carl Ameringer, when physicians dominated health care, "organized medicine set the agenda," here meaning state medical boards most commonly prosecuted physicians who "ventured outside the professional mainstream—abortionists, drug addicts, and 'unorthodox' providers" such as an acupuncturist or massage therapist. The agenda began to shift in the 1980s and 1990s when state medical boards received more money to hire more staff and became more accountable to "the media, consumers, insurers, government bureaucrats, and politicians." Boards then began to focus more on "incompetent practitioners because states linked medical malpractice with lack of physician discipline," Ameringer wrote.[18]

According to the *Plain Dealer* story, Ohio, unlike most of the states at the time, did not view "gross negligence, professional incompetence or adverse malpractice judgments as grounds for disciplinary action." Although as part of a national effort to curb the rising expenses of malpractice insurance, the AMA had recently recommended that state boards engage more actively in finding and disciplining incompetent physicians, Ohio had apparently made little effort to do so. As Webb wrote, according to former investigators with the state board with whom he spoke, "the board's investigators said they were rarely instructed to investigate malpractice judgments or complaints of poor medical practice." Investigators spent most of their time looking after doctors who needed drug or alcohol treatment or on cases where doctors were overprescribing, former investigator Michael Falleur told Webb. Doctors who were "plain old bad doctors, we didn't have time for," according to Falleur. He further noted that instead of investigating cases of bad doctors, the board turned them over to the local medical societies, which had no power over a doctor's medical license. According to Webb, of the "207 cases of substandard care the medical board has dropped since 1982, only 12% were dropped because they were groundless or lacked sufficient evidence of a violation. Eighty percent of the cases were closed by passing them on to medical societies or other organizations." Although board administrator Lee told Webb the board acted on any serious allegations against a doctor, the *Plain Dealer* investigation found this to be inaccurate.[19]

In two more shocking examples of the board's lack of disciplinary action against doctors, the board did not act to stop podiatrist Donald Pritt from operating, although in 1977, the board began receiving complaints about him. Pritt was accused of performing "unusual and excessive" surgeries in his office, resulting in "foot deformities, secondary infections, and, for one elderly patient, gangrene." Pritt, a West Virginia doctor with an office in Ohio, had his license revoked by West Virginia in 1983, ending a process that began in 1979 when that board filed charges against him. As of April 1985, when the *Plain Dealer* series ran, he could still practice in Ohio. In another case, the board began receiving complaints about Cincinnati gynecologist Meyer Fleischman in 1979, but, although investigators who looked at his medical office found it to be "unsanitary," with patient records being kept on "a few scraps of paper rolled up with a rubber band and stored in a broom closet," and that in 1984 a woman told the board, "he had given her a vaginal examination with dirty instruments," the board had not acted, according to the *Plain Dealer*.[20]

Gary Webb found only one case, that of George Gotsis, where the board cited a physician with a pattern of incompetence or negligence, but it took the board decades to do so. Jonathan Rosenbaum, a county prosecutor who worked to stop

Gotsis from practicing medicine, told Webb, "I'll give you an idea of how long it took the board to do something about George Gotsis, my father was president of the Lorain County Medical Society, and I remember him complaining about Gotsis." Jonathan Rosenbaum was nine or ten at the time. Records of Gotsis performing unnecessary surgery dated back to the 1960s; in 1973, the community hospital removed him from the staff, labeling his professional conduct as "criminal"; colleagues called Gotsis "an absolute disaster as a surgeon," a doctor who showed "contempt for the patient," saying he was careless and inept. But it was not until 1979, six years later, that the state board took any action, and, following an investigation by his malpractice insurance company Medical Mutual into his insurance claims, the board found that his infection rate was very high, with thirty of his patients having suffered "severe post-operative infections in one six-month period," infections attributed to "poor surgical technique and unsanitary operating conditions." Gotsis blamed the infections on his patients—whom he labeled as "alcoholics, drug addicts, prostitutes and psychotics"—for their inability to clean themselves. The board acted against Gotsis, although Medical Mutual officials said the board only acted because they provided the board with a fully documented case and pressured them to act against Gotsis. The board ordered Gotsis's license to be revoked, but this decision came three years after the board started looking into Gotsis's record, and Gotsis had been operating during the interim. By the time the board acted, it was moot: Gotsis was sent to jail in February 1983 for selling drugs to an undercover police officer and had voluntarily given up his license. A Medical Mutual official was quoted as saying the board's response to Gotsis was so discouraging, one did not even want to work to bring to their attention other cases. According to this unnamed official, it was a fallacy that in Ohio, "the medical board protects the public."[21]

Sociologist Horowitz, in her examination of medical regulation, found that when medical boards did discipline a fellow physician, it was "not so much on account of their incompetence as on the grounds of deficient moral character."[22] Professional medical associations in the 1970s and 1980s continued to support professional control of medical boards, defending the right to self-regulate because nonphysicians lacked the expertise to regulate doctors. But, as Horowitz also noted, although doctors "are trained to make an expert call in cases involving technical medical issues," this does not mean they can also "claim particular expertise to pass judgment on a problem physician's character or to assess the balance of anticipated and unanticipated consequences that a particular board holding will set in motion."[23]

One reason the board failed to act against doctors was that many members of the board never learned about them. Ohio, unlike several other states in the 1980s, did not require insurance companies or physicians to report to the medical board when they lost or settled a malpractice case.[24] Another reason was fear of a lawsuit. Michael Falleur, the former attorney investigator for the board, told Webb, "All you had to do was say the word 'lawsuit' and you'd see nine doctors grab their throats because they hated to see their names on lawsuits." According to Falleur, doctors on the board worried about their "annuities and the Cadillacs going out the window" and cringed "when they thought they were going to get sued." Although the board could be tough when it wanted to be—Webb reported that in October 1983, it suspended a $260-a-week clerical worker for fifteen days without pay for showing up repeatedly a few minutes late, an action Webb labeled "one of the stiffer disciplinary actions the board has ever taken"—the fear of lawsuits from other doctors was a major cause for inaction by the board against its peers. As Webb outlined, two months before the board suspended the clerical worker's salary, it had heard the case of a Dayton psychiatrist, Oreste T. Chiaffitelli. Chiaffitelli, who had been convicted of a drug felony and who was an admitted drug addict, appealed to the board for the return of his medical license, which he had voluntarily surrendered only months earlier. Chiaffitelli was examined, at the board's request, by another psychiatrist, who reported to the board that Chiaffitelli blamed his felony conviction on having seen "too many black welfare patients" and on "abusing amphetamines for years"; moreover, the doctor who examined him noted that Chiaffitelli "lacked the most rudimentary knowledge of psychotherapy" and had tried to bribe him for a good report. Nonetheless, although the board received the report on Chiaffitelli, it voted unanimously to reinstate his medical license, under threat of a lawsuit if it did not.[25]

The *Plain Dealer* articles in the spring of 1985 detailing the failure of the board to protect Ohioans from doctors like Chiaffitelli had some effect, at least initially. On the Thursday after the series began, the medical board asked for the resignation of William Lee, the board's longtime administrator; a week later, Lee resigned.[26] A few days into the *Plain Dealer* exposé, Ohio governor Richard Celeste sent a sharply worded letter to the medical board, saying he must "share with you my dismay and outrage at many of the specific incidents described in this recent series of articles."[27] On April 17, Ohio state representatives announced the formation of a special Ohio House subcommittee to investigate the state medical board, an investigation representative John Thompson Jr. promised would begin "in the not-too-distant future."[28] Thompson, a Democrat from Cleveland, had his committee meet for the first time less than a month later and began by hearing from acting medical board administrator Ray Bumgarner, who promised the committee the board's full cooperation with its investigation. In response to a question about the *Plain Dealer* series, Bumgarner replied that there were some inaccuracies in the articles but, when pressed, could not name any specifically.[29]

In subsequent meetings, lawmakers expressed their outrage at the medical board, with one state representative saying that he "could not believe that an institution in this state has done such a lousy job."[30] Others who testified to the subcommittee also expressed their dismay and frustration with the medical board's inaction. Said one witness, a former family practitioner who left the field to work in health promotion for businesses, having the majority of members of the board be other physicians was "like letting the fox guard the henhouse."[31] Herman Abromowitz, president of the Ohio State Medical Association, presented a resolution in June to the committee, one that sought stronger enforcement policies. The medical association recommended that the board strengthen its disciplinary measures by making it mandatory to revoke a medical license if a physician were convicted of a drug felony unrelated to his own drug use; beginning the process of disciplinary actions against doctors convicted of felonies when they were convicted, not after their appeals ended, as was the current practice; use of administrative law judges as hearing officers for disciplinary hearings instead of medical board members; mandated reporting of felony convictions of physicians to the board and hospitals to report to the board when a physician had lost staff privileges; and finally, reorganizing the investigation process of the board and increasing funding to raise the number of people investigating.[32]

But while the special subcommittee met, the *Plain Dealer* reported on June 26, 1985, that the medical board had "dramatically stepped up its use of secret disciplinary hearings," as indicated by internal board records. So while the medical board had been telling Thompson's committee they were making changes in the way they operated, the board seemed to be doing more of the same. When told of the increase in secret hearings, state representative Thompson was astounded. "You've got to be kidding. I had no idea," he told Webb. "It was my understanding that they wouldn't be holding any more of those . . . that during the investigation they would cease and desist." Officials from the medical board defended their actions, saying that while there was no definitive reason for their holding the secret hearings, it was largely due to a backlog of cases. The number of secret hearings, called "informal conferences" by the board, had been on the decline in the months leading up to the *Plain Dealer* series, but following publication, the number of the hearings "skyrocketed," according to the newspaper. On April 29, for example, the board held seven such hearings, and on May 7, the board held six, and all but one of them concerned doctors allegedly abusing, or incorrectly prescribing, drugs. "We're not making deals behind closed doors, I can assure you of that," an official with the board told Webb.[33]

The state house special subcommittee continued to meet through the summer. In August, the state medical board began overhauling its process of disciplining doctors, proposing sentencing guidelines and rules about administrative hearings.[34] In December, the special house subcommittee issued its report to the full Ohio House, blasting the medical board for not protecting the public from dangerous doctors and issuing recommendations for the board to take. Under the proposed legislation, hospitals and medical societies would be required to report suspensions, revocations, or reductions of doctors; insurance companies would be required to report all malpractice claims, settlements, and judgments; and the board would have the power to suspend a doctor's license before a formal hearing if the board felt there was a danger to the public.[35] Additionally, they proposed that reports to the medical board would be public information. But the medical board reform bill that came before the legislature in March 1986 was not nearly as strong. Tweaked after weeks of private meetings with lobbyists for Ohio's medical and hospital associations, amendments were added that kept much of the information about doctors secret. The bill still required hospitals, medical societies, and medical insurance companies to inform the board of any disciplinary actions and malpractice judgments, but medical and hospital lobbyists succeeded in adding amendments that kept these reports confidential.[36] The bill, as amended, passed the Ohio House 95–0 and the Senate 30–0.[37]

The law, however, proved futile when it came to being able to discipline James Burt. Even with the added investigatory powers of the board and the mandatory (if still secret) reporting of disciplinary actions and malpractice judgments, the medical board's inability to end the practice of Burt was, in effect, as though the board had changed little from its practices of the 1970s.

Janet Phillips, 1981–1984

Burt's office notes regarding a phone call made by Janet Phillips on November 21, 1981—about three weeks after her surgery—stated that Phillips felt "great." A little over a month later, Phillips called again, this time concerned about blood following intercourse, and in early January 1982, Burt's notes said the bleeding continued after sex, although her initial discomfort during sex had begun to lessen. In early February, Burt's case notes regarding Phillips indicated she had some incontinence, but he spent much more time discussing her ability to have sex without bleeding, enjoy sex more, and that she was "responding sexually much better and had noted her personality [was] better." In his notes, Burt wrote that other people also found her personality to have improved. But by March 1982, he noted "the patient states consciously that she is depressed" and that small amounts of urine were being trapped in her vagina after she went to the bathroom, which resulted in a "very minimal" amount of moisture, although enough to "moisten the underclothes a little." Burt wrote he provided the "usual advice" following his love surgery: to "participate more and more as sex is becoming more and more pleasurable and in spite of the intensity of clitoral feeling to get used to the intensity."[1]

By the summer of 1982, Burt's notes indicate his surgery had worked, and sex was more pleasurable for Phillips, although "there are some sexual positions where there is some discomfort." However, Burt wrote in April 1983 that Phillips had a "very low grade, low intensity bladder and vaginal area discomfort and sometimes voids with relatively sizable amounts of urine and sometimes has lesser amounts of feeling of post voiding urgency sometimes." He diagnosed her with fungus vulvovaginitis (inflammation of both the vulva and the vagina) and cystitis (urinary inflammation) that month and treated her for the conditions, to which he reported she responded to, and by September was "asymptomatic and in good health."[2] But in April 1984, Burt noted Phillips described to him "what could be some vaginal trapping of urine, deflected from the inner lips and occasional urgency incontinence which keeps to a lesser frequency by not letting the bladder get overly full." He wrote that if the issue continued, he "might have to take the perineum down a bit."[3] Phillips later recalled Burt assured her the complications she developed after her surgery were "normal" and "all my problems were due to bladder complications that occurred during my [hysterectomy] surgery."[4]

Although Phillips and Burt later disagreed on many aspects of her care, condition, and symptoms while he was her physician, both agreed she stopped going to him in 1984. But Phillips, perhaps still scared about Burt's warning another physician could tear her and make her bleed, possibly bleed to death, did not go to another gynecologist for a year. However, she was seeing chiropractor Carol Loechinger for lower back pain stemming from repeated kidney infections as a result of her surgery. Loechinger advised Phillips to see a gynecologist.[5] In late 1985, Phillips finally told her fears to Loechinger about Burt's warning that she could bleed to death, and Loechinger made an appointment for Phillips with gynecologist Michael Clark, but, scared, Phillips did not keep the appointment. When Loechinger learned Phillips had failed to see Clark, she made another appointment for her patient and told Phillips if she did not go, Loechinger would take Phillips to the gynecologist herself. Phillips kept the second appointment.[6] Phillips later recalled she finally agreed to see Clark when "the pain was so bad that I *could not* stand it anymore."[7]

When Phillips saw Clark, she was suffering from urinary stress incontinence, was voiding into her vagina, and often had to stand up in order for the urine to leave her body. After meeting with Clark, Phillips decided to let him examine her, an examination that was painful for Phillips and somewhat difficult for Clark to conduct. It was after this exam in December 1985 when Phillips first learned the extent of her hysterectomy. Clark informed Phillips her clitoris had been circumcised and there was a good deal of scar tissue in the clitoral area, that her labia had been removed, and that her urine was collecting in a little pouch that resulted from the operation. He also told Phillips her vagina had been redirected.[8] To help her better understand what had been done to her, Clark drew pictures of typical female genitalia and then contrasted these drawings with her genitals.[9] Years later, Phillips recounted how she heard the gynecologist she saw in 1985 (presumably Clark) say, as she cried in his office, he did not "know where to begin with this mess."[10]

The day after he examined Phillips, Clark reportedly wrote to Loechinger, thanking her for "having the confidence in me to participate in the care of this very kind patient" and telling her "a great deal of discussion would have to take place before we attempt any type of surgical correction" on Phillips.[11] Phillips later recalled it was then she knew the hysterectomy "was not the cause of all my problems," as Burt had repeatedly told her, and she "would never be the same again." It was this appointment with Clark when Phillips became aware of all that happened to her body "and that Dr. Burt had lied to me about my bladder and lots of other things" and, moreover, that "Dr. James Burt had *not* told the truth about why I *should not* see another doctor." It was then when Phillips decided to contact an attorney.[12]

Chapter 6

Turn on Your Radio for the Love Surgeon, 1978–1988

Dayton is known for having survived two natural disasters in the twentieth century. The first was in March 1913, when the rain swelled the Miami River to a record crest of 44 feet, resulting in Main Street lying 20 feet below water and people camping out on rooftops.[1] The second occurred in January 1978. On January 17, more than a foot of snow fell on the city, and a few days later, an additional 15 inches came down on Dayton within thirty-six hours. On January 25, a blizzard blowing winds of nearly 70 miles per hour ripped across the city, causing 23,000 people to lose electricity.[2] Snowdrifts reached 25 feet high.[3] That winter reached record-low temperatures, and the loss of electricity to thousands resulted in the closing of schools, stores, and businesses.[4]

During that brutal January, health insurance companies stopped paying for love surgery. At first it was just Blue Shield, but Metropolitan Life Insurance soon followed, and both companies cited as their reason the opinion that the operation in question was experimental, unproven, and medically unfounded—language found in the county medical society's statement and later that year in the special consent form required by St. Elizabeth. When Burt learned that the insurance companies would no longer pay, the news "extremely distressed" him.[5] He tried to make the companies resume paying for love surgery, first by filing a complaint with the Ohio Civil Rights Commission, claiming as his wife, Joan Burt, had that paying for love surgery was a matter of women receiving equal medical treatment as men. When that got him nowhere, he filed a lawsuit calling the insurance companies' actions a restraint of trade and a breach of contract.[6] In the suit, Burt contended that he had lost at least $3 million because the companies had not paid him.[7] The court granted the insurance companies motion for summary judgment, and Burt's cases against them were dismissed in 1984.[8]

By the late 1970s, then, insurance no longer covered love surgery as a non-elective medical procedure. The lack of insurance coverage must have been a financial blow to Burt. Rumors of Joan and James Burt's debts began to be more than speculation. In late September 1980, a local art gallery sued the couple for not paying for a bronze sculpture and two paintings delivered to the Burt home in January 1979. The Burts contended that the pieces were left at their home on an approval basis; the gallery contended, and the court agreed, that the Burts needed to pay the gallery $6,972.50, with interest, for the art.[9]

In 1981, James Burt filed for bankruptcy, but it was dismissed.[10] Yet although the Burts' economic situation had apparently begun to unravel, James Burt continued to promote his surgery. He reportedly taught love surgery to several doctors during the early 1980s.[11] And starting on Wednesday, October 22, 1980, Burt appeared on a local radio show every other Wednesday for an hour as the "Love Doctor." The show aired at 11:30 a.m., taking listeners' calls on "sex, sexual and gynecological problems, as well as 'his work in female reconstructive surgery and its effects on sexual performance, marriage, and self-concept.'" Writing a review of the upcoming show for the *Dayton Journal Herald*, commentator Bob Schumacher noted that "it should make for provocative talk radio," adding "not the least of the reasons is the controversy over Burt and his surgical techniques." As Schumacher stressed, "Burt's work is extremely controversial, and many gynecologists question if it is proper to use the surgery for the purposes Burt espouses," citing the Montgomery County Medical Society's labeling of love surgery as "non-standard." Burt, however, seemingly embraced this label when speaking to Schumacher, saying, "'Gynecology is deficient in covering the area of problems related to a woman's vagina,'" a deficiency he was trying to address by raising the standards. Schumacher interviewed two local physicians, who asked that their names not be used, regarding Burt and love surgery. One of them said Burt had not developed a new surgery but had rather modified "some acceptable surgery and applied it in a very controversial way." Schumacher ended with a quotation from the radio station program director, who said the station wanted Burt to talk about sexual problems in general. "We are not endorsing this surgery," Steve Hall, the program director said, "but then again we are not condemning his surgery."[12]

In his comments to Schumacher, Burt stressed that his book, *Surgery of Love*, had been "very much misinterpreted by causal readers" and that it was "'way behind the times' with regard to his research." Burt told Schumacher that he and Arthur Schramm had been collaborating for several years to, as

Schumacher wrote, "learn if a couple's non-sexual personality and marital problems can be improved by surgery which improves sexual function." According to Burt, "we are beginning to be able to show . . . that wherein a mechanical happening—surgery—has enhanced intercourse response."[13]

Continuing in his efforts to publish the results of his surgery, Burt with Schramm wrote several articles about love surgery, including "Change in Structure of Psyche Resulting from Plastic Surgical Redirection Extension of Vagina" and "The Restructuring of Personality Resulting from Redirection Extension Vulvo-vaginoplasty in Women with Coitally Pathologic Pelvic Anatomy," but neither of these was apparently published.[14] However, in 1983, Burt finally published an article about love surgery in a professional, peer-reviewed journal, albeit one not published in the United States: a Finnish medical journal published his and Schramm's research on the positive effects of love surgery. Calling the surgery vulvo-vaginoplasty, Burt's and Schramm's article began by noting that "male coital dysfunction" was "generally recognized as often being primarily anatomic in etiology and amenable to surgery."[15] So too, they argued, was female coital dysfunction primarily a physiologic condition, "with personality and marital dysfunction then being secondary to the anatomic defects."[16] Although unclear whether they felt men also had these as secondary defects, what was clear was that they felt surgery provided women with an increased ability to orgasm during heterosexual, penetrative sex.

Burt and Schramm indicated that the patient material in the report came from Burt's thirty-two years of medical practice, and they noted that most of the women in the study "would not satisfy the usual criteria for candidacy for standard sex therapy." The women, Burt and Schramm wrote, were nearly all reluctant and embarrassed to discuss their sexual problems, although once they finally spoke about their sexual dysfunction, sometimes "after much time," the women all felt "relief" at having done so. The two men further noted that "all patients were informed in detail about the therapeutic options available" and, for "legal reasons," all of the women were "required to read and sign a special informed consent" document that contained, according to Burt and Schramm, "a strong negative placebo influence."[17] Here the two men are, presumably, referring to the consent form St. Elizabeth mandated Burt use.

Burt and Schramm outlined the details of Burt's vulvo-vaginoplasty, including the excision of the clitoral hood, which Burt "excised to prevent retraction of the glans under the clitoral hood during high levels of sexual tension." They concluded that the women received positive benefits from love surgery based on evidence from three studies they conducted: the first study was based on the questionnaire they developed in the 1970s and mailed to 209 patients Burt had operated upon between 1976 and 1979, the second study involved looking at the overall results of 100 patients Burt had operated upon beginning in 1977, and the third study was, according to Burt and Schramm, a "prospective study of personality structure change caused by surgery." The last study was the only one that began after 1979, when the consent form was required and when St. Elizabeth asked for documentation of the safety and efficacy of the surgery.[18]

Burt and Schramm found that the "effects of the surgery on structure of the psyche and pair bonding capacity have been superior to that which could have been expected from traditional psychotherapy." They further reported that prior to love surgery, 80 percent of the women "needed moderate or great amounts of effort in prolonged foreplay and/or coitus to achieve maximum response," something they estimated 20 percent of the husbands failed to provide, while after the surgery just over 47 percent of the women "needed very little effort" to reach orgasm. Seventy-five percent of the women reported an increase in the sensitivity of their clitoris, just over 80 percent stated they felt more sexually aroused during intercourse, and 80 percent indicated their ability to reach orgasm with intercourse had increased to a degree important to them. After surgery, Burt and Schramm also reported that women lied less to their husbands about whether they had indeed reached orgasm, couples had sex more often, and women reported gaining an "increased emotional satisfaction with coitus." According to Burt and Schramm, women increased their sexual assertiveness and men increased their attentiveness "romantically and sexually" to their wives' nonsexual needs. But in addition to the increased sexual satisfaction of both the women and the men following love surgery, Burt and Schramm reported that the surgery had an additional benefit: it reduced marital violence. According to their article, nearly 27 percent of those who participated reported "wife beating" before the surgery; after the surgery, Burt and Schramm claimed there was a 100 percent decrease.[19]

After the article's publication, Burt began telling his patients the special consent form was incorrect: love surgery had indeed been published and documented in a medical journal, meeting the ordinary standards of medical reporting. But although the publication of this article undoubtedly gave him some vindication, Burt began to cut back on performing love surgery. He may have been prompted to do so because of four lawsuits filed against him between 1985 and 1986.[20] Moreover, sometime in 1986, Good Samaritan Hospital and Health Center in Dayton dropped Burt from their courtesy staff because he did not meet that hospital's minimum standards of malpractice insurance coverage. Kettering Medical Center had already rescinded Burt's courtesy staff privileges earlier in 1986.[21] Additionally, he may have been under pressure to stop by a requirement that physicians operating at St. Elizabeth now had to carry malpractice insurance. The lawsuits, together with his lack of malpractice insurance, may have pressured Burt to quit performing love surgery altogether. In addition, there may have been a patient complaint to St. Elizabeth regarding love surgery, a complaint that prompted the executive committee to once again reconsider his hospital privileges, although no action was taken. Physician Walter Keyes, a member of the executive committee at the hospital from 1982 to 1988, recalled Burt performing fewer and fewer love surgeries during that time, perhaps only five, and it was decided that love surgery "seemed to be dying a natural death," he stated.[22] In January 1987, Burt apparently completely stopped performing the surgery he had worked for years to perfect and to promote.[23]

Two months after Burt stopped performing love surgery, the State Medical Board of Ohio would later claim it received its first complaint against him. The complaint did not come from a physician, a nurse, or a patient but rather from then-state congressman and later U.S. representative, David Hobson.[24] Carol Rolfes, a member of the state medical board, said the board did not hear about Burt from physicians in Dayton or from the local hospitals; instead, Rolfes said, "It was a senator who finally brought it to our attention." Hobson apparently was prompted to write to the state medical board after he learned about the surgery from a constituent. This person's sister had undergone love surgery and had later gone to a physician in California who, Hobson recalled, had said to her, "My God, who did this to you?" The constituent asked Hobson to look into what could be done, and according to Hobson, "I gave the medical board the information and they took it from there."[25]

In April of that year, the Montgomery County Medical Society suspended Burt's membership for failure to pay his dues.[26] As this indicates, the Burts were apparently in financial straits. The next year, on May 11, 1988, the court ordered the Burt home at 7152 Paragon Road to be sold within three days at a sheriff's auction unless the Burts made the mortgage payments.[27] In June, Burt again filed for bankruptcy protection for himself and his medical clinic, claiming more than $6 million in debts with assets less than $500.[28]

During the same month that James Burt filed for bankruptcy, Sidney Wolfe, a physician and director of the Health Research Group, a public interest organization based out of Washington, D.C. that monitored state disciplinary actions taken against doctors, wrote to the State Medical Board of Ohio about Burt.[29] Wolfe had been serving as the co-chair of the Medical Committee for Human Rights' Washington, D.C. chapter in 1970 when consumer activist Ralph Nader met him. Together, Wolfe and Nader founded the Health Research Group. As the medical division of Nader's Public Citizen, the Health Research Group conducted research on health care issues, used its research as a basis for lobbying and advocating for consumer health, and quickly assumed a major, visible presence regarding these issues.[30] Physicians performing unnecessary surgeries had been a longstanding problem, one that the Health Research Group had been calling attention to for over a decade.[31] In his June 14 letter to the state medical board, Wolfe wrote that Burt "has for many years performed unnecessary, nonstandard and potentially injurious gynecological surgery on thousands of women." Wolfe urged the medical board to revoke Burt's license, saying he was dangerous. If the board did not "immediately remove from practice a physician such as Dr. Burt, whose actions lie far outside the realm of acceptable medical practice and pose a significant threat to patients," Wolfe further wrote, "then we seriously question the board's commitment to protecting the health and safety of Ohio's citizens."[32] Four months after Wolfe sent the letter, he still had not received a response from the board.[33]

With so many financial problems, let alone the professional and ethical ones charged by the state representative and Wolfe, one can surmise why, when a national television show called to say it wanted to interview him and find out more about his surgery, Burt accepted the opportunity to appear before a national audience. But on the day before the program was to air, Burt issued a statement saying that the claim made by CBS's *West 57th* show that "I performed experimental surgery for 22 years without patients' consent and authorization" was "totally false and untrue." When approached for comment by the *Dayton Daily News*, St. Elizabeth declined but issued a statement saying the "procedure, though controversial, is a combination of medically accepted procedures."[34] On Saturday, October 29, 1988, thousands of people in Dayton went to the city's historic Oregon District to be part of the annual Halloween costume parade, watching witches, Grim Reapers, and monsters walk past.[35] But those in Dayton who stayed home that evening, sitting through *Simon and Simon* for the news magazine show *West 57th* at 10 p.m., watched a local doctor and hospital paraded before a national audience.[36]

Chapter 7

The Women and the Surgery, 1970–1986

In the 1970s, both Barbara Demick and Linda Murray wrote articles in which women spoke in glowing terms regarding the benefits of love surgery. These women were satisfied with the outcomes and effects of their surgery: for them, better sex lives and happier relationships with their male partners. But this was not the case for all the women, even those who elected for the procedure. On May 9, 1978, Judith Romer, who learned about love surgery from the article in *Playgirl*, traveled to Dayton from New Jersey to see Burt and have the surgery. Six days later, Romer flew home with a bottle of the painkiller Percodan and a bottle of the sedative Quaaludes, the latter to help reduce any tension she might feel during sexual intercourse. Less than a month later, Romer returned to Dayton for the first of what ended up being three corrective surgeries because of "vaginal wound dehiscence," meaning her closed surgical wound ruptured.[1] It is unclear from the available record who performed these surgeries.

Other women, however, did not know they had elected for the surgery as part of their care. In 1976, Ruby Moore consulted Burt regarding urinary incontinence.[2] A year later, on November 1, 1977, Burt performed love surgery on Moore, who did not know this was a component of the surgery she had agreed to undergo. Six days later, due to complications, she had a second surgery. On November 28, Moore underwent yet another corrective surgery, and nearly two months later, she had a fourth surgery, this one called "vaginal revision." Between February and March 1978, Moore had six more surgeries for complications as a result of love surgery. On April 25, her vagina was resutured.[3] In total, Moore underwent sixteen surgeries to correct a surgery, as she stated years later, she "did not ask for."[4] (Again, it is unclear from the available record who performed these corrective surgeries.) Following her multiple surgeries, Moore developed, she later said, a variety of physical problems, including repeated kidney infections and incontinence as well as depression. When she asked Burt, she recalled him telling her she had "inferior tissue" but that with time she would heal. As part of her consideration of suing Burt in 1980, Moore contacted the Montgomery County Medical Society to see if there were any complaints against Burt, but Moore recalled being "given the impression that no complaints had been registered" against him. So she decided not to pursue legal action.[5]

Similarly, Liz Sanders did not know love surgery would be part of the surgery she agreed to undergo. According to Burt's chart, Sanders was a "coital cripple." In 1975, when she was forty-one, Sanders went to Burt for a hysterectomy and was not asked about love surgery. "Before I had the surgery, he told me that because I had had such large babies, I was torn up inside and had to have some reconstruction done" in addition to the hysterectomy. It was only during a postoperative follow-up examination that Burt informed Sanders about love surgery. She recalled Burt telling her that the surgery "should make my sex life fantastic." But Sanders was not then worried about her sex life; she was worried about cancer. Her sex life, however, did not become "fantastic"; instead it was painful, a pain she blamed on her own body. Sanders recalled Burt telling her she "should feel like a 16-year-old virgin, that if I didn't something was wrong with me psychologically."[6]

Like Sanders, Beverly Yearyean and Theda Hanks each agreed to a hysterectomy and ended up having love surgery too. In 1978, Yearyean went to see Burt about her painful and heavy menstrual periods. She decided to see Burt based on a friend's recommendation. At her initial visit with Burt, he recommended a hysterectomy, and she agreed to the procedure. However, Yearyean also recalled Burt then asking her about her sexual experiences—about how pleasurable sex was for her and about her partner's genitals. During the discussion, Burt showed her pictures of surgeries he had performed in order to, he told her, improve the pictured women's sex lives, and he wanted to know if she would also like him to do so for her. Yearyean recalled thinking the photographs were "disgusting" and that she told Burt she wanted "nothing to do with that." Yearyean went ahead with Burt for the hysterectomy and following the surgery was home from work for more than two months because of the pain and complications. She recalled thinking at the time that this was normal, a thought reinforced by Burt. Three months after the surgery, when Yearyean first attempted intercourse, she found vaginal sex to be impossible and "horribly" painful. Although she tried to engage in penetrative sex again in 1982, it again did not occur, and she again experienced burning pain. After that experience, Yearyean stopped trying to have romantic relationships with men.[7] Theda Hanks, in June 1984, underwent a hysterectomy performed by Burt, although he also performed love surgery upon her, without her consent. Following the surgery, Hanks experienced multiple physical problems, including painful sex, nausea, vaginal itching, and incontinence. When Hanks told Burt of these problems, Hanks recalled Burt telling her they were "normal after a hysterectomy, and that they would improve over time."[8]

Burt told Norma Kennard she needed a hysterectomy to take care of her frequent fibroid tumors. At the time, Burt also suggested he would "tie [her] bladder up." Kennard agreed and in May 1975 had surgery. Following the surgery, she required a catheter to urinate—and needed one for several weeks—and found, once they resumed having sex, intercourse with her husband to be very painful. In addition, Kennard became incontinent and suffered from chronic pain in her pelvis. Upon examining her vulva, Kennard recalled seeing that the entrance to her vagina was "almost completely" closed. Six months after the surgery, Kennard went to other physicians in the Dayton area, some of whom, she remembered, noticed she had been "sewn up" and "cut" and that the physicians commented to her that she must have undergone surgery with Burt.[9]

Sometimes the women who had unwittingly undergone love surgery noticed a difference in their vulva area themselves. On November 19, 1974, James Burt delivered the child of Dianna and James Lewis. The couple lived in Otway, Ohio, and at home about a month after giving birth, Dianna Lewis complained of being in severe pain in her genital area. Examining herself, she determined that her labia had been stitched together from the opening of her urethra to her anus. Burt, however, claimed her pain was the result of muscle spasms. Lewis sought other doctors to correct the surgery.[10]

Like Lewis, other women, after having had a surgery performed by Burt, noticed their vulva looked "different": Judy Dresher, who was attended by Burt for the birth of her child in 1970, noticed soon after her child's birth that her clitoral area had stitches.[11] Similarly, Lydia Eiford, who had a hysterectomy performed by Burt in 1978, was also told by Burt that during the surgery, he would "tighten" her vagina. After the surgery, when she examined her vulva area, she recalled seeing a distinct difference from what it had looked like prior to her surgery. Embarrassed by what she regarded now as an abnormal appearance of her vulva, she stopped having annual gynecological examinations.[12] Burt operated upon Litha Ann Jeffery in March 1976 in an effort to stop her heavy vaginal bleeding. However, following the surgery, Jeffery experienced a host of physical problems, including pelvic pain, urinary incontinence and infections, and pain during intercourse. Upon examining her vulva, Jeffery recalled

thinking she looked "different." Jeffery stopped going to Burt shortly thereafter because she "didn't appreciate" what he had done to her body and her
inability to have sex.[13]

Jeffery was far from the only woman who experienced problems having sexual intercourse following love surgery. Along with performing a hysterectomy
on Bonnie Ginter in 1970, Burt suggested Ginter also have her vagina reconstructed, which led to her inability to have vaginal intercourse and her subsequent divorce in 1976.[14] Similarly, Patricia Chappell, who was one of Burt's
patients in the 1960s, had him deliver her child in September 1969 and shortly
thereafter, when intercourse was attempted, experienced pain. She stopped seeing Burt in 1974 and divorced a year later because of her inability to have pain-
free intercourse.[15]

Linda Cook went to James Burt in 1982 for relief of her pelvic pain. He told
her he could stop the pain by suspending her dropped uterus, but he also performed love surgery. Following the surgery, Burt prescribed Percodan for her
pain, to which Cook became addicted. The pain and the Percodan left her unable
to think clearly, and Cook lost her job and then her home. A divorced mother of
two, Cook lived with her daughters in a shelter until a local church assisted her
in finding a new place to live. Several months after the surgery, Cook had to go
to the emergency room, where she later recalled the examining doctor saying,
"Good Lord, how do you have sex?" It was another four years before Cook went
to see a gynecologist, this time at the Ohio State University Medical School in
Columbus. This gynecologist had seen other former Burt patients and had performed corrective surgery on them, which he also did on Cook. She sued Burt
that year for malpractice.[16]

Cook was not the only woman who began speaking out publicly about her problems by suing. And in this way Boyles—the president of the Montgomery
County Medical Society in 1982—had been correct in suggesting that patients
need to raise criticism of a physician before actions could be taken; the actions
of patients are part of the system that regulates doctors. Sometimes that regulation comes in the form of telling another doctor, as in the case of Maria discussing Burt's recommendation of love surgery with Donne Holden. And sometimes
it comes in the manner of a letter, as in the case of Nancy Houston writing to
the hospital administration. But criticism of an errant physician and his inap-
propriate, substandard, or indeed harmful care can also come through another
form: the malpractice lawsuit. But this action needed confirmation from a physician in order to proceed.

According to an early 1980s text on the practice of gynecology and the law, "malpractice" referred to any professional misconduct "that embodies an unreasonable lack of skill or fidelity in carrying out professional or fiduciary duties." The purpose of a medical malpractice suit was to provide recovery for damages "sustained as a result of a physician's failure to exercise ordinary practice and reasonable care in the diagnosis and treatment of a patient." Malpractice suits against obstetricians primarily centered on labor and delivery, negligent care after surgery, and failure to test in a timely manner.[17] In addition, physicians could also be sued for performing unnecessary surgery.

During the second half of the 1970s—just when Burt was both marketing and beginning to come under pressure for performing love surgery—the extent of the performance of unnecessary surgeries had once again arisen as a critique of medicine.[18] This perennial concern that physicians were performing surgeries unnecessarily arose in the 1970s through a series of books and articles meant for consumers. For example, in his 1971 book, *How to Avoid Unnecessary Surgery*, surgeon Lawrence Williams asserted that around one-sixth of all surgeries were unnecessary. His book was followed by others, urging patients to obtain a second opinion before undergoing surgery. That same decade, John Bunker, a Stanford anesthesiologist, published in the *New England Journal of Medicine* his research showing that American physicians operated more than their British peers, who, despite not operating as often, had patients with equally good outcomes. His study, historian Nancy Tomes argued, "confirmed what lay and medical critics had been saying since the late 1930s: the economic structure of American medicine encouraged physicians to operate when doing so might not be necessary."[19]

In 1977, the fears of an increase in unnecessary surgeries (and those unnecessary surgeries sometimes happening at public expense now under Medicare and Medicaid) resulted in the Department of Health and Education (HEW) launching a new and, as they termed it, "major effort" to reduce the number of such surgeries. Although noting there were no studies to estimate the number of unnecessary surgeries that occurred in the United States, Hale Champion, a HEW undersecretary, told members of the House Oversight and Investigations Committee, which had been looking at the problem since 1974, that there were some data from individual cities showing a rise in unnecessary surgeries. Some cities, for example, saw between 1970 and 1975 an increase of commonly overused surgeries, like hysterectomy, by 200 percent, a figure dramatically larger than the 25 percent increase in surgeries in that same time period nationwide.[20] By 1977, hysterectomy had become the most commonly performed major surgery in the United States. Testifying before a House Commerce subcommittee in May 1977, Kenneth Ryan, chief of obstetrics and gynecology at Harvard, and John Morris, chief of gynecology at Yale, agreed that the operation was overused.[21] As historian Tomes noted, feminist health activists warned women against "hip-pocket operations" (so called because the surgery was seen as more beneficial to the wallets of the physicians than the patients—also an indicator of the gender of the majority of physicians at the time) such as hysterectomies.[22]

In a series of exposés on the practice of medicine written in January 1976 and appearing in the *New York Times*, journalist Jane Brody reported on a major, five-year-long study sponsored and conducted by the American College of Surgeons and the American Surgical Association on surgeries in the United States. With approximately 18 million Americans undergoing surgery each year and 80 percent of surgeries elective, the study found at least "some surgeons 'make work' for themselves by doing operations that are unnecessary." Researchers who reviewed the data found that the medically questionable surgeries were performed, Brody reported, for a variety of reasons: "the doctor exercises poor judgment, because the patient insists on or expects surgery, because the doctor wants to protect himself from a possible lawsuit, or simply because a doctor—on whose recommendation the patient depends—earns nothing for the operation he recommends against." Moreover, other studies found that one- to two-thirds of some procedures performed, such as hysterectomies, "may not have been in the patients' best medical interests," Brody wrote. George Zuidema, chief of surgery at Johns Hopkins School of Medicine and coordinator of the study, told Brody that "uncertified [meaning not board certified] surgeons tend to do most of the operations that are controversial—hernias, tonsillectomies, hysterectomies and so forth."[23]

The study uncovered the extent to which doctors' decisions to treat were not always in the patients' best interests. The increase in the number of lawsuits, and in the amount plaintiffs demanded, reflects one way in which some patients responded to the rise in unnecessary surgeries. In 1971, only about 17 percent of doctors had been sued at least once in their medical career; in 1975, that percentage had risen to 26.[24] In addition, a host of cultural and economic issues also gave rise to the increase in medical malpractice suits against doctors in the 1970s, including the erosion of a relationship outside a medical context between physicians and their patients, the increasingly impersonal world of health care, and an emerging patients' rights movement, as well as an increasing public perception of health care as a commodity.[25] These changes in perceptions about medical practice played out in the legal realm with increased numbers of lawsuits and increased compensation. To illustrate: in 1957, a suit resulting in $100,000 for a patient was nearly unfathomable; by the late 1970s, awards began reaching the million-dollar mark.[26] Although the malpractice cases concerned individual practitioners and patients, the rise in the number of—as well as the costs associated with—malpractice lawsuits reflected larger dissatisfactions with the way physicians were increasingly being seen as unresponsive to patient needs and as not being responsible in regulating their peers.

Burt, of course, regarded love surgery as a necessary surgery—an opinion, it would seem, not shared by the majority of his peers nor some of his former patients. Linda Cook was not the first to sue Burt over love surgery: Dianna and James Lewis, the couple from Otway, Ohio, sued Burt for $525,000 in 1976, claiming that love surgery—which Burt performed on Dianna Lewis without her consent after childbirth—prevented them from having sex and ruined their marriage. Their suit was dismissed, however, on the grounds that the compensation the couple demanded was excessive.[27] As noted above, a more than half million dollar compensation for malpractice would have still been uncommon in the mid-1970s.[28] Given that malpractice suits themselves remained relatively uncommon in the 1970s, perhaps it is not surprising that between 1976 and 1986, only nine women—including Dianna Lewis, Judith Romer, and Linda Cook—sued Burt for malpractice.[29]

But Burt seemed impervious to lawsuits. Linda Cook asked the Ohio State University gynecologist who examined her and performed corrective surgery upon her to testify, but he refused.[30] To proceed, she needed his testimony. To pursue a medical malpractice suit at the time, a patient needed to have an expert testify for her in order to establish what the standard of care was and that the physician being sued failed to meet this standard of care, resulting in adverse effects. Doing so thus required a medical expert.[31] With no medical expert willing to testify, Cook ended up settling for $1,500, with nearly half going to cover her legal fees.[32] Anna Mitchell, who went to Burt in 1973 for delivery of her child and upon whom he performed love surgery, sued Burt in 1975 and settled two years later for $5,000 because no doctor would testify on her behalf.[33] She later recalled how frustrating it was that "no one would testify for me" and that Burt had recorded the procedure in his surgical notes as a routine episiotomy.[34] Judith Romer, along with her husband John, sued Burt and St. Elizabeth in May 1980, claiming love surgery left her unable to have sex and that the hospital was negligent in allowing the surgery to occur as it was not considered standard medical practice.[35] In their suit, the couple maintained that Burt did not tell them the surgery was "experimental" and "not within normal and anatomical confines."[36] Moreover, the Romers stated that as a result of the surgery, Judith

Romer had suffered serious physical and psychological injuries and that the results of the surgery had negatively affected their marital relationship.[37] Burt, however, said that Judith Romer had an infection after the surgery and called their lawsuit against him "a malicious prosecution."[38] The Romers' case was dismissed in 1981 when she failed to appear at the trial.[39]

Perhaps more of Burt's patients experienced problems following love surgery, but only a handful publicly claimed such by suing him in the 1970s and early 1980s. Indeed, many of Burt's patients remained with him for years, even some women who experienced adverse effects of a surgery they were unaware he had performed. As an example, Coney Mitchell started going to Burt in 1967 when he delivered her third child. In addition to delivering her baby, Burt also apparently performed love surgery on Mitchell, and she developed chronic bladder, urinary tract, and vaginal infections. Mitchell continued to go, however, to Burt, and twelve years later, he performed a hysterectomy on her. In 1985, Mitchell was still going to Burt and again he operated on her, this time to repair her bladder problems.[40] Perhaps it was Burt's reported persuasiveness that kept women like Mitchell returning to him, even when they experienced problems—perhaps he told his patients their problems were typical, or perhaps his also reportedly gentle—and at times threatening—manner kept women going to him. Or perhaps it was fear of going to another doctor or simply habit that kept women returning to Burt even if they had complications such as those Mitchell experienced.

Years later, in the popular coverage of the Burt story following his exposure on *West 57th*, some of the reporters asked why more women had not sued Burt. Of course, one answer to this is that not all women were dissatisfied with the surgery—recall the eight women Barbara Demick interviewed who said they were happy with the results of love surgery—a surgery they elected to undergo. In addition, probably not all women experienced the severity of postsurgery complications in the same manner or to the same degree as Romer or Cook. An additional possibility is that the intimate nature of the surgery and the postsurgery complications regarding sexual intercourse perhaps silenced some women who possibly did have poor outcomes. Beside a host of physical problems ranging from urinary tract, vaginal, and bladder infections to chronic yeast infections, the reduced size of the vagina—even in some cases the near closure of its entrance—made vaginal sex, if not impossible, very painful. For those women who experienced sexual problems and pain during intercourse, a fear of publicly discussing their problems may have prevented them from coming forward against Burt with a lawsuit. "That a large malpractice suit has not been filed against this man can only be attributed to the nature of a sexual inadequacy complaint," stated one of Burt's critics, who spoke anonymously to Demick in 1978. "It's like a rape case. A woman—and especially these—doesn't want to give her private sexual history to the courts, public, police, and newspapers." She would be asked, this anonymous source continued, "why she thought she was sexually inadequate in the first place, why she was stupid enough to give this man $1500 for voluntary surgery, and why it didn't work."[41] This physician was assuming all the women elected and consented, or even knew, about the surgery, but not every woman who underwent love surgery elected for it, and even those who did perhaps still did not want to publicly discuss the post-surgery problems they were experiencing on a very private part of their bodies and lives.

Additionally, ignorance about their bodies and what had been done to their bodies may have kept some women from suing Burt or even from ceasing to use him as their physician. When Gerry Harness examined her genitals after her bladder surgery, she knew they looked different, "but I assumed this was due to the repositioning Dr. Burt described" of her bladder from her surgery.[42] Unlike Harness, not all of Burt's patients may have realized their genitals looked different. Even though the 1970s was a decade when some women were encouraging each other to examine their own genitals with a hand mirror, a large number of women who responded to sex surveys during that decade expressed a good deal of ignorance about their bodies—for example, some women did not know they had a clitoris.[43] Other women were hampered from exploring their genital area because they felt, as more than one woman put it in responses to sex surveys in the 1970s, "dirty down there."[44] Often their male partners were just as ignorant about female genitals. For example, in 1981, Shere Hite followed up her study on women's ideas concerning sex and sexuality by publishing one on men, some of whom told Hite that they did not know where the clitoris was on their wives or girlfriends. While a few knew it was located in the upper vulva area, other men were even more vague, and some were just confused, believing the clitoris was in the vagina.[45]

Finally, though, there is also the possibility some women, even those who had physical problems, were simply uncomfortable challenging the medical authority of their physician. Although in some ways extreme in what happened to the women, the relationship Burt had with his patients reflects the uneven nature of many doctor–patient interactions. In general, patients have less power than physicians, and this imbalance of power is, to some extent, the natural result of the reason for their relationship: patients seek medical attention when they need care. They are often upset, confused, and probably anxious about the symptoms that are disrupting and possibly threatening their lives.[46] Patients,

limited in their ability to assess their physicians' medical knowledge and evaluate treatment options or need, are dependent on the judgment of their physicians.[47] In need of their physicians' expertise and advice, patients willingly
submit to being told what to do and also submit to questions and procedures
some find embarrassing, confusing, or undignified, all in the hopes that they
will regain health. Patients' need and acknowledgment of the physician's ability to treat them empowers the physician. While patients are able, and were in
the 1970s and early 1980s increasingly expected, to ask questions and seek an
understandable or detailed explanation, and if unhappy with the advice of one
physician to seek that of another or to refuse all treatment options, for most
patients the desire to reduce pain or extend their life meant they willingly
deferred to the doctor's decision.[48]

Sociologist Sue Fisher spent six years in the early 1980s observing the interactions between doctors and patients regarding hysterectomies and Pap smears
in two teaching hospitals. When she spoke with patients, she discovered that
they were often neither too emotional to understand medical information nor
too passive to ask questions. She found the problem in communication more
subtle. "Patients *believed* that the doctors had more information and skills they
lacked," Fisher wrote. "They believed, therefore, that the doctors should be the
ones making the medical decisions," and they believed the "doctor knew best
and would act in their best interests." The women's actions "flowed from these
beliefs," according to Fisher.[49] The women Fisher interviewed believed in and
trusted their doctors. The women who went to James Burt, and who continued
to go to him even after he failed to adequately explain or alleviate their pain
following surgeries many did not know they had undergone, were acting from
this socialization. They trusted Burt because he was the physician.

Janet Phillips, 1986–1987

Soon after her appointment with Michael Clark, Phillips contacted attorney Mary Lee Sambol and on April 4, 1986, filed a malpractice lawsuit against Burt.[1] But Phillips did not just sue Burt; she also sued St. Elizabeth, accusing the hospital of failing to review Burt and his surgery and of failing to establish guidelines to "prevent experimental and detrimental excessive and outrageous surgery on non-consenting females."[2]

Although Clark examined Phillips, in March 1986, Phillips traveled to Cincinnati to see obstetrician gynecologist Bradley Busacco.[3] Phillips was not the first former Burt patient Busacco examined or, eventually, treated. Busacco, who obtained his medical degree from the University of Florida in 1979 and moved to Cincinnati for his residency in obstetrics and gynecology, remained at the University of Cincinnati following his residency as a faculty member during the 1980s. It was during the mid-1980s, shortly after he completed his residency, that he saw his first former Burt patient. This woman came to his attention after she went to the Wyoming Family Practice Center, a clinic where Busacco saw gynecology patients.[4] That March night in 1986, the nurse warned Busacco that the woman he was about to examine had a strange story.[5] When Busacco examined this woman, who had gone to the clinic for help alleviating painful sex, he initially thought she had undergone a rather extreme version of a vulvectomy—the total removal of the vulva, including the inner and outer labia and clitoral area—a procedure that is generally considered a last resort to remove cancer in the area. But what he saw looked beyond a vulvectomy. The woman told him the surgery was not to remove cancer but had been done as part of another procedure she had undergone and that apparently it was supposed to improve her sex life. When he spoke with me, Busacco stated he did not believe this first woman's story about the reason for the surgery. She, in turn, told him that she could bring other women who had had the procedure for the same reason she was giving him.[6]

Other women started to go to Busacco shortly after this first woman, sent to him by word of mouth, recommended by other former Burt patients. During the mid-1980s, he recalled sometimes seeing two or three of Burt's former patients per week, and he estimated that during the 1980s, he saw a couple hundred women who had been Burt's patients. These women asked Busacco similar questions, wanting to know what had been done to their bodies. The women further told Busacco that they felt different, that their genitals felt different. Busacco would hand these women a mirror and explain to them what was different about their anatomy from typical female anatomy. He recalled most of the women being alarmed and surprised by what they saw and asked him, most often crying, why it had been done and reiterating that they had not agreed to the surgery. They also told similar stories: they did not have prior knowledge about love surgery before having undergone it, they did not consent to it, and that Burt often asked them how their sex lives were after he had operated upon them. The women also often expressed to Busacco their hatred for Burt for what he had done to them, and their anger was also against the medical system, which they felt had let them down. Finally, they also had similar complications: chronic urinary tract and yeast infections, pain when walking, and pain having vaginal sex with their male partners. Busacco did not recall ever seeing a woman who had knowingly elected for the surgery.[7]

When I spoke with him, Busacco described how the surgery disfigured women: it removed the labia minora, and the clitoris was both circumcised and moved downward toward the vaginal opening by around 1 centimeter or so. By pulling the clitoris down, it also meant the urethra was then pulled into the vagina (as Busacco described: think of the letter C, with the top the clitoris and the bottom the urethra: pulling the top of the C down impacts the location of the bottom of the C). With the urethra in the vagina, when a woman urinated, the urine collected in a small pool inside the vagina, often causing urinary tract infections. In addition, the perineum overlapped with the vaginal opening, creating a small fold of skin. When I told him Burt claimed love surgery arose out of his modifying episiotomy repair, Busacco said he could not see how this surgery had developed from that, for it was such a large departure from episiotomy repair.[8] Note that Busacco's description regarding moving the clitoris differs from Burt's, who claimed to raise the vaginal entrance rather than lower the clitoris; although they disagree regarding what was done, both saw the distance between the clitoris and entrance to the vagina as shorter.

It was not just by word of mouth that former Burt patients found Busacco; Sambol had heard he was seeing former Burt patients and she started sending some of her clients to him. Busacco recalled speaking with Sambol, how she told him physicians in Dayton were nervous about seeing these women, and that she—and they—were looking for a champion for their cause: a physician who could both treat the women, complain to the state medical board, and testify in a malpractice lawsuit against Burt. Busacco, still fairly new to medical practice and an untenured assistant professor at the University of Cincinnati, thought about and discussed with his wife what to do.[9] In an interview he gave in 1991, Busacco said that after speaking with his wife, Peggy, he decided he had a duty to report Burt to the state medical board. He told the reporter, "I decided it would be very difficult for me to live if I didn't do it," and that ethically, "I wouldn't have been able to live with it, to know there were patients who needed help. I couldn't turn my back on them." Peggy and Bradley Busacco then, as the reporter wrote, "steeled themselves for what was to come."[10] When I spoke with him, Busacco remembered conversations with his wife about what to do, the concerns that if he spoke up, he risked being sued, but he ultimately decided the only "Christian thing to do would be to go forward."[11] Busacco agreed to notify the state medical board about Burt, and he signed a complaint to the board.[12] He also agreed to be a medical expert for the women's lawsuits.

Before a trial starts, witnesses provide their testimonies, under oath, during depositions. The purpose of a deposition is for all parties in the suit to know what the witnesses are going to say—to know all the facts that will be introduced during the trial, so that there are no surprises once the trial starts—and to preserve the testimonies of the witnesses. During his deposition in March 1987 for the Phillips lawsuit, Busacco said he had not looked at the surgical records for Phillips, although Sambol stated for the record that he was unable to do so because Burt "has failed to provide us any." Because Busacco had not been provided with her medical records, he based his comments on his own examination of Phillips and on the surgical record of Cheryl Sexton, another former Burt patient whose records he was able to see. According to Busacco, Burt deviated from standard practice when he performed love surgery and, by doing so, had performed malpractice. Busacco stated, "Dr. Burt is the only one who does this surgery and that there really is no standard of care really to speak of other than Dr. Burt being the sole practitioner of this surgery."[13]

During his time to question Busacco, Howard Krishner, an attorney for St. Elizabeth, asked the doctor how, since he had "no idea how many women he [Burt] has performed this procedure on," would Busacco have any idea how many of the women "have had good results and who have reported good experiences to Dr. Burt?" Joseph Walker, an attorney for Phillips, objected to the question. Krishner, however, pressed for an answer from Busacco, whom he said was assuming all the results of the surgery were negative. Walker jumped in, moving to strike the question, and added "that is bullshit" as he did so. With tension obvious among the attorneys, Busacco finally replied he had not assumed that and agreed with Krishner that it "would be important to know and I'll leave it at that." Krishner pressed again by asking that if 200 women had had the procedure and less than 10 percent had negative outcomes, "would that make any difference to you in formulating and expressing the opinion which you earlier did in terms of being critical of Dr. Burt?" Busacco responded, "I still feel that Dr. Burt has deviated from the standard of care even if 90 percent of his women state that they were better off." Krishner continued to pursue the issue. If, he queried, "a physician says to the patient, nobody else does it this way" but "I believe in this procedure and in this technique" and if the physician tells the patient "I have had good results on other people," even with that sort of disclosure, the hospital attorney asked, was it "still malpractice for Dr. Burt to go forward and perform the procedure?" Busacco responded, after an objection to the question by Sambol, "the way that Dr. Burt has done that, I believe, it is malpractice." Busacco continued, saying that because Burt performed his surgery "without the backup of the literature and peer review" and because it was not "approved for human experimentation," it was "basically Dr. Burt's invention that he has put into practice." Burt's practice of love surgery, Busacco felt, constituted unfettered human experimentation.[14]

Chapter 8

Tabloid Headlines, 1988–1989

The television program *West 57th* was not exactly well regarded. When it debuted in August 1985, John Corry reviewed it for the *New York Times* and said the show was not really television, "and it certainly isn't journalism; it's video, and it's a mess." Corry called it a "supermarket tabloid set to music."[1] CBS designed the show to feature fast cuts and lots of flash; it strove to be hip and new and was aimed at audiences younger than those who watched the more staid and established *60 Minutes*.[2]

Many who critiqued the media considered it a prime example of the "trash TV" genre, a controversial label thrown around quite a bit in the late 1980s by television and cultural critics.[3] And October 1988, when CBS aired the program concerning James Burt, was considered one of the trashiest months of all for television. During that month, talk show host Geraldo Rivera's nose was broken during an on-stage brawl among his guests when one of them threw a chair during an episode called "Teen Hatemongers." That incident came barely a week after Rivera hosted a two-hour special on NBC concerning devil worship that included, according to a report in *Newsweek*, "blood-soaked orgies, dismembered corpses," and "ritualistic child abuse." NBC and Rivera were far from alone. On Fox's *A Current Affair*, viewers watched episodes on pornography, grave robbing, and grisly reenactments of murders.[4] The majority of the content in the television news magazines shows concerned violence and crime, especially rape, murder, and child molestation and abduction, according to Teresa Keller in her critique of the genre written in the early 1990s. Keller singled out the *West 57th* segment on James Burt, saying the program lacked the "dignity" of the network's older program *60 Minutes*, "exemplified" in its airing of "the

Figure 4   James Burt, c. late 1980s. Reprinted with permission from the *Dayton Daily News*.

story of a doctor who did experimental surgery on women's vaginas without their permission." The story, Keller wrote, "told about the atrocities and mutilations the doctor was engaged in," although the "postscript revealed that he no longer practiced medicine." There was, Keller concluded, "no news value— only shock value" in the story.[5]

    And shock it did. On the morning of Saturday, October 29, it was not the local *Dayton Daily News* that broke the story of Burt's upcoming exposure that evening on national television but rather the Cleveland *Plain Dealer*. Under the lead story headline "'Love' Doctor under Attack," reporter Judy Grande wrote about Joy Martin, a woman who gave birth to a son in 1973 with Burt as her obstetrician and then spent the next fourteen years going from doctor to doctor trying to find a reason and treatment for her chronic bladder and vaginal infections. Martin finally found the reason in 1987 when she learned Burt had performed love surgery upon her. Martin, Grande wrote, was one of several women who were coming forward against Burt on a television show that evening.[6]

The CBS show came to Dayton to do a segment on James Burt because Mary Lee Sambol had contacted them. In addition to lawsuits, Sambol had decided to try and pressure Burt in a myriad of ways: she informed the State Medical Board of Ohio about him and, as she put it, she "griped" to the AMA, the Montgomery County Medical Society, the local newspaper, and St. Elizabeth, but "nobody would help us."[7]

Although Sambol reportedly reached out to the local media, she also sought coverage from media outside of Dayton with the hope of exposing Burt and his surgery and in that manner eliciting a reaction to stop him from practicing. The media, as Sambol apparently recognized, can play a significant role in the regulation of the medical profession—recall the exposé written by Gary Webb in the mid-1980s that resulted in action by the Ohio legislature. Webb's exposé illustrated what sociologist Ruth Horowitz found was the media's role in medical regulation: that "investigative reporting not only spotlighted hidden problems but also helped clarify the issues and identify key players responsible for the problems and their solutions." Media attention, she wrote, was "an important source for generating public discussion."[8] So despite that some considered *West 57th* to be "trash TV," it still managed to spotlight the problem of Burt and his practice of love surgery.

Burt and four of the women suing him for malpractice—including Janet Phillips—made appearances on *West 57th*. Although the women appeared angry and depressed, they were also shown as compelling victims. Burt, on the other hand, was portrayed as a vile manipulator of these and other women. And while reporter Karen Burnes interviewed Burt and the four women, she was quite noticeably more sympathetic to the women's stories of not being asked about love surgery and of their descriptions of the complications they suffered.[9]

Burnes introduced the program as an "extremely disturbing and, in some cases, shocking" story about "a group of women, a doctor and a hospital." She then cautioned those watching that in order to tell the story, it was necessary to use some "clinical language, which may make you uncomfortable." But, she stressed, "we have done so because what happened to these women in Dayton, Ohio is something that can happen to anyone." It is, she continued, a "story of a system that many believe had allowed a doctor to harm—and in some cases, to shatter—lives. The doctor is still in practice, the hospital still in business. And the women are devastated."[10]

The introduction was then followed by the four women all making short condemnations about Burt. Joy Martin said Burt "shouldn't be walking the streets, let alone having a scalpel in his hand." Phillips told Burnes, "I went to him for help. I didn't want to be his guinea pig." Cheryl Sexton said that she felt as though Burt "created a new sex organ for me, like he would for a man that had a sex change." Lastly, Sandy Shockey told Burnes, "This man reminds me of someone who did experimentation in Auschwitz." His practices were "unchecked, and no one could stop them," she stated.[11]

After this introduction, a Burnes voiceover followed footage of Burt walking into his clinic, with Burnes saying, "Twenty-two years ago, he began to surgically alter the anatomy of women." Burnes told her viewers:

> Burt has spent these last years trying to perfect his technique while women were asleep under anesthesia. He does this, he says, to make women "better sex partners," and he's called it "love surgery." But some women call him a butcher. Dr. Burt has been sued repeatedly for performing an operation that no other doctor has ever done. He remains in practice for reasons which we will explain, and he remains convinced that women are born with their sexual organs in the wrong place.

With this as her introduction, viewers saw Burnes sitting with Burt and Burt agreeing that he regarded himself a pioneer. The show, shifting rapidly between topics and between speakers, quickly moved to Burnes speaking with Bradley Busacco, who said, "I hate to use the term 'Frankenstein,' but it's almost like we're creating a new anatomy here, and in order to do that, some are falling by the wayside." In a voiceover, Burnes informed her viewers that Busacco had been sought out by some of Burt's former patients because doctors in Dayton refused to treat them. Busacco told Burnes he had never seen a surgery comparable to love surgery, and he could not see a medical benefit for it. According to Burnes, "When he spoke off-camera, Busacco expressed horror and outrage. Before he appeared on-camera, the doctors in his community told him to keep quiet. He agreed to talk to us despite that, and despite his fear of legal repercussions."[12]

The show then returned to Burnes speaking with Burt and challenging him regarding the specifics of love surgery. Burnes asked why Burt circumcised women, saying, "This is a procedure that in Africa is considered punishment." Burt, however, interrupted her and disputed this statement. Burnes in turn interrupted Burt, saying, "Sorry, it's considered a form of punishment to women in Africa." Following this brief and tense discussion, the show shifted to Busacco stating perhaps removing the clitoral foreskin could enable more sensitivity but that this may not be desirable. The audience then heard from Phillips, who emphasized Busacco's point: "The hood that he cuts off from over the clitoris is there for a reason, for protection. And it's easier for me to understand how important that is because now mine is exposed. And to wear jeans, if you get bumped there, if you're—during sex, foreplay—if you're touched rough, it is very painful." "I feel," Sexton added, "like he's just taken everything from me."[13]

Burnes then turned back to the four women, seated in what appeared to be a legal library, stressing that none of them had gone to Burt for the surgery or its supposed sexual benefits. But they did all recall for Burnes how, when Burt spoke with them about the medical reasons for their visit to him, he kept returning to their sexual lives. According to Phillips, "he kept asking me about being able to climax," and she kept telling him, "I have no problem." Burnes is then shown asking Burt about his book, *Surgery of Love*, and asking what he meant when he wrote about women as "horny little mice." Asked Burnes, "Isn't that a degrading phrase for someone who says he's a champion of women?" Burt, who had earlier told Burnes he felt his book was "very misunderstood" and that he had been trying to write in the way people spoke "in the privacy of their own life," now said that he thought he was "probably" "a very poor writer."[14]

The second portion of the show turned to how Burt was allowed to practice love surgery or, as Busacco stated, how Burt had found at St. Elizabeth "a way to do experimental surgery without close supervision." Burnes, once more in a voiceover, noted that as a Catholic hospital, St. Elizabeth did not allow vasectomies, tubal ligations, or elective abortions, yet allowed Burt to perform love surgery. She told her audience that there were "no federal laws which regulate experimental surgery, or prohibit a doctor from practicing, no matter how many times he's been sued." But, she added, "in Dayton, where hospitals are desperate to fill beds, someone like Dr. Burt can be an asset." Busy obstetrician gynecologists, she noted, could bring the hospital where they delivered nearly $1 million in income annually. But she also added a more direct financial need for St. Elizabeth to allow Burt operating privileges, suggesting it did so because Burt owned land the hospital wanted for a parking lot, land Burt sold to St. Elizabeth in 1981 when they were both subjects of a lawsuit. St. Elizabeth, Burnes noted, refused to comment for the show or allow *West 57th* to shoot any footage in the hospital.[15]

Not to be so restrained, the program used a hidden camera to take pictures inside St. Elizabeth. The producers of the show also managed to obtain interviews with, as Burnes noted in a voiceover, "several high-level personnel" at the hospital who spoke anonymously to give *West 57th* background information. "They told us," Burnes continued in a voiceover as the hidden camera went through the hospital, "that many of the staff wanted Dr. Burt removed, going so far as to call him 'crazy' and 'a mutilator.' But the hospital's attorney decided nothing could be done."[16]

Although Burnes asked the women about the complications that resulted from the surgery and challenged the motivation behind the surgery, the themes of consent and the pain these women had experienced as a result of the surgery were central to the show. As Joy Martin stated, "I didn't have any control, I didn't have any say so," in having the surgery performed upon her while she was under anesthesia. Phillips reiterated this feeling, saying,

> You have to keep trust someplace, especially a hospital. You go in there and you're put to sleep. Your family isn't in that operating room and saying "Now, wait a minute. I don't think you should cut right there." Your attorney isn't standing there, saying, "Well, that's against the law, to cut there." I mean, you're asleep.

The women, including Phillips, also told of the pain they had experienced since the surgery and how it had interrupted their sexual lives. Shockey told of the "extreme" pain during intercourse, what she described as "sharp, piercing, knifelike pain that feels like something is tearing inside you." She added, "What little joy you do feel during sex, it just doesn't seem worth it." Phillips felt as though she could not go on dates because she did not want to explain her problem to a man. Although the women all signed the special consent form St. Elizabeth began requiring in 1979, a consent form Busacco described to Burnes as being a sign that the hospital was "deficient in policing this particular physician with regards to this particular surgery," they all stated they did not really know what it meant.[17]

Burnes introduced the show as being about something that could "happen to anyone," and this was a theme throughout. Toward the end of the show, Burnes asked Busacco if the women who went to Burt were naive. He agreed they were to some degree, "but no more than most patients who come in the office." An unscrupulous physician, he said, "could take advantage of the majority of patients who walk into your office." The *West 57th* segment ended with a voiceover from Burnes telling her audience, "Dr. James Burt continues to practice, and the system continues to let him. He believes he has made a contribution to mankind, and that one day history will vindicate him. No matter what, he says, he'll fight to keep his work alive." With the voice of Burt and an image of the door to his clinic office, the show ended by his saying to an unseen patient, "Think over the options, and if you wish to go ahead, we'll set it up."[18]

On the Sunday morning after the show aired, the *Dayton Daily News* carried excerpts from it and quoted Burt as well as Sexton and Sambol, the latter of whom told the newspaper, "All these women have become nervous wrecks." The *Dayton Daily News* also took information from the *Plain Dealer* regarding Sidney Wolfe's letter to the state medical board questioning Burt, a letter that had still received no response from the board.[19] Burt, who had presumably hoped the television show would provide a positive forum for his surgery, instead called the show a "conspiracy of lies" and the women who appeared on the show "well-rehearsed liars."[20] James Makos, acting president of St. Elizabeth, issued a statement saying the hospital would conduct a "thorough re-evaluation" of Burt's surgery and of his relationship with the hospital, although St. Elizabeth was "not aware" of Burt performing any surgery without a patient's consent. Makos further noted that Burt was licensed by Ohio and that the state medical board "has not taken any action against Dr. Burt or restricted his license to practice medicine." However, the medical board confirmed to the Dayton newspaper that day that it was "looking into" Burt. According to a spokesperson for the board, the board's confidentiality policies prohibited her from saying why it began the investigation into Burt, although she did say the investigation had begun months before the airing of the CBS show.[21]

In the coming weeks, numerous people would publicly respond to the CBS show. One person who did so fairly quickly—and one of the few who did so in defense of Burt—was Arthur Schramm, who wrote a two-page letter to Makos. According to the *Dayton Daily News*, Schramm's letter to the president of the hospital accused the CBS show of misrepresenting Burt, who, Schramm stated, was one of the few physicians who was technically skilled, clinically competent, and dedicated to his patients. He further stressed to Makos that Burt was working to correct a common condition in women, one that few other clinicians diagnosed.[22]

But Schramm was decidedly in the minority on these points. On Tuesday, November 1, the governor of Ohio, Richard Celeste, received a memo providing him background on the State Medical Board of Ohio's investigation into Burt. According to the memo, there was one complaint filed with the state board in July 1987, but the "woman complainant moved to California and declined to testify," so the investigation on that front ceased. The governor's memo, written by Paul Goggin, further noted there were "additional complaints" brought forth in February 1988 "and the case is currently under investigation," though, Goggin noted, he had "not received a satisfactory answer on why the investigation is taking so long, but its probably a result of St. Elizabeth dragging their feet as well as the Board's own deliberate process." However, Goggin wrote, "Burt and several witnesses have been deposed, and the Board is seeking experts in human experimentation to give testimony." But this, Goggin noted, "was proving to be difficult due to doctors being reluctant to testify against other doctors."[23]

Goggin further informed the governor, "It appears that many of the patients signed releases for the surgery, particularly in more recent years; but, it is clear that Burt performed unauthorized operations as well." It appeared to Goggin that both Burt and the hospital were beginning to "treat this case from a strict legal perspective." The hospital, Goggin reasoned, was "probably concerned because Burt has successfully undergone peer review, and was permitted to perform his 'procedure' for more than 10 years. I expect they both see serious liability in the future." Goggin ended by noting that Henry Cramblett, the supervising physician of the Burt investigation for the board, had not "recommended a summary suspension of Burt's license because he sees no 'clear and present danger.'" But Goggin told the governor in the memo, "I'm not sure how he arrives at this conclusion given the situation, but at this point Burt can continue to practice until the case is fully investigated and presented to the entire Board." Goggin, however, found this situation "absurd" and suggested the governor demand "that the Board take some action," stressing, however, that "it would probably be a good idea if Nap looked into the legal implications" of doing so first.[24]

The "Nap" Goggin referred to was Napoleon Bell, legal counsel to Celeste, and Bell, in a memo dated two days later to Celeste, informed the governor he had phoned "a classmate of mine at Mt. Union College" to discuss the Burt matter with him. The classmate, referenced only as Cramblett in the memo but presumably the Henry Cramblett on the state medical board, told Bell that the board had been conducting an "intensive investigation" of Burt, "with the hope of obtaining hard evidence that would allow the Board an opportunity to severely discipline him and/or revoke his license to practice." Cramblett further "confirmed the fact that there have been no similar 'surgical procedures' performed by Dr. Burt at St. Elizabeth Medical Center, in Dayton, for the past 2 years." Bell believed that Burt had been requested to surrender his license, but Burt refused. Bell further found as part of his investigation that "the medical staff at the hospital" or the hospital's board of directors "could take decisive action, and remove him from the staff. Further, the Joint Commission on Accreditation for Health

Care Organizations could investigate this matter, and depending upon their findings, could place the accreditation for St. Elizabeth's Medical Center in jeopardy." Bell ended his memo by recommending that the governor's office "contact the Joint Commission on Accreditation and request an immediate investigation with a complete report to this office."[25] On his copy of the memo, Celeste wrote "OK" next to his initials.[26] Bell contacted the Joint Commission and reported back to the governor on November 9 that the commission was aware of the current investigation of Burt by the state board, that the commission had visited St. Elizabeth, and that the Joint Commission "is in the process of concluding their investigation" and would be finished in the next thirty to sixty days. The commission's results, however, would only be released to the hospital, Bell reported, unless the investigation resulted in a "withdrawal of accreditation." If that happened, it would become public knowledge.[27]

On Thursday, five days after the CBS show aired, the chairman of the state medical board received a letter, copied to the CEO of St. Elizabeth, from governor Celeste, who expressed he was "gravely concerned" about the "recent news revelations" indicating Burt "performed a questionable surgical procedure on hundreds, perhaps thousands, of patients entrusted to his care." If, Celeste continued, Burt had indeed performed an operation that was "an 'unproven, nonstandard practice of gynecology' on women who, in fact, had not consented to his questionable technique," it was an "unconscionable breach of medical ethics that needs to be dealt with swiftly and severely." He urged the board to "get to the bottom of these allegations as quickly as possible." The governor asked that the board "expeditiously" discover "the extent to which Dr. Burt's procedure was performed on unconsenting and uninformed women." Celeste further asked the medical board to obtain written agreements from Burt and St. Elizabeth that love surgery would not be performed pending the board's investigation into the practice of the surgery.[28] The governor was reportedly "outraged" to learn that the board had begun investigating Burt in February 1988 but had failed to take any action against him.[29]

Timothy Stephens, president of the state medical board, hand delivered his response to the governor later that same day. In his letter, Stephens announced that the board was going a step further by investigating not just Burt "but also the actions of the local medical community which may have permitted this situation to go unchecked for years without acting or reporting information to this board." But Walter Reiling Jr., who was the immediate past president of the Montgomery County Medical Society and who became a sort of spokesperson on the Burt matter for the society during this time, called the state board's actions a "cop-out" because only the state board possessed the power to restrict and discipline doctors.[30] Lauren Lubow, the spokesperson for the board, in turn said that all licensed doctors have a legal responsibility to report to the board a physician in violation of the law.[31] Reiling responded to Lubow, saying the board was making an "unfair indictment of physicians in this community."[32] Richard Tapia, the county medical society's executive director, called the charges that his society had been silent regarding Burt "political," one that outraged him, and, like Reiling, called the board's response a "cop-out." The board, Tapia complained, "is acting as though they never heard a thing about this guy," when in fact Tapia recalled at least twenty anonymous complaints women had made regarding Burt since 1978, complaints the society had passed on to the board.[33]

Celeste also received a prompt reply from James Makos, then the acting president and CEO of St. Elizabeth. In a letter sent express from Dayton to Columbus the day after he received the letter from Celeste, Makos wrote that he agreed the state medical board should proceed with an investigation into Burt, "and we will cooperate fully." Makos continued, assuring the governor that "the allegations raised are of grave concern to St. Elizabeth Medical Center." He then informed the governor that the hospital's "surgical records show that the procedure in question has not been performed here since January 1987, and none are currently scheduled." Moreover, Makos stated that "Dr. Burt has assured me and the Medical Center that he will refrain from performing the procedure in question until this matter is resolved." Makos ended by saying he would "personally monitor the situation closely" and that the governor had his "assurance that St. Elizabeth Medical Center remains committed to providing high-quality health care to our Dayton community and that our re-evaluation will be thorough."[34]

The *Dayton Daily News* coverage of the Burt story continued into the following weekend after the show aired, with a lengthy article in the Sunday paper by reporter Julia Helgason titled "He Hurt Us, Physically and Emotionally, Burt's Ex-Patients Say." Under the headline, before the start of the article, an advisory to readers appeared, stating "the following story contains graphic descriptions that some readers may find offensive." Helgason interviewed the women who appeared on the CBS show, and one told Helgason how her ten-year-old daughter was now refusing to go to school because of harassment following her mother's appearance on the television show. "She's so hurt and humiliated, she can't even bring herself to tell me what they said," the unidentified woman stated. In addition to speaking with the women who appeared on the CBS show, Helgason noted that at least a dozen other women had come forward saying Burt had hurt them as well by rearranging their anatomies. The women, wrote Helgason, "who say they've been hurt by the procedure say their vaginas are so tight after surgery that intercourse is excruciatingly painful for them and often for their husbands as well."[35]

In addition to speaking with a number of women who had undergone love surgery, Helgason also interviewed Dayton obstetrician gynecologist Robert Hilty, chair of Kettering Medical Center's gynecology department for the past eighteen years. As Hilty told Helgason, "Obviously, I can't say all their stories are true because I don't know that," although most gynecologists in Dayton, he continued, "would agree that a number of them do have significant problems." These problems included, according to Hilty, that when they urinated, it went into the vaginal sac created by the surgery, resulting in leakage. Moreover, "for many of them, intercourse is painful," in part caused "by the altered course of the penis, and the exposed clitoral area." Of the men Hilty said he had spoken with, intercourse was often painful for them as well as for their wives.[36]

The following day, November 7, the *Dayton Daily News* editorial asserted that both the state board and local doctors were to blame for not acting to stop Burt. "Nobody—not the state medical board, not the hospitals, not the doctors, not nurses, not the news media, not his dissatisfied patients—ever really went to work to shut the man down," the paper blasted. "The outrage from everybody is too late."[37] Readers responded to the paper's editorial. Monica Kittle Schiffler thanked the paper for its coverage, including this particular editorial, regarding Burt. "It is infuriating and terrifying that no serious investigation of this man was initiated until he was exposed on national television," she wrote. Moreover, "if this is the quality of protection we can expect from our hospitals and our medical societies, perhaps we should keep in mind this modified version of an old saying: Let the patient beware."[38]

A week and a half after the airing of the *West 57th* episode, on November 10, Burt reached an agreement with the state medical board to limit his license, prohibiting him from performing love surgery, or indeed any surgery, while the board's investigation was under way.[39] Signing the agreement, however, did not mean Burt admitted to doing anything wrong; "the agreement," the document read, "shall not be construed as an admission by James C. Burt, M.D., of violations of Ohio laws relating to the practice of medicine or surgery."[40] According to the front-page story on the *Dayton Daily News* the following day, the state medical board "stopped Dayton gynecologist Dr. James Burt from performing surgery in Ohio." Although Burt declined to comment, the president of St. Elizabeth, James Makos, said his hospital was "pleased the State Medical

Board has joined the medical center in securing additional restrictions on Dr. Burt."[41]

In her AMA newsletter article, Laurie Abraham wrote that "when Burt went down, he dragged Dayton's medical community with him," with a public demanding answers as to why the hospital as well as "the city's physicians" could have allowed Burt to experiment "on unsuspecting women for more than 20 years."[42] As this article highlights, Burt and St. Elizabeth were not the only ones to endure media scrutiny following the CBS show; the state medical board indicated it planned on speaking with local physicians in Dayton, and Dayton doctors were questioned as to their role regarding Burt.[43] Reporting on this, newspapers across Ohio ran stories with headlines like "Doctors Aware of 'Love Surgery.'"[44] Indeed, Charles Young, a former investigator for the state medical board and the only one assigned to Montgomery County from 1975 to 1984, contradicted statements by Richard Tapia, telling the *Dayton Daily News* that he did not "remember the medical society talking to me about Burt doing any surgery," and if they said they had, "they were sorely mistaken." Young's former supervisor, Edward Valentine, agreed, saying although he "used to talk to Dick Tapia several times a week he never mentioned it—not once—to me." Valentine, who was retired at the time of his comments, further told the newspaper that if the board had been told, "we'd have done something."[45]

The implication was, of course, that Dayton doctors had acted defensively to either protect one of their own, or to protect themselves, and failed to contact the board regarding Burt. Although ultimately the board did not pursue any local physician as part of its investigation, Dayton doctors saw the very idea of it as shocking.[46] Physicians in Dayton interviewed by the *Dayton Daily News* said it was "ridiculous" to suggest that they were acting under a "conspiracy of silence." Ohio, however, had twelve years earlier enacted a law requiring doctors to file a complaint with the state board if they suspected a peer of violating the state's Medical Practices Act—the so-called "snitch law"—and no Dayton physician filed such a complaint, according to an official with the state medical board.[47] As Dayton gynecologist Robert Hilty told the *Dayton Daily News*, perhaps he and other local physicians should have written a formal complaint—in hindsight what he called a "technical error" on their part—to the state medical board, but local doctors did say they informally complained, thus, in Hilty's opinion, doing their duty.[48]

A physician's obligation to report a peer for bad medical practices is the lynchpin to viable peer review. But another part of the problem with stopping Burt, doctors told the *Dayton Daily News*, was that some found it difficult to call Burt incompetent. "It's hard to take away somebody's right to practice medicine unless he's incompetent or impaired," physician Stephen England told the newspaper. "You can say Burt was misguided. You can say consent wasn't always obtained. But I don't think you can say he's incompetent or impaired."[49]

Additionally, doctors in Dayton claimed they were prevented from reporting Burt because not every woman got bad results from love surgery. While some women suffered serious negative outcomes, the *Dayton Daily News* reported doctors anonymously as saying that "many of Burt's patients—perhaps as many as 90 percent, by one estimate—were satisfied." Although the paper did not specify who provided them with that estimate or where they obtained the number, an anonymous physician reportedly said, "I've talked to women who thought the surgery was pretty neat."[50] England, who had seen about a dozen of Burt's former patients, couldn't recall one who was unhappy with the surgery. Shortly after the CBS show aired, a woman who had been one of Burt's patients for nearly three decades told England that she and a few other women were quite happy with the surgery. "This woman," England noted, "had about 60% of the full love surgery in 1970 along with a vaginal hysterectomy" and she told him "she had great sex ever since." England said the woman told him the surgery "saved her marriage."[51]

Some physicians never spoke up about, or even questioned, Burt because they never saw bad outcomes from his surgery—or even, as England claimed, only saw women satisfied with the results. That at least some women were pleased with love surgery was repeated in a letter to the editor by Dayton physician Charles Johnson. In his letter, Johnson wrote that he had seen "none who was dissatisfied among the hundreds that I have examined," nor had he found any "patients who were critical of Dr. Burt, and I have seen many who were extremely defensive of this physician and his medicine." Burt, Johnson stressed, was probably encouraged by the "support of his satisfied patients." So why, Johnson asked, "can't the media reach out and hear from the thousands of women who have been happy with Dr. Burt for years or reach the many whose benefits have enriched their lives?"[52]

But perhaps the biggest reason local doctors did not speak out, the newspaper found, was fear of lawsuits. Gynecologist Robert Hilty said that Dayton physicians were not "protecting each other like the Mafia" when they did not report Burt; rather, he said, the reason physicians did not speak up was "to protect themselves" from lawsuits.[53] Most physicians the newspaper talked to acknowledged that the possibility of a lawsuit was a great deterrent to speaking out against Burt. The *Dayton Daily News* contacted seven obstetrician gynecologists on the staff of St. Elizabeth, but after a week, only two physicians returned the phone calls. One, Stephen England, consented to being named while the other spoke only on condition of anonymity. The two gave conflicting accounts on what the hospital did in regard to Burt. The anonymous physician said the administration of St. Elizabeth ignored the recommendations of the hospital's obstetric and gynecology staff "completely" when they advised the hospital to rescind Burt's staff privileges. England, however, said the administration tried to stop Burt and sought doctors from Cincinnati or Ohio State University to give their opinions regarding Burt, thus sparing local peers, but no one would do so even from outside the city. Robert Hilty, the Dayton gynecologist, told the *Dayton Daily News* that the underlying problem for doctors in such cases involved the strict ethical standards on complaining about local peers who were competitors. "Obviously, a physician can't go to the press and say 'Hey, I've got a hot story on another doctor," Hilty said. "If I could do that, I could ruin an excellent physician for no better reason than I didn't like him."[54]

Physicians could then, as now, disagree over the manner in which a peer practiced, disagreements that could be over therapies or over how a peer interacted with patients. When this occurred, many physicians, rather than disparage that physician in public or report the physician to the state medical board, simply stopped referring patients to the questionable physician. In a profession reliant to a good degree upon referrals, to not refer was regarded as a significant rebuke. Further, just as there was the ethical (and legal) requirement to report incompetent and impaired physicians, there was also the professional ethical requirement not to complain about peers, as Hilty stressed to the *Dayton Daily News*. Physicians felt they needed evidence that Burt was treating patients in a manner that was below the standard of care, that his practice was incompetent or impaired. And recall that this is what Walter Reiling Jr. stressed to me: evidence of poor outcomes as a result of the nonstandard practice of love surgery took time to become apparent to other physicians in the community.

Possibly under pressure—from the media, from the governor—the State Medical Board of Ohio began investigating some Dayton-area physicians in November.[55] Although the investigation was secret—with board spokesperson Lauren Lubow declining to tell the newspaper which physicians the board was investigating—the newspaper found through publicly available county and federal lawsuits the identity of five physicians who had worked with Burt: Max Blue Jr., a urologist in a suburb of Dayton; Sukhdev Rai Singla, a general surgeon; Shaikh M. Badrul Islam, a general surgeon in a suburb of Dayton; Francis J. Seiler, an anesthesiologist based at St. Elizabeth; and Bassam Nakfour, an obstetrician gynecologist in a suburb of Dayton. Four of the physicians—all except Singla, who had committed suicide in July 1987 after being investigated for allegations he traded drugs for sex from prostitutes and offered a bribe to two police officers who were investigating the case—spoke with reporters Julia Helgason and Dave Davis. Nakfour and Islam both said they had assisted Burt with hysterectomies but never with love surgery; Islam told the reporters he left the operating room once the hysterectomies were finished and said it was up to Burt's fellow obstetrician gynecologists at St. Elizabeth to prevent Burt from performing love surgery, not him. Nakfour, who in 1980 Burt claimed had watched him perform love surgery, said he had only assisted Burt with vaginal hysterectomies. Nakfour, who had moved to Dayton from his native Lebanon in 1976, told the paper he came to Dayton "a foreigner with no patients and no connections," so he "helped anybody who asked me to help them." But, he told Helgason and Davis, he always left the room once the hysterectomy had been completed and that he quit assisting Burt entirely once he learned the extent of Burt's surgeries. As a recent immigrant, however, Nakfour felt that any challenge to the surgery should have come from an established local physician.[56]

Sieler, an anesthesiologist, confirmed he sometimes had administered anesthesia to Burt's patients, but, he said, he had no "input" into what Burt did. "We are taking care of the patient," Sieler was quoted in the newspaper as saying, and "that type of surgery is done with the patient's legs up, so we see very little." Max Blue, the final physician to be implicated as helping Burt, was in a position to see more than a little. Blue, a urologist, told Helgason and Davis that he began working with Burt when some of Burt's patients began experiencing urological complications, and he offered to assist Burt as a means of preventing those complications from arising. But Blue said he had not been assisting Burt for the last four or five years because of a dispute over the management of a patient. Around the same time, Blue told the reporters, he also discovered he could be liable for any mistakes Burt made during surgery, as Burt was no longer carrying malpractice insurance but he was. Blue further told Helgason and Davis that although he had reservations concerning some of the procedures Burt performed, he did not consider it his responsibility to prevent Burt from performing them. "This is a society where people want things on demand," he told Helgason and Davis, and so if a woman signed a consent form, she is able to have whatever procedure she wants.[57] Blue's last point here again brings forth the difficulty physicians see of working to stop a peer from performing a surgery that, while unnecessary, is elected and opted for by the patient.

Did Dayton physicians fail to say anything to the board, or did the board fail to act on physicians' reports? Did the board start an informal investigation that never proceeded because of lack of evidence or lack of staff time? Discovering what happened is made more challenging not just by the passage of time but also because the state board's records on Burt—despite the passage of time—remain closed; an investigation into a physician was, as seen by the exposés in the *Plain Dealer* published in the 1980s, private and confidential, and remain closed.

The state board, however, following those exposés in the *Plain Dealer*, stepped up its actions regarding incompetent and/or impaired physicians. By the time the Burt affair erupted in late 1988, the State Medical Board of Ohio had acted against sixty doctors in the state, thirteen of whom lost their licenses, a much higher number than the twelve total between 1980 and 1984. According to the board's guidelines, there were nine categories in which loss of a license was mandated: conviction of a felony, obtaining a license by fraud, practicing under a suspended license, a drug-related conviction, and for drug misadministration. While the board claimed to investigate all the complaints it received, investigations took months or even years, as there were only twelve investigators for the state's 22,000 practicing physicians. But critics of the Burt exposure were not only concerned with the ratio of investigators to doctors or the amount of time it took to carry out an investigation; they were also concerned about the secrecy of the investigations, just like the findings of the *Plain Dealer* stories published only a few years earlier. The public, according to the *Dayton Daily News* story that ran the same day as the story in which doctors told the paper they should not be blamed for not stopping Burt, "can only find out a brief history of physicians, such as where he or she graduated from medical school and whether any formal action had been taken by the board." People who called the board about a doctor could not find out if that doctor was under investigation. Ray Bumgarner, the board's executive director, said this was so that the board could first finish an investigation and discover whether the complaint against the physician was founded.[58] Bumgarner here expressed a fear that if a complaint was found to be warrantless, posting the complaint publicly would needlessly harm the physician's reputation.

Because an investigation took so long and was so secret, patients might never become aware that a physician whose care they were under was being investigated. Such a process was in the physician's favor. Consumer advocates and other critics of the medical board review system regarded the Burt case as an illustration of just how ineffective the Ohio board was when it came to disciplining doctors, even after the reforms made just a year earlier, reforms intended to give the board greater power to discipline doctors. "The reforms obviously weren't enough to catch even this bad example of bad medical practice," asserted Sidney Wolfe of Public Citizen's Health Research Group.[59]

A week after stories about Burt's peers' culpability for his actions appeared in the Dayton newspaper, Burt was again on the front page, this time speaking out against the media and the women confronting him. "The media has accepted lies as truth, and the lies have had an intense emotional impact," he told the *Dayton Daily News* during a phone interview. The women accusing him of malpractice, he said, "are very convincing in their sales job." "What you have to realize," he continued, "is that this is a debate between dissatisfied women who may have had complications, who may be lying, who may have had positive feelings turn negative when forced to pay the bill, and women who stand to make a lot of money from the lies." Although acknowledging that he could not perform love surgery any longer, he told the Dayton reporter he still believed his work was "significant" and that others should practice it. "But if you write anything about me, write that I care about women," he said. He now had, he told the reporter, "more compassion for women and their problems than I've ever had." He stood behind his surgery, maintaining that women benefited from it. The newspaper, however, noted that since the scandal began unfolding a month earlier, no woman had come forward testifying to the benefits of the surgery, while "more than a dozen unhappy women had called the newspaper" during that time. The problems experienced by these women included "lack of informed consent, excruciating pain during intercourse, chronic bladder infections and devastated lives."[60] These complaints, and the overarching theme of a lack of consent, paralleled those made during the *West 57th* show.

Nearly a month after it was criticized on the CBS show alongside Burt, St. Elizabeth took out a full-page advertisement in the *Dayton Daily News*. Running on Sunday, November 27, the "statement to the community from St. Elizabeth Medical Center" reminded readers that the hospital, known locally as "St. E.," had been serving that community for more than a century. The ad read, "St. E's 2,300 employees are honorable, capable people who care for the ill and injured," which was why the hospital was "extremely distressed by the experiences expressed recently by former patients of James Burt, M.D., a physician on the medical staff." The women's allegations "deeply sadden us not only because of the traumas they have described, but because of our own commitment to women's health." St. Elizabeth was "re-examining and re-evaluating our peer-review system" and applauded the State Medical Board of Ohio for following "our lead" by obtaining an agreement with Burt not to perform any surgery in Ohio. The statement, signed by the hospital's acting president, James Makos, acknowledged that the community had questions "that need—and deserve—honest, straight forward answers" but also that, although wishing the hospital "could provide answers today," the "current litigation restrains us." "More importantly, these questions should be answered not in this message, nor in the media, but rather in the courts where justice is best served."[61]

The hospital's attempts to control the backlash against its role with Burt, however, did not appease everyone, including members of the local NOW chapter, who called for a protest of St. Elizabeth on Saturday, December 3. Donna Oblinger, speaking for the local chapter, told the newspaper that the group wanted to publicly protest the hospital for allowing Burt to perform surgery there for more than twenty years.[62] About fifty people demonstrated that Saturday in front of the hospital, carrying signs reading "Burt is a four-letter word," "Don't mess with my urge to merge," "Save our bodies, Stamp out Burt," and "No more quacks."[63] Oblinger, quoted in the *Dayton Daily News* coverage of the rally, said Burt was "using women for his research and all of St. Elizabeth was aware of it and let it go on." Curtis Christian, one of about six men at the protest, told reporter Jim Bland that he was there because, having only recently heard about the Burt controversy, it "kind of upset me badly. I'm not upset so much by the type of surgery he was doing, but the fact he carried it our apparently without the patients' consent."[64]

In the days and weeks following the show's airing, the hospital's public relations staff fielded hundreds of phone calls from other people angry over what they saw on national television. After days of intense media coverage, Brenda Zimmer Gibson and Kari Harrell, women who then worked in St. Elizabeth's public relations department, later recalled "the entire medical center staff" feeling "rather beat up" by the experience. So Gibson and Harrell and their colleagues "decided to hold a candlelight vigil outdoors on the patio just outside the cafeteria." They organized the vigil and notified the media and, they later recalled, "while the weather wasn't all that cold that day, a front moved through in the early evening and it was bitterly cold with wind chills near zero." Adding to their worry that no one would come due to the bitterly cold weather, the media showed up an hour prior to the event. However, according to Gibson and Harrell, more than 500 people came to stand outside and listen to emotional speeches by the hospital president, the chief of staff, and others about "the good works of the hospital and its staff." In hindsight, the two women saw the event as a reaffirmation of the "loyalty and pride of the St. Elizabeth staff and its friends."[65]

But while many now rallied around the hospital, few, it appears, publicly came out to support Burt. Indeed, during this time, it appears only one local woman came forward to talk about how love surgery benefited her. Kathy used only her first name for fear, she told Roger Snell, the *Columbus Dispatch* reporter who interviewed her, that "people who complained about Burt's surgery might criticize her for defending him." Burt delivered both of Kathy's two children in the 1970s, and she traveled from Columbus for him to do so because he seemed to her to be "a genuinely caring person." Now forty-one and still living in Columbus, Kathy recalled that Burt did not ask her permission before he performed love surgery following both of her births, but he did tell her afterward, explaining to her how what he did was done to enhance her sexual experiences.[66] She recalled that Burt did not explain "a whole lot" when she saw him for her six-week postbirth checkup, but that she did recall Burt asking her husband if he "liked" his "new playpen." Kathy said she felt the surgery was successful for her, and she felt she had to speak up after seeing the CBS program.[67]

In the months to follow, two other women followed Kathy's lead and publicly spoke up in support of Burt. Following Burt's appearance on CBS, Deborah Linville came forward to say she requested and liked love surgery. A Dayton woman, Linville called the surgery "fabulous" and wholeheartedly endorsed it.[68] According to Linville, before the surgery, she did not have vaginal orgasms, "and now I have three to four orgasms nine out of ten times I have sex."[69] Linville lamented that she was "the only 'Miss Positive.' God, I wish other women would speak out."[70] Another woman from Dayton, Jeanne L. Johnson, wrote a letter to the editor of the *Dayton Daily News* to say that while Burt "may have become very creative and transcended his expertise to mania proportions," he did not "murder, molest, rape or deserve to be whipped to the point that he supplicated God to fill him in on whether he should shoot himself!" Johnson felt Burt deserved "credit where it's due" and noted that he "graciously and diligently saw me through a late-in-life pregnancy and delivered a beautiful and healthy baby girl in 1965." The care after delivery was "excellent," and Johnson concluded her letter by saying that she hoped God would give him the strength to "find peace."[71]

Peace, however, continued to elude Burt. On Thursday, December 8, 1988, the State Medical Board of Ohio sent Burt a letter notifying him that the board "intends to determine whether or not to limit, revoke, suspend, refuse to register or reinstate your certificate to practice medicine" based on his performing surgery that "was actually far more extensive than merely closing the episiotomy" on women and that he performed this surgery without their informed consent. The board issued forty-one violations against Burt, charging him with offenses such as gross immorality, overprescribing painkillers, and performing unnecessary surgery without informed consent. While five of the violations regarded his practice of love surgery in general, thirty-six of the violations referred to individual, although unnamed, patients. For patient 1, for example, the board charged Burt with performing "on or about November 1, 1976," "coital area reconstructive surgical procedures and clitoral circumcision," procedures that "were not appropriate treatment for the problems indicated." Many of the cases dated from the 1970s, although there were a number from the 1980s, such as patient 33, who, the report stated,

> suffered post-operative problems including pelvic urinary-like pressure, vaginal infections, urinal bleeding, vaginal irritation, heavy discharge, cystitis, dysuria, constant urinary tract infections for one year after the surgery, bladder tenderness, urine trapping in vagina, dyspareunia, bleed-ing after intercourse, backache, excessive sensitivity of clitoris, decreased sexual function, and marital problems.

The board called Burt's surgery "unproven" and "not scientifically validated with respect to safety and efficacy, and . . . thus experimental or investiga-tional."[72] The state board informed Burt that he was entitled to appear at a hearing regarding the matter, where he or an attorney for him could "present your position, arguments, or contentions in writing, and that at the hearing you may present evidence and examine witnesses appearing for or against you." But, if Burt declined to request such a hearing within thirty days, the board could still determine whether or not to revoke or limit his ability to practice medi-cine.[73] In his memo updating Governor Celeste on the Burt investigation, Napo-leon Bell wrote that "it would appear that this matter has been favorably concluded."[74]

Many critics, however, accused the board of acting late, especially since Burt had been public about both his surgery and his habit of not fully inform-ing his patients since the 1970s. Lauren Lubow, speaking for the board, would not comment on whether the board knew about Burt's 1975 book *Surgery of Love*, in which he admitted to performing the surgery without obtaining consent, nor would she confirm when the board began its investigation of Burt. "It's very easy for people to be righteously indignant in a situation like this," she said. The board, she said, was in a situation where they had to "prove all the charges" against Burt before taking any action and that "takes a good deal of time."[75]

Although Burt refused to comment to the newspaper about the board's charges against him, he appeared on a local television show the night the state board released the report, saying in a live interview he would review all of the forty-one charges and answer each of them. He also said he was looking at pos-sibly suing CBS over the *West 57th* program because it "so strongly and abruptly impacted the governor and the medical board and caused them a great deal of apparent distress." Calling the CBS program "inaccurate," Burt said he thought a lawsuit might be necessary because of "all the lies aired through the media."[76]

With the charges made by the state medical board, the Burt investigation attracted the national media again. The violations against Burt appeared in newspapers from the *New York Times* to the *San Jose Mercury News*, running across the wire on the Associated Press.[77] Perhaps not surprisingly, the *Dayton Daily News* ranked the James Burt story as one of the top ten stories of the year for the city, alongside Dayton's crack epidemic and the murderer Theodore Sinks, a *Dayton Daily News* employee charged with killing his forty-four-year-old wife, who had also worked for the paper, and hiding her body inside concrete on the top floor of the newspaper's building.[78]

As if being ranked next to a murderer and a drug epidemic were not enough, Burt learned at the end of the year he and his wife were going to lose a condominium through foreclosure. They were also informed one of their homes and his office were to be foreclosed. The sheriff would auction the house, with four bedrooms, four fireplaces, a pond, and a gazebo, all enclosed behind an electric gate, if the Burts failed to make payments.[79] These foreclosure notices came shortly after a federal judge rejected Burt's bankruptcy request from the previous June, thus allowing for the malpractice lawsuits against him to move forward.[80]

At the beginning of 1989, Burt decided to fight the board's charges and requested a hearing regarding charges he "totally denied." It was legally his right to request such a hearing, and the burden of proof regarding the charges lay with the state medical board.[81] Burt may have been heartened by the news that St. Elizabeth, after its internal investigation, announced it would not act against him, although it would not reinstate his ability to practice surgery at the hospital. The hospital's investigation found no operation had been performed without patient consent, and "contrary to what others are saying, there were no unusual complications involved in the 170 cases we reviewed," James Makos, president of St. Elizabeth said. Asked if it would reinstate Burt's privileges at the hospital if the medical board did not revoke his license, Makos replied it would consider doing so for some surgical procedures.[82]

In its editorial, however, the *Dayton Daily News* took Makos to task on the number of cases reviewed, saying it was an apparent attempt to "downplay Dr. Burt's involvement at St. E's." According to Makos, the hospital review found 170 cases of love surgery performed by Burt between 1975 and 1987, but this number only counted "the instances where people were *signing up* for 'love surgery,'" noted the newspaper—not the times Burt performed it on women who were having a baby or a hysterectomy. By not including this distinction, the editors wrote, it left "the impression that Dr. Burt was doing only on average of 15 'love surgeries' a year between 1975 and 1987," something the *Dayton Daily News* concluded was "an unconscionable distortion."[83]

But Burt apparently was not able to wait to see what the state medical board's actions would be regarding his ability to practice, for on January 12, he closed his medical office.[84] Shortly thereafter, he offered to surrender his license to the State Medical Board of Ohio.[85] As Bell explained to Celeste in his memo keeping the governor abreast of the Burt investigation, an offer to relinquish a license "is a usual strategy for doctors and lawyers facing serious charges, with the possibility of losing their licenses to practice, permanently." If the state medical board accepted Burt's offer and did not go forward with the hearing on January 30, "it would be possible," Bell wrote, "for Dr. Burt to, at some future date, request the privilege to practice medicine again, either here or possibly in some other state." Bell concluded his memo by writing that, in his opinion, "the medical board would impose permanent revocation of Dr. Burt's license, which possibly would prevent him from practicing anywhere in the future."[86] The state medical board rejected Burt's offer and set a hearing for January 30.[87] Although he seemed poised to fight to keep his license only weeks before, rather than appear before the board, Burt voluntarily surrendered his medical license.[88] On Wednesday, January 25, Burt sent a letter notarized by his attorney, Earl Moore, to the state medical board, notifying it that he "voluntarily, knowingly and intelligently surrendered all rights to practice medicine." His voluntary surrender of his license was effective immediately and enforceable throughout the United States.[89] Moore told the *Dayton Daily News* that by avoiding the hearing, his client would not have to produce evidence and testimony that would be public information and thus available to former patients suing him.[90]

The board accepted Burt's surrender of his license because, as spokesperson Lubow stated, "it essentially does the same thing that we could have done through a formal hearing." But even as he surrendered his license, Burt admitted no wrongdoing and defended love surgery in a two-page statement that accompanied his letter. According to the statement, Burt surrendered his license to protect his family and friends from "unjustified abuse." Burt stated his "practice of medicine and surgery has always been in accordance" with Ohio's laws and with the "tenets of ethics as published by the American Medical Association." He further wrote that he prayed "everyday that the Sisters of the Poor and the Catholic Church can be protected from the malicious greed of those who have incited this tragedy, that is based on the bearing of false witness."[91] Once again, Burt made headlines both regionally and nationally, with papers such as the *New York Times*, the *Philadelphia Daily News*, and the Associated Press carrying the story of his license "surrender-revocation."[92]

On the evening Burt sent his surrender letter, some of his former patients called each other to let them know about the agreement reached between Burt and the state medical board. Nancy Houston, the new mother who wrote to St. Elizabeth following her painful and unpleasant interaction with Burt when he delivered her daughter in 1975, told the *Dayton Daily News* that she was confused about what happened. "I thought the board said it wouldn't accept his license without an acknowledgement that he's guilty," she said, disappointed. Although Houston was not one of the women suing Burt, Janet Phillips was, and she told the press she had spoken with other women and none of them knew what to make of Burt surrendering his license, but they were all "disappointed" by his action. "We are telling the truth, and he didn't have a leg to stand on. We wanted a hearing and we feel [that by not defending himself] he is admitting guilt."[93]

Burt, however, did not admit guilt. Instead, two days after he surrendered his medical license, Burt said he intended to stay in Dayton, working to promote his surgery and teaching it to other doctors. He also announced his intention to write about love surgery for publication in medical journals. Earl Moore, speaking for Burt, claimed Burt had been asked to teach at medical schools, although Moore declined to provide the names of the schools.[94]

Following Burt's surrender of his medical license, St. Elizabeth announced it had rescinded all his medical privileges and removed him from the medical staff.[95] But two months after signing an advertisement defending the hospital and the actions it had taken to curtail Burt and his practice of love surgery, St. Elizabeth president Makos said he would consider letting other physicians perform love surgery at the hospital. "I would look at it," he told the *Dayton Daily News*, "and I would reserve judgment on that in the sense that I would like to have the ability to look at it and see if we want to continue to permit that or not." Makos made the comments during a news conference the day after Burt surrendered his medical license. During the conference, Makos stated he was not convinced Burt did anything wrong at St. Elizabeth. Moreover, in contrast to the advertisement that ran two months prior, Makos now stated that St. Elizabeth was not planning to review its peer-review system, saying he felt "our procedures are adequate and that we have very good people who are participants in that process."[96] Saying the hospital had reviewed all of Burt's love surgery patients' records between 1975 and 1987, Makos again stressed that the hospital's internal review found Burt's patients did not have unusual complications.[97] Although Burt had rescinded his ability to practice medicine,

St. Elizabeth still faced lawsuits with the former gynecologist, so the hospital president was, one can assume, keeping this in mind.

Shortly after Burt voluntarily surrendered his medical license at the end of January, Makos sent workers to Burt's office to obtain medical files. Makos was concerned because Burt had threatened to destroy the files when he closed his office, apparently telling Makos that if St. Elizabeth did not take the files, he would burn them, an act the *Dayton Daily News* noted was not, "oddly enough," illegal.[98] So the hospital took possession of thousands of pages of Burt's patient files. Burt told a reporter the press had "totally destroyed me and I don't have the money to store the records and to copy them for the patients," who were suing him and who wanted copies of their medical records from him. On February 3, Makos obtained the records, although he noted that it put the hospital in a difficult position of holding on to records that were part of a lawsuit in which it was a co-defendant.[99] The hospital reportedly approached both the Montgomery County Medical Society and the Ohio State Medical Society, as well as the State Medical Board of Ohio, about taking the records. The county society declined, however, because it felt it, like the hospital, had a conflict of interest. The state medical society also declined, partly, the *Dayton Daily News* stated, because Burt was not a member (a "bizarre" reason, according to the paper). And finally, the state board would not accept the files because it said it did not have jurisdiction over them, as Burt had given up his medical license. As the local paper editorialized, "the case that began by falling through the medical community's cracks has ended up between the cracks."[100]

That St. Elizabeth possessed the patient files troubled some of Burt's former patients, one of whom went to the hospital to try and get her records for her new gynecologist and was refused.[101] Attorneys Sambol and Walker had also demanded the records of more than thirty of Burt's former patients as part of their lawsuits against Burt. They claimed to have their clients' approval to have access to their records, but St. Elizabeth did not hand the records over, claiming them to be in disarray.[102] The records, however, were soon taken by a bankruptcy trustee, because, as John Ducker, one such trustee, told a local newspaper, "no one else was available to do so." Although the hospital would keep the records, locked, on its premises, only the trustee had a key. Those wishing access to them needed a court order.[103]

With the airing of the CBS show in late October and the extensive local media attention following it and the surrender of Burt's medical license, many women discovered they were not the only ones with complications following a surgery they were unaware they had undergone. Gerry Harness saw Burt in the early 1970s when she was thirty-three for relief from heavy periods. Burt told Harness her excessive bleeding was from uterine cysts and he advised removing the uterus and recommended additional corrective surgery on her bladder, which, he told her, had dropped as a result of her three pregnancies. So in 1972, Harness had surgery, which lasted twelve hours. After surgery, Burt informed Harness, who was in terrible pain, that he had also taken her ovaries upon discovering they were diseased and prescribed the hormone Feminone. Believing her pain would subside and she would bounce back after surgery within a short amount of time, Harness became frustrated and saddened when her pain in fact became worse, especially when she and her husband attempted sex. Burt's answer to the couple's complaints was to try different positions and for her husband not to take "no" for an answer. But the sex was always painful, she had frequent migraines, and, after quitting her job, Harness slipped into depression, for which in 1973 she was committed to a psychiatric hospital and given electroshock treatment. Not getting any better and having no idea what was going on, her husband took her home, against her doctor's orders. It was then that she discovered the side effects of Feminone were migraines and depression, and, going off them, her headaches disappeared. In 1975, she read about love surgery in the local newspaper and wondered if the surgery had also been performed upon her and spoke with an attorney about suing Burt for malpractice. Her attorney, however, informed her that unless another doctor testified against the surgery, she had no case. Her family doctor refused, so Harness decided she would just try and get on with her life, although by now that did not include sex with her husband. It was not until the fall of 1988 when Harness and her husband were both watching Burt on television that she felt her pain was legitimized, after listening to the women on the show speak of their pain as the result of Burt's surgery. "Thank God, I'm not the only woman going through this!" Harness thought. Following the show, Harness contacted Sambol and filed a $3 million lawsuit against her former gynecologist.[104]

Harness was not the only woman to discover by watching the CBS show in October 1988 that her pain and problems stemmed from surgery Burt had performed. Recall that Liz Sanders went to Burt in 1975 for a hysterectomy and ended up also having love surgery, which resulted in her inability to have sex. After seeing the CBS show in 1988, she recalled thinking, "My God! There's nothing wrong with my mind, it's my body!"[105] At least one woman found out by watching the show as a rerun in the spring of 1989.[106] Others heard that they were not alone through other routes. Lydia Eiford, who had moved to Florida, learned from newspaper stories clipped by her mother, who still lived in

Dayton.[107] Ginger Tripoli, also living in Florida in the late 1980s, read an article in late 1988 in the *St. Petersburg Times* discussing how Burt had been accused of malpractice and that the state medical board was looking into his practice. After reading the article, Tripoli recalled contacting Janet Phillips, who recommended she see Bradley Busacco.[108]

In the months after the CBS show aired, many women came forward with similar stories regarding Burt and the negative effects of love surgery. These women had all trusted Burt. He delivered the child of Mary Peters, for example, but following the birth and reconstruction surgery, she experienced pain during urination and bladder, kidney, and vaginal infections; sex was also painful for her.[109] Similarly, recall how Lydia Eiford went to Burt in the late 1970s for "excessive vaginal bleeding," for which Burt recommended a hysterectomy, and how Burt also told Eiford he would tighten some of her vaginal muscles.[110] Also recall the story of Litha Ann Jeffery, who went to Burt for treatment for heavy vaginal bleeding and infertility and how Burt told her a minor surgery would take care of her problems, a surgery she underwent in March 1976. Shortly after surgery, Jeffery experienced pelvic pain; bladder, urinary tract, and vaginal infections; and painful intercourse. She also noted that her vulva area looked different.[111] Burt also operated on Marva Hopkins in 1976, telling her she needed a hysterectomy because of a precancerous growth. Following surgery, urinating was impossible for Hopkins (she required a catheter for weeks), and when she began having sex again with her husband, it was painful; she tore and bled.[112] Barbra Roberts underwent surgery to correct a problem with her bladder in 1981, but shortly following it, she experienced problems with her kidney, bladder, and intestines, as well as difficulties having intercourse.[113] There were more women who sued, and they often had the same problems following love surgery. Sambol recalled that probably half the women who contacted her claimed they were unable to have vaginal sex.[114]

By mid-February 1989, six women had filed suit against Burt.[115] Earl Moore, Burt's attorney, stated that most of the suits filed by these women would be dismissed because of the statute of limitations. Sambol, however, disagreed, arguing that the statute of limitations "starts when a patient knows or should know that a doctor did something wrong which injured her." The clock started ticking, according to Sambol, when the CBS show aired. Until *West 57th* aired, many of the women, Sambol argued, "didn't connect the problems with Dr. Burt. They felt it was their body's reaction to surgery that had been done correctly. They didn't know that their anatomy had been rearranged."[116]

In addition to seeking redress through the courts, former patients also reached out to each other. Many women called Janet Phillips directly or called the *Dayton Daily News* or the local television station for her phone number following the airing of the CBS show, and she became the center of a group of former Burt patients. Phillips recalled so many phone calls that she bought an answering machine so that instead of answering the phone all night, she "could help her daughters with their homework" and cook dinner; she would then "return whatever calls I could." Phillips and other women gathered to support each other informally in small groups at one another's homes, and a larger group of Burt's former patients came together and met at a local hotel, the Cambridge Inn, at a gathering organized largely by Phillips and Cheryl Sexton.[117]

In early 1989, other women in the Dayton area—including those who did not say they had undergone love surgery—publicly responded to Burt. Some women did so through letters to the editor. Kathleen Hopson wrote in to challenge James Makos, who claimed love surgery did not conflict with Catholic teachings. According to Hopson, "I was taught that the human body was the perfect creation of God," and, therefore, through his surgery, Burt was seeking to "improve on the works of God," something that was "dead wrong" according to the church's teachings. Makos's defense of the surgery made Hopson "feel ashamed to be a Catholic," and she ended by saying that "Dr. Burt, the CEO, and St. Elizabeth are reflecting a very poor image on the Catholic Church."[118]

Other Dayton women commented on the sexual nature and the sexism of the surgery. Laura Lee Frye wrote that "if it had been male anatomy Dr. Burt had been rearranging, you can bet the medical community would have been screaming a long time ago."[119] Nancy Grisby commented in her letter to the editor about the claims Burt and Schramm made in their article that love surgery reduced domestic violence because it "'made women' 'easier to live with.'" Citing the rates of domestic violence in the United States, Grisby wrote such ignorance was harmful, particularly when it came from "professionals who should know better." Shame on them, she concluded.[120] In another letter to the editor, Suzanne Rosen wrote that there was "something radically wrong with Dr. Burt." If a woman is having "sexual problems, it is because she is with a lousy, insensitive lover." What she needed was not surgery but rather a new partner. "St. Elizabeth Medical Center, as well as Burt's colleagues, should have chased this man out of town years ago," but instead, Rosen concluded, "they have been protecting him."[121]

Rosen's conclusion was similarly reached by the national television and print media when it again descended upon Dayton in the spring of 1989. In late

February, the Fox network television show *The Reporters* aired a segment on the Burt story focusing on Burt's former patients, what producer Suzanne Mitchell said was a "story of human tragedy more than a medical story."[122] The *Oprah Winfrey Show* did a segment on Burt and his former patients that ran in May.[123] Some of the women spoke to *People* magazine in a story that appeared in late March. Coney Mitchell told the magazine she "had all the faith in the world in Dr. Burt" and that he "never told me he was going to do 'love surgery' on me. I don't know why he did that, unless he hates women." Linda Cook said she saw Burt "as if he were a spider with a fly. From the first time I walked into his office, he was scheming to get me into the operating room so he could perform this love surgery of his." Judy Mack told *People* she "did not go to Dr. Burt for love surgery." Following the surgery she did not request, she suffered from bladder infections and pain during intercourse. Mack said that before the surgery, she "had no problems at all sexually. If I had requested it, I would have been able to accept the consequences. Right now I feel I've been raped." Another woman, quoted anonymously, told *People* she worried that Burt was going to get "away with this unscathed."[124] *People* magazine also interviewed and quoted Sidney Wolfe. He told the magazine the Burt case represented a failure of the system at every level. Local doctors, medical groups, St. Elizabeth, "any one of these groups could have easily turned off this guy 15 or 20 years ago," *People* quoted Wolfe. Burt, Wolfe said, "is a butcher."[125]

People was just the first of many popular national magazines in the first half of 1989 to run articles on Burt and question the lack of accountability of local doctors and the hospital. Dayton physician Robert Hilty, who was quoted by several of the magazines, told *Woman's Day* that "everyone knew that a lot of his patients were having problems," and while no one wanted to protect him, "nobody talked either because they're all afraid of being in court." But that, said George Annas, an expert on medical law and bioethics then at Boston University School of Medicine, was a "flimsy excuse." It was, Annas told the magazine, "a way of saying 'I don't want to get involved.' So what if it's time-consuming and costly to defend a libel suit? Would they rather have more and more women butchered by this man?"[126] In June, *Savvy Woman* ran an article called "Crime against Nature" and in it asked if "anything can be done to prevent similar cases from happening." According to bioethicist Arthur Caplan, then director of the University of Minnesota's Center for Biomedical Ethics, there was very little that could be done. "Doctors can do what they want when they want as long as they get permission from the subject. And that's relatively easy to get," said Caplan. Although Caplan suggested the peer-review system needed some repair, such as a way to relicense physicians every few years in a manner similar to what was done for airplane pilots, George Lundberg, the editor for *JAMA*, called the system "damn good" and contended that changing it would mean restricting "human creativity and professional experimentation and application."[127]

But where the medical community of Dayton was really taken to task in print was in a story that appeared in the July issue of a magazine geared toward physicians and the business of medicine, *Medical Economics*. In a long article titled "Why Was the Love Surgeon Allowed to Keep Cutting?" senior editor Mark Holoweiko questioned why Burt's colleagues failed to intervene effectively, writing that doctors, and especially the hospital, could have "prevented 'love surgery' from becoming another lurid example of medicine's ineptitude at self-policing" by simply denying "Burt permission to do his pet procedure."[128]

Shortly before this article appeared, Sambol sought expert assistance from outside the state to help with her cases against Burt. In the spring of 1989, Sambol enlisted New York plaintiff attorney Harvey Wachsman, a high-profile malpractice lawyer who appeared with regularity on CNN as a malpractice expert and who, prior to becoming an attorney at age forty, had been a neurosurgeon.[129] On May 4, 1989, Wachsman and Sambol, representing Sheila Wilson, filed a malpractice suit against Burt, but this time they also named as defendants an additional eighty-two doctors in the Dayton area—including members of St. Elizabeth's peer-review committee, members of the local medical society, and local obstetricians—for allegedly not reporting Burt to the licensing board.[130] Wachsman declared that the eighty-two additional defendants were involved in a "conspiracy of silence no different than Nazi Germany."[131] People in this country, Wachsman stated, "deserve to be protected from individuals like that."[132] According to Wachsman, "if we left out anybody this time, we'll name them next time," although he added that he expected some who were initially named would be removed following depositions when it could be determined they were not liable.[133] The lawsuit demanded $50 million in punitive damages.[134]

Wilson, alongside about a dozen former Burt patients, attended the boisterous news conference held by Sambol and Wachsman in the Montgomery County Courthouse announcing the lawsuits.[135] Judge Carl Kessler, irate, kicked the attorneys out of the courthouse, ordering them to hold their news conference outside.[136] Kessler called the use of the county courthouse for the news conference improper, and Wachsman told reporters he intended to apologize later to the judge. Prompted by their news conference, Frank Woodside III, a Cincinnati attorney representing St. Elizabeth, called Wachsman's comments "bombastic, grandstanding" and of a "New York style" and not representative of what he regarded as the Midwestern style: rational and low key.[137]

Despite the numerous articles about him and multiple lawsuits pending against him, Burt maintained his innocence, saying the media had "destroyed my life" and that he was a victim of an "unjustified crucifixion" and an "avalanche of yellow journalism."[138] And indeed Burt must have felt like an avalanche was bearing down upon him. In early February 1989, a judge granted one of the women suing him, Coney Mitchell, a default judgment because of Burt's failure to respond to her lawsuit. While the judgment awarded no monetary damages, Sambol said Burt's failure to respond to Mitchell's lawsuit "tells me that Dr. Burt is not going to deal with these women," that the doctor was, in essence, "admitting that he treated them negligently by refusing to defend the claims."[139] That same month, on Friday, February 3, Burt's former clinic was sold at a sheriff's auction and was set to become an insurance office. Also sold at auction that day was a condominium owned by the Burts and their house at 7152 Paragon Road. The four-bedroom house was appraised at $210,000 but sold to North Carolina National Bank for $170,000. This bank, as well as Society Bank, both had liens on the house. Society Bank foreclosed on the house and the other two properties when Joan Burt, who owned them, defaulted on the loans.[140] Further, James Burt's attempts to start a new career in real estate were thwarted when Florida revoked his real estate license, citing his failure to disclose the charges before the State Medical Board of Ohio and the multiple lawsuits against him.[141] In addition to his financial and legal stresses, in early March, Burt underwent surgery for prostate cancer.[142] Although Earl Moore, who released this information, declined to say where Burt would be undergoing treatment, a month later, when Moore stated Burt had been released from the hospital, he did say Burt was "back in the States now."[143]

Moreover, Burt's attempts to strike back at those he felt wrongly accused him were stifled. On September 24, 1990, federal judge Walter Rice dismissed a portion of Burt's $250 million libel lawsuit against CBS, ruling that Burt had no private right of action under the Federal Communications Commission's personal-attack rule. However, Rice did not dismiss the entire lawsuit, saying he would consider further arguments on whether the statute of limitations had expired on the CBS broadcast of the show, thus redirecting Burt and his lawsuit. CBS argued that Burt's suit should be dismissed because the former gynecologist failed to file it within one year after the episode aired. Burt, however, claimed the statute of limitations had not run out because the show was broadcast a second time and he had filed the lawsuit within a year of the second broadcast. Rice gave Burt twenty days to file this lawsuit.[144] Burt managed to squeak just under this deadline, refiling his $250 million suit against CBS the third week of October.[145]

While Burt was seeking redress through the courts regarding the CBS show (a redress that ultimately failed when his case was dismissed in 1991), St. Elizabeth, listed as a co-defendant with Burt in the malpractice lawsuits, asked Richard Dodge, the judge in those cases, not to allow the State Medical Board of Ohio's letter to Burt outlining the gross immorality charges against him to be used in the malpractice trial because, the hospital attorneys said, it was hearsay and would be highly prejudicial and misleading to the jury.[146] On Thursday, October 11, Judge Dodge began ruling on what evidence could be admitted in the upcoming malpractice trials, saying the state medical board letter charging Burt with "gross immorality" could not be introduced as evidence against him because it was hearsay and therefore inadmissible. Additionally, Dodge said the jury might confuse the charges made in the twenty-one-page letter with actual findings. "Unfair prejudice," Dodge said, was "bound to result" if the board's letter was allowed as evidence. Because all parties in the lawsuit were barred from discussing the upcoming trial to the media, neither side commented on the ruling.[147]

In addition to their lawsuits against Burt, some of his former patients sought to have their voices heard about what happened to them by testifying in support of new legislation regarding what physicians needed to disclose about other physicians. Soon after the spring 1989 meeting of former Burt patients at the Cambridge Inn, some of the women met with state representative Rhine McLin to discuss what Burt did to them.[148] Following this meeting, McLin, along with state senator Linda Furney of Toledo, introduced legislation to strengthen the powers of the state medical board.[149] In their announcement of their proposed bill to the press, a bill the *Plain Dealer* said in its reporting of the announcement would "keep patients safe from incompetent or unscrupulous doctors," Furney commented on the uneven nature of the doctor–patient relationship. "We are taught at an early age that doctors are awe-inspiring men and women with the power to cure sickness," and although over "90% of the time this trust is warranted," Furney stated, "what happens when that trust is betrayed?" The only thing protecting patients, she commented, was the state medical board. And, "right now, that board is understaffed, underfunded and up against the silence of the doctors themselves."[150]

An aspect of their proposed bill provided the state medical board with the power to fine physicians failing to report medical abuses up to $50,000.[151] A vocal critic of the board following the outing of Burt on the CBS show, McLin would also have increased the investigatory powers of the board, increased penalties for incompetent doctors, and increased the number of nonphysicians on

the board.[152] In an editorial, the Cleveland *Plain Dealer* supported the bill, one
it noted had been "spurred in part by the overwhelming silence over the alleged
abusive practices of Dr. James C. Burt, the Dayton gynecologist known for his
self-described 'love surgery.'" The bill, the editorial further asserted, would
hopefully break the silence about any future physician who "endangers the
patient and shames an entire profession."[153] The State Medical Board of Ohio,
however, asked the legislature to wait on McLin's bill, because an increase in
its state budget appropriation had recently allowed it to hire more investigators,
and the board hoped this would better enable it to perform its job at protecting
the public from doctors such as Burt.[154] The board did receive an increase in its
budget, which the board said would be used to double the number of staff attorneys, add six more investigators, and start operating a consumer complaint
database.[155]

Representative McLin's legislation was scheduled to be first heard before
the Health and Retirement Committee on Wednesday, January 10, 1990, and witnesses who gave testimony at the second hearing on February 6 in support of
the legislation included Sambol and four women who had undergone love surgery: Phillips, Ruby Moore, Coney Mitchell, and Phyllis Ann Eckenrode.[156]
Whispering her testimony, Eckenrode told the committee that Burt "hurt me so
bad" she was "afraid to go to any doctor." Mitchell told the panel about a constant pain in her vagina—something she said she later learned was because of
constant infections, the result of a small pocket formed as part of love surgery
where urine collected and caused infection.[157] During their testimony, the
women sat on pillows.[158]

Although one panel member, Representative Robert Hagan, commended the
women for speaking "about something so sensitive" to the panel, the representatives were, at best, incredulous toward the women. Representative Paul Jones,
chair of the committee, questioned why they had gone to Burt. "Weren't you
aware of the questions surrounding Burt's surgeries?" Jones asked the women.
Moreover, during the women's testimony, members of the all-male committee
walked in and out of the room and spoke loudly with lobbyists, and one member, State Representative Patrick Sweeney, closed his eyes during their testimony.[159] Sandy Theis, a reporter who covered the women's testimony, recalled
the chair being rude to the women—indeed, she called their treatment by the
committee as "one of the meanest things I ever saw."[160] Opposed by the state
medical association, McLin's legislation ultimately failed.[161]

Chapter 9

Love Surgery on Trial

Medicine is a self-regulating profession; as the sociologist Eliot Freidson argued in his analysis of medical self-regulation, "to be granted freedom from supervision is a mark of being trusted, of being autonomous; in short of being professional."[1] However, it is not the only means by which medicine is regulated—it is also regulated socially, economically, and legally. And the primary means by which physicians are legally regulated is through medical malpractice litigation. As Timothy Jost noted in his analysis of medical regulation, although such litigation is "commonly viewed as a means of compensating victims of medical error," it is also a form of ensuring the quality of—that is, regulating—medical care.[2]

In late January 1991, Judge Richard Dodge of the Montgomery County Common Pleas Court announced that the malpractice suit filed by Janet Phillips against James Burt and St. Elizabeth would begin on May 6.[3] Phillips's case would be the first of dozens filed against the gynecologist.[4] During that spring, Phillips submitted pages and pages of medical records to be introduced as evidence in her trial. As further evidence of her injuries suffered at the hands of Burt and, by extension, St. Elizabeth, Phillips provided a statement of her medical bills for the corrective procedures she had undergone through March 20, 1991. The list included Burt's charge of $6,492.50 for the surgeries, as well as for painkillers, visits to multiple doctors, and several hospital stays, totaling $18,686.52.[5]

Because of all the local as well as national media attention covering Burt and his surgery, there was concern a jury would be difficult to seat, so preparations began for the trial to be moved to Toledo on May 17 in an effort to find an

impartial jury pool if one could not be found in Dayton.[6] But in late April, before
the jury selection process even began, Judge Dodge imposed sanctions against
Earl Moore, James Burt's attorney, and attorneys for St. Elizabeth, for their "friv-
olous conduct" in seeking to suppress evidence Phillips planned to introduce
at trial. Dodge fined St. Elizabeth $13,391 and Moore $3,500. Moore was cited
because Burt failed to appear for his deposition on March 25.[7]

In a final attempt to stall or prevent Phillips's lawsuit against him, on Thursday, May 2, just days before jury selection was to begin, Burt moved to withdraw from the case by petitioning the Supreme Court of Ohio, saying he was
physically and financially broken, and did not want his love surgery to garner
further negative publicity. Burt said that if he would be allowed to withdraw,
he would accept a default judgment. In what the *Dayton Daily News* described
as a "rambling, six-page motion," Burt reiterated his belief in the benefits of love
surgery. "Even though I have been professionally, economically, and personally
totally destroyed by misrepresentations, I desire not to expose further those
concepts, which I feel will benefit generations of women when given valid professional attention sooner or later," he wrote. There has been, he complained,
"a massive unrebutted publicity campaign mounted against me and my concept
of adding to female surgery a detailed consideration of female physical sexual
needs and problems from the woman patient's point of view in the media for
over two years," and he did not want to subject himself or his surgery any longer to what he believed was the unfairness of the media. Thomas Moyer, the
chief justice of the Supreme Court of Ohio, denied Burt's request, saying Burt's
motion to withdraw appeared simply like another tactic to delay the lawsuit.
"I denied it because there didn't appear to be any merit to what he was arguing," Moyer stated.[8] Burt's motion before the Supreme Court of Ohio was not
signed by Earl Moore, and the *Dayton Daily News* wrote that it did not appear
"to have been written with the help" of an attorney.[9]

As part of his motion, Burt also complained that Judge Dodge was prejudiced. Dodge, Burt wrote, "has already found me guilty from my trial by media."
But in addition to asking the Supreme Court of Ohio to enable him to withdraw,
Burt appealed to Dodge, thus also asking the lower court for permission to withdraw from the lawsuit, a petition Dodge had already denied once. On the same
day, however, a possible reason why Moore had not signed onto Burt's motion
or helped him craft it became apparent: Moore had asked Dodge for permission
to withdraw as Burt's counsel.[10] Within a day, Dodge refused both Burt's and
Moore's requests. Although it was unclear if Burt would return from Florida for
the trial, Dodge ordered Moore to appear, even though Moore had told Dodge
he had lost touch with his client. While Dodge lacked the legal capacity to

require Burt to attend, he did have the power to make Moore attend the trial.[11] Ultimately, Burt did not attend what came to be a trial that took over a month; because it was a civil, and not a criminal, trial, Burt was not legally required to be present.[12]

On that following Monday morning, the day jury selection was scheduled to begin, the *Dayton Daily News* editorial blasted Burt. "Dr. James Burt may be a disgraced, broken, and sick man" but that did not "mean he can just ignore people who sue him." Both the trial judge and the chief justice of the Supreme Court of Ohio, the editorial noted, said "Burt can't just walk away from his accusers." The law, "and justice," the paper concluded, "requires that much of Dr. Burt."[13]

In Dodge's courtroom, more than 200 potential jurors were summoned to appear, and all sides expected it would take at least a week to fill the jury pool.[14] Harvey Wachsman, the head litigator for Phillips, staring intently at the first juror he queried, asked, "If the law was such that to punish the hospital, to put it out of business, would you be able to do that?" The juror, the *Dayton Daily News* reported, stared back at Wachsman and, after a moment, answered yes. But Dodge wanted none of that sort of questioning, so before the next potential juror, the judge told Wachsman to stop asking questions about destroying hospitals. Instead, twenty-five men and women were asked about their knowledge of the case, their ability to serve on a jury for a trial that was expected to last at least five weeks, and if they could award a large amount of money to Phillips. Several of the women in this initial group were disqualified after revealing that their knowledge of Burt made it impossible for them to set aside their prejudice, although a man who revealed that a nurse at St. Elizabeth once complained to him about Burt was permitted to stay. By the end of the first day, eight men and three women had made it through the preliminary cut.[15] But by Wednesday, three days into jury selection, only a handful of jurors had been selected, and that prompted Dodge to order sheriff deputies to hand-deliver summons to twenty people who had been called for jury duty but failed to appear or contact the court.[16]

It took a day longer than expected to seat a jury, but the first malpractice suit against Burt to go to trial began on May 14, 1991, and stayed in Dayton. The jury consisted of five men and three women.[17] Bailiff Shirley Freeman, who had worked in the county courts for more than twenty years, told the *Dayton Daily News* the jury selection process was the longest she could recall.[18] Dodge, in an attempt to have an even balance of women on the jury, or at least to not allow it to be male dominated, put the names of the prospective jurors on index cards, shuffled them, and drew. The first seven cards Dodge pulled, however, were all men, and the jury breakdown ultimately had more men than women.[19]

On Tuesday, May 14, the trial began, and immediately attorneys for St. Elizabeth told the jury that the hospital should not even be part of the trial. "This is an issue between Janet Phillips and Dr. Burt, not the hospital," K. C. Green, an attorney for the hospital, said in his opening remarks. St. Elizabeth, Green continued, did not fail in its responsibility to regulate Burt during the years he performed love surgery. Moreover, Green argued, the surgery in question was not experimental. "It's not experimental to vary standard medical techniques," Green stated, "that's good medical practice." But Wachsman disagreed, saying in his opening remarks that dozens of women were "mutilated in an illegal operation" by Burt and that the hospital permitted it. "The review process (at the hospital) was in place," Wachsman asserted, but "they did nothing about what they knew." Reading from Burt's book *Surgery of Love* about the ways his surgery transformed women from quiet housewives to "horny little house mice," Wachsman told the jury in his opening argument that Burt was "using these women literally as rats or mice." And, Wachsman asserted, the hospital knew. Green, however, countered that it was Phillips who knew and characterized Phillips as "unhappy with the procedures she knowingly agreed to undergo." In his opening remarks, Burt's attorney, Earl Moore, chimed in, saying Phillips knew about and consented to the operation.[20] Although lawyers for the hospital would argue for the duration of the trial that the hospital should not be part of the lawsuit—and that, regardless, Phillips had filed past the statute of limitations—these lines of argument that opened the trial—whether Phillips's consent was informed, whether love surgery was experimental or a variation on standard surgeries, and what the role of the hospital was to oversee the practice of a physician on its premises—were the three central points around which the trial revolved.[21]

The first central point of argument concerned whether love surgery was different from standard gynecological obstetrical procedures. Wachsman argued that "there was malpractice year after year" and that the hospital "disregarded the safety of others" and allowed Burt to perform an experimental surgery.[22] On the second day of the trial, former St. Elizabeth's nurse Nancy Goodman took the stand and testified that Burt's episiotomy repair surgery was not a standard episiotomy repair.[23] Goodman testified that nurses referred to what Burt did as "special repair," because it was "different from routine episiotomy repair." Within months of her beginning to work in the obstetrics department and observing what Burt was doing, Goodman testified she felt the procedure was different enough that it warranted an additional consent form, and she made this suggestion to her superiors, Sister Ellen Durso and Ethel Goecke. According to Goodman, Durso and Goecke told her there was nothing they could do about it. Goodman also testified that she complained to the director of the obstetrical practice residency program at St. Elizabeth on several occasions, and while supportive, he also told Goodman there was nothing they could do about Burt's surgery. "He was always very supportive," Goodman testified, but told her "there was not a whole lot that we could do about it, since we did not have complaints from the patients at the time."[24]

Yvonne Curington, a nurse who worked alongside Burt in the delivery room in the 1970s, testified that Sister Ellen Durso, who was then the director of nursing, listened to a group of nurses express concern about Burt. We were all "upset," Curington testified, "and Durso's response was 'as long as he isn't killing patients, we have to put up with him.'"[25] Similarly, Beatrice Busse, who worked as a nurse-anesthetist at St. Elizabeth during the 1970s, testified that she recalled Burt performed love surgery on all of his obstetrics patients and that this was well known among her fellow nurses. She recalled that the nurses scorned Burt's work but believed nothing would be done to stop him unless he killed one of his patients.[26]

Curington, who received her training at St. Elizabeth's nursing school, got her first job in labor and delivery at the hospital in May 1971. In her position, she witnessed Burt perform episiotomy repairs that were, as she testified, "drastically different" from the ones performed by other physicians. During her cross-examination by Moore, Curington stated what she meant by drastically different: "Everyone else was doing an episiotomy repair where the perineum was incised and then resutured by approximating the edges of incision back together again and stitching them together." But, Curington testified, "Burt's episiotomy repair was not like that" as it changed "the angle or axis of the vagina" and tightened the walls of the vagina, thus "creating a thicker perineum" and also resulting in the "opening to the urinary bladder which was inside the vagina not on the outside."[27]

Bradley Busacco, the Cincinnati gynecologist who treated many of Burt's former patients and who appeared on the CBS show, told the court that as a result of the surgery, Phillips may never recover feeling in her bladder, and he was uncertain if this loss could be corrected. As a result of this loss of feeling, Busacco stated that Phillips could not be certain when her bladder was full and thus needed to relieve herself every two hours. Moreover, he had never, Busacco testified, seen a vagina like the one he saw when he first examined Phillips.[28]

In addition to the testimonies of Goodman, Curington, and Busacco, Phillips's attorneys brought in medical experts from outside Dayton to argue that love surgery was far from standard practice and, moreover, that it had no therapeutic value. Stanley Wiener, testifying for Phillips, called love surgery "a procedure that has absolutely no value."[29] Wiener, a medical expert brought in from New Jersey, called love surgery "false, fictitious and fraudulent" during the third day of the trial. Wiener based his opinion upon reviewing the medical records of thirty-one of the patients Burt performed love surgery on from 1969 to 1981. Additionally, St. Elizabeth, Wiener stated, should not have allowed the unorthodox surgery or at the very least done better with their consent form by outlining the surgery. During his time on the stand, Wiener, a practicing obstetrician gynecologist for twenty-five years, said he had never seen a procedure like love surgery, and stressed that both Burt and St. Elizabeth were negligent in their care of Phillips.[30] Emanuel Friedman, a retired professor from Harvard University who also provided expert testimony on behalf of Phillips, called love surgery "experimental, unverified, and lacking proven results."[31] No expert testimony was given on the merits of love surgery.

The second central point of argument was whether the hospital should have provided more oversight of physicians performing surgery on its premises, specifically whether physicians were providing the standard of care. During the trial, it emerged that Burt had kept two sets of medical records for his patients, with the set kept at the hospital describing Phillips as in need of a hysterectomy and a candidate for love surgery because during sex she experienced "disabling pain" while the set he kept in his private clinic described Phillips as "functioning sexually quite well." Friedman testified that the existence of these two sets of records regarding Phillips, as well as the records of thirty-one other women he looked at, showed the hospital had failed to monitor Burt's surgeries over the years.[32] Friedman testified that one possible reason St. Elizabeth did not oversee Burt as tightly as it should have was economic: according to the financial documents he examined, Friedman claimed Burt generated about 5 percent of patient revenues generated by the hospital between 1971 and 1973, making him, out of 500 physicians who practiced at St. Elizabeth, the leading one for those years, although it was also noted that his productivity (and thus economic revenue) significantly declined afterward.[33]

Questions about the oversight of the hospital regarding Burt were also heard through the testimony of former nurses who worked at St. Elizabeth in the 1970s. Although Goodman and Curington said they brought up concerns about Burt and his practices in the 1970s, the two they claimed they spoke with testified they never heard any concerns from nurses regarding Burt. Sister Ellen Durso, who from 1968 to 1979 had been director of nursing services, and Ethel Goecke, who had been assistant director of nursing between 1974 through 1980, both testified at the trial. Durso told the jury that Yvonne Curington did not talk to her about Burt and that she never responded to Curington by saying "that as long as Dr. Burt wasn't killing patients, there was nothing that could be done to stop him." When asked how she could be so sure she never responded to Curington in such a manner, Durso responded that she would never have made a statement like that since "patient care was uppermost in my mind." Similarly, Goecke denied that Nancy Goodman protested to her about Burt's unusually extensive episiotomy repair. Indeed, Goecke said she could recall only praise from nurses about Burt. However, when pressed, Goecke also said that, as she had been retired for more than a decade, she had "blocked out" most of her memory of her time when she worked at St. Elizabeth.[34]

The third central line of argument between the parties centered on informed consent: first, whose role it was to obtain consent and, second, whether Phillips had given it. To the first point, Raynald Lane, a physician and senior vice president of medical affairs at St. Elizabeth, testified that the consent letter Burt's patients were required to sign was the only one of its kind at the hospital when he started there in 1979. Speaking before a large blowup of the consent form for love surgery, Wachsman read the letter out loud, adding that the "form speaks for itself" about the role of the hospital in the Burt affair. Lane, however, disagreed, saying it was not the hospital's responsibility but the individual clinician's to obtain informed consent.[35] Glen Hait, a plastic surgeon from Scottsdale, Arizona, and an expert witness for St. Elizabeth, testified that the hospital did an adequate job of ensuring Phillips gave informed consent. Under questioning by Wachsman, however, Hait also said that the consent form seemed to say "Watch out and see what you're going to have done to you before you have it done."[36] Moreover, Hait also said he had never before seen a consent form like the one used for love surgery.[37]

Stanley Wiener, as a medical expert for Phillips, testified that St. Elizabeth should not have allowed love surgery as it was unorthodox or should at the very least done better with its consent form by outlining the surgery. Although attorneys for St. Elizabeth objected and the judge upheld their objection, Wiener characterized the consent form as "fictitious and fraudulent," and "a 'stamp of approval' by the hospital."[38] "I believe a patient would be misinformed by this form," he said.[39]

Since Phillips's signature was on the consent form, the trial principally centered on whether Phillips had been sufficiently informed when signing the form. To prove their points, attorneys for the hospital and Moore had testimony from people who claimed Phillips indeed knew about love surgery prior to having it. Vivian Helbling, Burt's former secretary, testified that she gave Phillips a separate consent form for love surgery and recalled her signing it. "I reached up, handed her a document, asked her to sign it—give it back to me and I would witness it," Helbling testified, thus contradicting Phillips's claim that the consent form for love surgery was one within a stack of documents where she could only see the signature line at the bottom for all of them.[40]

In addition to Helbling's testimony, Jennifer Baker, a former coworker of Phillips in the 1970s at a company called Kadon, testified that she recommended Burt to Phillips when Phillips needed a second opinion regarding a hysterectomy. But according to Baker, Phillips also knew she would undergo love surgery when she elected to have Burt operate on her. "I knew that she was going to have the love surgery," Baker testified, because the two women had discussed the surgery in the late 1970s. Moreover, Baker also said Phillips told her that following love surgery, even wearing tight jeans was sexually stimulating. "I was under the impression she was pleased with the surgery," Baker told the jury.[41]

When Phillips took the stand, she denied all of what Baker said, stating she never discussed love surgery with Baker and that, moreover, wearing tight jeans was painful, not pleasurable. "It was just like hitting a raw nerve," Phillips testified, "I couldn't even wear pantyhose, much less jeans." Moreover, under cross-examination by Wachsman, Baker told the jury that after leaving Kadon, she was fired from her next job, a job where Phillips knew the owner. Baker apparently asked Phillips to intervene, but Phillips refused to do so, telling the jury that because she refused, Baker had said she would get Phillips back. Baker denied this charge, saying she never threatened Phillips, and was prompted to call Burt to offer to testify on his behalf after she saw the CBS show. "In the show it stated that Janet did not know what surgery she was going to have," Baker told the jury, "and I knew that that was not true."[42]

Although Phillips testified, James Burt never did; indeed, he never even attended the trial.[43] In an editorial, the *Dayton Daily News* lamented the fact that Burt did not appear, writing, "It might have been good for this community—not to mention former Burt patients—to hear from the 'love doctor' in some detail about what he thinks of the surgery now, and about how he would defend what he did."[44]

The Burt trial ended up taking a little more than five weeks.[45] Part of the reason it took so long was that there were three parties involved. Another was the pace of the questions. Wachsman, the *Dayton Daily News* stated, "plodded along at a snail's pace" in his questions of his witnesses, with some of his questions taking as long as three minutes to pose. The slowness of Wachsman's questioning was exacerbated by the frequent objections made by Moore and the hospital's attorneys. Dodge expressed concern about the fairness of the trial because of Wachsman's pace, saying the trial was "going to appear to be not real fair pretty

soon," although he did not go so far as to accuse Wachsman of deliberately trying to slow down the trial. Because of the slow pace, Frank Woodside III, an
attorney for St. Elizabeth, worried that once it came time for him to cross-
examine the witnesses, the jury would find it difficult to follow.[46]

Wachsman did not endear himself to the judge or to the jury, which strug-
gled to stay alert during some of his long and repetitive questions. But because,
with the exception of Busacco, the physicians Wachsman had on the witness
stand had not actually seen any of Burt's former patients, only their medical records, they could not be asked directly for their opinions. Wachsman had to
elicit these through a list of assumptions about Phillips's condition and, on the
basis of those assumptions, could then ask their opinions. While this was legally
necessary, it also resulted in very long and detailed descriptions of Phillips's
postsurgery anatomy and medical problems. As Martin Gottlieb wrote in his
opinion piece for the *Dayton Daily News*, Wachsman "told a horror story again
and again and again," a story Gottlieb believed the jurors "will not forget—ever,
for as long as they live."[47]

Possibly the most graphic parts of the trial occurred when Bradley Busacco
testified. During his time on the witness stand, Busacco stated that while some
of Phillips's injuries could perhaps be corrected with additional surgery, possibly costing $10,000 or more, some of them might never be corrected. Accord-
ing to Busacco, Burt had severed the nerves leading to Phillips's bladder that
signal when the bladder is nearly full, and as a consequence, Phillips had to
relieve herself every two hours. Moreover, until he examined Phillips, Busacco
said he had never seen a vagina constructed like Phillips's. To illustrate the differences, Busacco used a series of drawings contrasting a typical vulva and vaginal area with what that area looked like after Burt's love surgery on Phillips.
During this time, Phillips sat quietly, crying. When pressed about why it took
her more than four years after the surgery to seek out another opinion, Busacco
said, "I feel a woman is not capable of examining her own vagina." But, as importantly, Busacco also said he believed Phillips had very little understanding of
what had been done to her.[48]

Phillips sat for days as people described her body and its functions in, as
one observer put it, "breathtaking explicitness." On the day Busacco testified,
an area high school class was in the audience. And it was on that day, with teenagers watching, that the trial became very explicit. Using large drawings of the
female genital area propped up on an easel, Busacco described the location of
the vagina, clitoris, and the hood of the clitoris. He also described what Burt
did to Phillips, pointing out where he sewed back the hood of her clitoris and
explaining that a photograph showing two fingers sticking inside a vagina was

meant to show how Phillips had to urinate. The photographs were of Phillips's own body, the fingers her fingers, as they opened the vagina in order to allow the urine to leave her vagina (recall that Burt had redirected the urethra so that it emptied into the vagina) to reduce the chance that the urine would accumulate and cause a painful and, as the jury heard repeatedly, "odiferous" infection. Busacco explained how Phillips had to stand to urinate. *Dayton Daily News* opinion columnist Gottlieb said that, while the jury "had been restless at points in this trial," when Busacco testified, using the drawings and photographs, he had their rapt attention.[49]

As Janet Phillips listened to Busacco describe her inability to feel a full bladder, listened as he used a series of drawings from the perspective of a doctor examining a woman in stirrups to explicitly describe to the jury what had been done to her, comparing her body with that of a typical female body, she cried.[50] During her time on the witness stand, she was reduced to tears when Moore questioned her about how the surgery affected her present sexual life.[51] She frequently cringed, according to the journalists observing, as intimate parts of her body were discussed in the proceedings.[52] In addition to hearing about her body and the toll of the surgery upon it, Phillips listened as her attorneys detailed the repercussions to her relationships following the surgery, including divorce from her husband, Edmund Phillips, in 1984.[53] Moreover, during the trial, supporters of Burt loudly whispered disparaging innuendos about her.[54] Gottlieb wrote that despite what must have been painful for Phillips—indeed, he considered her being victimized again by the proceedings—she sat with quiet dignity.[55]

Although Phillips may have sat with "quiet dignity," the courtroom itself was full of tension, in particular between the attorneys.[56] The growing animosity probably was not helped by what the local newspaper called a "sweltering" courtroom, the result of the air conditioning breaking down.[57] And although this tension between the attorneys and increasingly the judge bubbled at the surface during the beginning of the trial, by the third day, it had already burst, the rupture point coming when Wachsman read from the cover letter of Phillips's medical records. The hospital letter stated that the patient records were complete, "with the exception of the nurses' notes—which were destroyed." Wachsman changed the inflection of his voice while reading the section about the nurses' notes, an inflection that stressed that sentence, and Frank Woodside III, the hospital's attorney, vehemently objected, moving for a mistrial. Dodge excused the jury and asked Wachsman if what he had just done was necessary. Wachsman pointed out he was simply reading a letter from the hospital, but Dodge chided him by saying, "That was obviously done with vocal inflection to indicate some form of wrongdoing by somebody." Such behavior, Dodge warned all the attorneys, would not be permitted before the jury. Dodge fined Wachsman $100 in an effort to control the growing animosity.[58]

This would not be the only time during the trial that the judge reprimanded one of the attorneys for their remarks.[59] On more than one occasion, Dodge ended a squabble between the attorneys for the three parties. One morning Dodge had to break up a screaming match between Moore and Joseph Walker, one of Phillips's attorneys, when the two men called each other names during a hearing without the jury present. Dodge threatened to both summon the sheriff's deputies and fine both of them if such behavior continued.[60] During the third week of the trial, the tension had obviously begun to wear on everyone. In response to a curt objection made by attorney Woodside, Wachsman muttered "of course" in a voice loud enough to be heard by all in the courtroom. Dodge immediately ordered the jury to leave the courtroom and called Wachsman up to the bench, demanding he explain himself. Wachsman apologized, saying he was fatigued and "overtired." "It was not my intention to embarrass him," Wachsman told Dodge.[61]

Although the trial was covered daily in the *Dayton Daily News* and presumably also on the local televised news, it did not appear to be a media circus. Indeed, there were often empty seats.[62] Five weeks after the start of the trial, the jury listened to closing arguments.[63] Heard on Wednesday, June 19, the arguments lasted more than five hours. Woodside, arguing for St. Elizabeth, stressed Phillips's signing of the consent forms, including the one specific to love surgery, that Phillips continued to go to Burt for more than two years after the surgery occurred, and that Phillips waited years after the surgery to file a malpractice claim. Moore, arguing on behalf of Burt, stressed in his closing arguments that the "4,000 other women who had the surgery" were satisfied and belittled Phillips's claims she had suffered recurring infections and pain following love surgery. "You people have had more pain and suffering sitting through this trial than she has," Moore contended. Finally, during his closing argument for Phillips, Wachsman contended that St. Elizabeth had protected its pocketbook instead of its patients and that Burt was "almost the devil incarnate in a white jacket."[64] He also stressed to the jury that by their decision, they could send a message not just to St. Elizabeth but to all hospitals about the role of the hospital to protect patients.[65]

Despite the vitriolic closing arguments, in an editorial the next day, the *Dayton Daily News* praised Richard Dodge for keeping "the proceedings orderly and civilized, a task somewhat complicated by the presence of lawyers for three sides." Moreover, the editorial stressed that those watching—including former Burt patients "who have strong emotions about the issue"—respected the need to have restraint during the trial. Finally, the editorial noted that Wachsman "had a point" asking jurors to send a message to all hospitals about their role in protecting patients, even though Dodge was correct in sustaining the lawyers' objection that the jury should rule only on the actions of St. Elizabeth.[66]

Dodge had the jury sequestered so they would not be exposed to press coverage of the trial. The sequester was unusual for Montgomery County—indeed, Dodge could not recall the last time a jury had been sequestered.[67] At 5:30 that afternoon, after the jury had left to debate at a hotel, Dodge watched Burt interviewed on WDTN-TV, a local television channel. He watched it again that night at 11. After watching both broadcasts and deciding that they were "outrageous," Dodge concluded it was necessary to issue a nationwide warrant for Burt's arrest for contempt of court because the interview violated Dodge's ban on all parties from contact with the media. The interview, which was run in six parts by the local ABC affiliate, began that Wednesday afternoon and evening, continued the following day at the same times, and concluded that Friday.[68] In the interview, Burt denied any wrongdoing and, during a portion of the interview broadcast Thursday night, said he had received Phillips's permission to perform the surgery.[69]

During the interview, Burt claimed he did not attend the trial because he thought it "very prejudiced." Had he attended, he believed he would "have been interrupted constantly and my message, quite possibly, [would] not have received the attention I would have liked it to."[70] The whole country, he claimed during the interview, "has been brainwashed for 2 ½ years without rebuttal and without any significant investigation of facts." Moreover, Burt claimed he did not think he would have had the stamina to speak to the jury due to his recent cancer treatment.[71] He was, however, interviewed in Los Angeles, where he was reportedly visiting family, having flown from his home in Florida to do so.[72] Dodge ordered Burt arrested for violating his ban on speaking to the media, finding Burt in contempt of court. Florida, however, refused to honor Dodge's civil warrant for Burt's arrest, as police in Lee County, where Burt lived, could do so only if the suspect had been issued a civil warrant by a Florida judge.[73]

Phillips had asked for $10 million in compensatory damages and $20 million in punitive damages from Burt and St. Elizabeth.[74] But just after 3 p.m. on Friday, June 21, two days after the jury left the courtroom to deliberate, they came back with a unanimous verdict in favor of St. Elizabeth.[75] The jury contended they could not award damages against the hospital because Phillips had waited too long to sue. Woodside told reporters that the ruling was "significant," and Green, another hospital attorney, said he did not think "it will ever be any sweeter." James Makos, president of St. Elizabeth, called the decision a "victory for the hospital and the whole medical community."[76] An editorial in the local newspaper, however, disagreed, saying the hospital "has gotten off very lucky" and was "pressing its luck with a public claim of 'exoneration'" since the jury concluded "that the hospital was 'guilty of negligence.'"[77]

Although unanimous in its decision regarding the hospital, seven of the eight jurors decided Burt was negligent and awarded Phillips $5 million in damages. In a statement made through his son, James C. Burt III, in Los Angeles, Burt told the press that "I am pleased that the hospital has been exonerated, as I expect to be on appeal." Phillips, Burt's statement continued, "has not told the truth from the beginning and has been believed by almost everyone."[78]

Phillips showed no emotion as the verdict was read and left the courtroom, declining to speak to the gathered reporters.[79] Speaking later that day, Phillips stated she felt "like we had a victory in that we did what we set out to do": they removed the "scalpel" from Burt's hand. Phillips also felt her trial meant hospitals were on notice: "The next time nurses say a doctor is doing funny stuff in the operating room, I'll bet money they'll listen."[80]

Although her initial comments were few on the day of the verdict, the following day Phillips spoke with Julia Helgason, a reporter with the *Dayton Daily News*, telling Helgason she doubted she would ever see a penny of the award. Moreover, she stated that the trial was "more than painful." It was, Phillips stressed, "humiliating." The trial cost her, she stated, "thousands and thousands of dollars" paid to "doctors and lawyers and investigators," and "for what?" She never dreamed, she told Helgason, "it would end like this." She won, she said, "but I didn't win."[81]

The *Dayton Daily News*, in its editorial the day after the verdict, noted that while Phillips had expressed "some satisfaction with a verdict against" her "victimizer," the ruling got St. Elizabeth "off on a technicality" and the "jury awarded Ms. Phillips $5 million in damages from a man who claims to have no money." Taking its own editorial position from the previous day to task, the newspaper, which on June 21 had "suggested that the legal process looked pretty impressive in the trial," now doubted the efficacy of the proceedings since the jury "was never told that Dr. Burt claims to have no money." Instead, the editorial pointed out, they "heard over and over that he was St. E's best-grossing doctor in the early 1970s." The editorial asserted that Phillips had, once again, been made a victim.[82] Indeed, it soon became clear that Burt would be unable to pay—his attorney, Earl Moore, reported the Burt had no assets and that he was living on Social Security, with help from his family.[83]

Jurors interviewed by the local paper after the trial also felt that Phillips was a victim and felt badly about their decision. According to juror Steve Lodge, he and his peers debated, sometimes heatedly, over the course of their two days together and had some regret that they felt unable to hold St. Elizabeth financially liable. "We felt bad about the decision," Lodge stated, "I feel I can speak for the rest of the jury because we felt bad about what we had to come up with," although he also said he felt the hospital did not act against Burt because the physician made a lot of money for the hospital.[84]

Shortly after the ruling, Phillips appealed, arguing the evidence presented at the trial supported her contention that she did file within the time limit of the statute. Mary Lee Sambol argued that "the jury misunderstood the court's instruction, and the evidence showed that she did in fact file within the acceptable statute of limitations."[85] But Phillips was not the only woman suing Burt; her case was simply the first to go to trial. And in late August 1991, an Ohio appeals court ruled that although there was a one-year statute of limitations for suing a physician for malpractice, the time for suing a hospital was different. According to the appeals court ruling, as the Dayton Daily News reported, "hospitals become liable when a doctor with staff privileges develops a pattern of incompetence that the hospital knew about or should have been aware of through its monitoring system." Thus, the statute of limitations for suing a hospital began once a plaintiff discovers a pattern of incompetence.[86] With this ruling, the appeals court effectively removed the argument made by St. Elizabeth, finding that Phillips had not sued too late. The appeals court ruling was not about the Phillips case, however, but rather those of Jimmie Dean Browning and Coney Mitchell.

In 1980, Browning went to urologist Max Blue out of concern for bladder infections and difficulties urinating. Blue operated on Browning, but her condition failed to improve, and, two years later, complaining of pain during intercourse with her husband, Blue advised she see Burt. Burt, Browning recalled, told her the pain she was experiencing stemmed from her husband's penis hitting her bladder during vaginal sex and that this could be relieved by placing her bladder on what he called a "pedestal." He also apparently indicated to Browning he would improve her sex life. In February 1982, she underwent surgery, although she contended what the surgery would entail had not been fully explained to her. Following the surgery, she needed to employ a urinary catheter for six months, and when it was removed, she was unable to properly void, causing extreme pain and vomiting and necessitating hospitalization. She continued to have frequent bladder infections, and pain-free sex with her husband proved impossible. The last time she saw Burt was in 1983, when he, she said, left her a message telling her he was leaving town and she did not need to see him again. She did, however, continue to see Blue, who performed several more surgeries on her, including removing a kidney. Finally, in 1987, Browning sought another opinion from a urologist at the Cleveland Clinic, who, she recalled, told her there had been a "flaw" in her surgery. At that point, however, Browning had undergone sixteen surgeries, and she was unclear which surgery had the "flaw." Browning confronted Blue during the summer of 1987, accusing him of malpractice; Blue, Browning recalled, denied her accusation and suggested she see a psychiatrist. Browning was not aware that one of the surgeries that had been performed upon her was love surgery until she watched *West 57th* in October 1988.[87]

Recall that Coney Mitchell first went to Burt in 1967 when she was pregnant with her third child. In 1972, he had her hospitalized for a D&C after a miscarriage. In 1976, he told her she should not have any more pregnancies, and he performed a tubal ligation. Then, in 1979, she underwent a hysterectomy by Burt, and in 1985, he operated on her to reinforce her bladder—something she had been having problems with since the birth of her third child—telling her, she recalled, that it would enable her to again engage in sexual intercourse, which had been difficult and painful following that birth. During this whole time, she had repeated infections and pain and felt, she stated in her deposition, that she "lived on antibiotics." Four months after the last surgery, when Mitchell and her husband attempted to have sex, she recalled being "totally blocked . . . I was covered over." That first attempt proved "so painful" and she "started bleeding like everything and I was scared to death and I didn't know what was wrong so, of course, I looked down" and saw that the vaginal opening was basically covered. When she called Burt, he told her healing would take more time. Mitchell and Burt apparently got into what Mitchell recalled as a "heated argument." Despite this, Mitchell continued to believe Burt and did not go see another physician for fear that she would, as she remembered Burt telling her, "bleed to death," as another doctor would not understand what he had done. Moreover, Mitchell recalled Burt repeatedly assuring her that she would get better and, she later found out, also repeatedly told her husband not to "take no for an answer" when it came to sex. She stopped seeing Burt in 1987, although she did not fully understand what happened to her until she watched *West 57th* in the fall of 1988. She went to see Busacco, whose name she got from watching the CBS show, in late 1988 and, after that, Sambol.[88]

In their editorial in response to the ruling, the *Dayton Daily News* said the ruling in the Browning case "changes the rules in the Burt cases in a big way" by "wiping out" the defense of the hospital that Phillips, Browning, and the other women had waited too long to sue. Instead, the appeals court ruled, the one-year statute of limitations when it comes to hospitals begins "on the date a patient learns that the hospital knew or should have known about a 'pattern of incompetence'" regarding a physician. The editorial further noted that with its ruling, the appeals court was "breaking new ground" since it was different from previous Supreme Court of Ohio decisions.[89]

St. Elizabeth challenged the Browning ruling and appealed, thus sending it to the Supreme Court of Ohio. If the decision were to be upheld by the state supreme court, it would affect ten of the forty lawsuits that had been dismissed for having been filed too late, and it would undoubtedly influence the other thirty, since St. Elizabeth was challenging those as being similarly filed too late.[90] After the appeals court ruling, Phillips's attorneys went back to court, arguing that the hospital should be held liable for damages.[91]

In August 1992, Phillips's attorneys argued before Dodge that, based on the ruling that the statute of limitations for a hospital had not expired in the case of St. Elizabeth, Phillips should get a new trial. While Phillips's attorneys argued for her to get a new trial, the cases against Burt and the hospital that had been moving through the legal system were held, waiting for the Supreme Court of Ohio to decide whether it agreed with the ruling of the appeals court that the statute of limitations regarding suing a hospital did not begin until the plaintiff became conscious of an apparent pattern of incompetence.[92]

In January 1993, the Supreme Court of Ohio heard oral arguments in the Browning and Mitchell lawsuits.[93] That summer, with a vote of 5–3, the court ruled that Browning and Mitchell had a right to sue St. Elizabeth. As Judge Andy Douglas wrote in the majority opinion, "Perhaps now they, and others, will have their day in court where the conspiracy of silence in the local medical community which permitted the atrocities to be committed—and the atrocities themselves—can be fully explored." The ruling did not "pass judgment (on the claims of negligence), although it is tempting to do so given what the record shows has happened to these two women," Douglas further wrote. While not addressing the merits of the lawsuits, the court ruling enabled the suits to move forward, since the ruling supported the appeals court decision that the time the statute of limitations began was not when the women began experiencing problems but rather when they watched *West 57th* and learned about a pattern of incompetence. Moreover, Douglas wrote that the one-year statute of limitations did not apply to a hospital: "A hospital does not practice medicine and is incapable of committing malpractice," and thus, a two-year statute of limitations applied when it came to matters of a hospital's negligence.[94] The women, then, could sue the hospital under negligence laws, although the hospital was not liable under malpractice laws.[95]

St. Elizabeth appealed this decision, and the appeal went all the way to the U.S. Supreme Court. In February 1994, the Court declined to review the rulings from the Ohio courts, letting stand the rulings of the lower courts in support of a statute of limitations for a hospital being two years when it came to negligence.[96] The U.S. Supreme Court did not provide a written explanation—something a spokesperson said was routine regarding cases the Court did not want to hear. When asked for a response to the high Court's ruling, Sambol said she was "glad that these women are finally going to have their day in court." There is now, she also said, "no place St. Elizabeth can go."[97]

Sambol, however, was not the only one pleased with the decision of the U.S. Supreme Court: so was James Burt. Living in Fort Myers, Florida, he had recovered from prostate cancer and was trying to start a foundation for promoting love surgery. Because the U.S. Supreme Court ruling meant the lawsuits could proceed, it meant St. Elizabeth, he felt, would have to defend the surgery. In Phillips's trial, recall, the hospital did not defend love surgery but rather argued that the women had both filed too late and that the hospital should not be party to the lawsuits. According to Burt's son, some of the women, those who were among the "hundreds of cases with good results," would also be brought forward to testify in support of the surgery for the hospital. Moreover, Burt's son also said his father would testify that information from his "extensive scientific testing" regarding the surgeries would show "how greatly their [the patients'] quality of life improves when painful sex or no sex is replaced with good sex." Burt had thought he had lost this research, his son stated, but had recently found it in a storage space he had rented. The evidence in question were sets of questionnaires women filled out before and after the surgery. "Many of the plaintiffs in the cases against the hospital are going to have some real difficulty at trial because we have," Burt's son said, "in their own handwriting, what difficult sexual problems they were having before surgery and how happy they were with the good results, still, many months after the surgery." But while James Burt and his son said they had offered to help the hospital with the lawsuits by providing this information, they noted St. Elizabeth had not responded to their offer.[98]

The U.S. Supreme Court decision prompted the women suing Burt to drop him from their lawsuits—as he was bankrupt—and focus on the hospital.[99] And this is what other Burt patients did: in June 1994, a panel of judges heard arguments from twenty-five women seeking to have their cases reinstated against the hospital.[100] By early September, the appeals court looking at these cases had allowed five women to go forward. The judges threw out one woman's case, saying there was evidence showing she knew, or should have known, enough to have been "alerted" of the reasons for her complications from a 1978 surgery by Burt before the airing of the *West 57th* program.[101] A week later, though, a state appeals court allowed seven additional cases to return to the lower courts to be considered for their claims against the hospital. At that point, the court had dismissed two of the twenty-two cases it reviewed but allowed the others to proceed.[102]

Nearly three years after her first trial against James Burt, on March 17, 1994, Judge Richard Dodge agreed Phillips should have the right for a new trial against just the hospital, something her attorneys had been requesting for a long time. When asked, Green, St. Elizabeth's attorney, said he welcomed Dodge's decision. "We had originally sought a separate trial for the hospital," he told the *Dayton Daily News*.[103] In the middle of June 1995, an appellate court ruled that Phillips could pursue a new trial against the hospital with the claim that St. Elizabeth was negligent in allowing Burt to have staff privileges. Sambol called the decision "great" and that she was "anxious to get back in there and get Janet some justice finally."[104] Her suit, however, was put on hold in November, while waiting for the Supreme Court of Ohio to decide if she had filed her case in time.[105] The following November, the court heard arguments on whether Phillips—who underwent love surgery in 1981 but who did not know the extent of her surgery until more than two years later when, as her attorney, John Lancione, put it, Phillips went to a gynecologist who told her "I've never seen anything so horrible in my life and you better go to a lawyer"—had filed too late. Much of the argument presented before the high court revolved around when Phillips understood St. Elizabeth might be accountable for her injuries.[106] In January 1997, however, the Supreme Court of Ohio cleared the way for Phillips to sue the hospital by a vote of 4–3. When asked, Sambol said she was "pleased."[107]

Denied this appeal, the hospital began to settle the remaining lawsuits, including the one by Phillips.[108] Initially, before the Phillips trial began, Wachsman had asked the hospital for $100 million to settle all the suits—and had refused to settle the cases individually. During the trial, he reportedly lowered the offer to $25 million and then after the trial to $16 million. In November 1991, St. Elizabeth started working on settlements out of court with each woman individually, initially offering $2.4 million to do so—which would have amounted to between $25,000 and $100,000 per woman. Each side—Wachsman and the attorneys for St. Elizabeth—accused the other of acting inappropriately during these settlement talks.[109] In March 1995, Judge John Kessler consolidated the forty active lawsuits; settlement talks began again shortly after this consolidation.[110] By late January 1997, the hospital confirmed it had indeed settled thirteen of the forty-six lawsuits regarding Burt and his surgery.[111] By that fall, St. Elizabeth—which had been bought and renamed Franciscan Medical Center—reported that all but two of the cases had been settled. Although all involved agreed not to not disclose the terms of the settlements until 2030, using a source it called "close to the case," the *Dayton Daily News* reported the amount totaled about $20 million. Using information from the anonymous source, the paper stated that Phillips and Ruby Moore received the largest amounts of about $1 million each in April; the average settlement approached $400,000. Although it was a significant amount of money, Cincinnati attorney Green, who had long represented the hospital, said the settlement would "not put the hospital in a bad financial condition."[112] James Burt's son issued a statement regarding the settlements and the speculated amounts, saying if the amounts were accurate, "it is truly a shame." The statement further said the Burt family continued to believe the women's complaints were not true.[113]

Three years later, in the middle of July 2000, Franciscan Medical Center announced it would close in the fall. The announcement was not unanticipated and came on the heels of a potential buyer, the sixth since 1998, failing to make an offer. The closing meant the end of the area's oldest hospital and the loss of more than 1,500 jobs.[114] In part, the closing was a result of Dayton having had more hospital beds than it needed for more than two decades. In 1983, for example, because of the saturation of hospitals, the *Dayton Daily News* published a series called "The Hospital Wars" documenting the increased competition and the rise in beds.[115] In part, the closing was a result of St. Elizabeth having had too many empty beds, too little income, perhaps taking too many charity cases, and entering too late into the technological advancement competition. Combined with government cutbacks, one report estimated the financial losses of the hospital being about $1 million a month. But in part, the closing was a result of the Burt case.[116] Slightly more than a decade after the CBS show aired, Burt and the hospital had both been compelled—by the media, by legislation, by lawsuits, by patient activists, and by patients—to end their roles in medical care.

Stock Assumptions

In the late 1990s, around the time the Burt cases were beginning to be settled, some Americans started talking more publicly about female genitals not because of James Burt and his love surgery but, rather, because of a new trend in cosmetic surgery: designer vaginas. This surgery, which in some manifestations tightened the vagina by suturing the vaginal wall muscles together to reduce the circumference, was being performed by a handful of physicians for, they asserted, the sexual benefit of the woman. Surgeons who performed cosmetic vaginal surgeries claimed by the late 1990s that demand for the surgery had doubled within only a few years.[1] What came to be called female genital cosmetic surgeries (FGCS) included not just vaginal tightening but also reduction of the labia and removal of the clitoral hood, performed for reasons linked to sexual function and/or appearance.[2]

Burt has been connected with this emerging surgical trend.[3] Critics of FGCS have regarded Burt as an early practitioner of such surgeries, one who saw the female genitalia as "surgically alterable" with the intention of resolving the "'problems' of a sexual or psychological nature," as sociologist Virginia Braun wrote.[4] In contrast, some practitioners of FGCS have sought to distance themselves from Burt, arguing their surgery was distinct from love surgery in being elective—apparently either not knowing or not acknowledging that some women also elected for love surgery. As James Apesos, a plastic surgeon in Dayton, Ohio, wrote in his book *Vagina Makeover and Rejuvenation: Vaginal/Vulval Procedures, Restored Femininity*: "the old days of 'love surgery' are past. Unwanted misguided experimentation by a lone practitioner is not our subject matter."[5] And although some do argue for a distinction to be made between contemporary

FGCS and Burt's version, one can also argue for the strong continuation between those who market FGCS today with how Burt similarly asserted that women—if not all women, then the majority of women—were candidates for love surgery: both Burt as well as his peers today who promote FGCS regard the female body as inherently flawed and in need of surgical correction.

The story of Burt and his practice of love surgery has nearly always been framed as an isolated incident, as an aberration within medicine: as the "misguided" "lone practitioner," per Dayton physician Apesos, or as "one of a kind," as the *Dayton Daily News* labeled him in a 1991 editorial.[6] Positioning Burt and his practice as an outlier within medicine removes him and his practice from medical norms. But that same 1991 editorial asserted that, even though the "medical community would have everybody believe that he [Burt] was an aberration, a fluke," "many bad doctors [are] practicing today, and nobody is getting in their way."[7] This editorial followed one that appeared earlier that same month, when the newspaper called the Burt case "an egregious example of the medical profession not policing itself—to the detriment of many, many women."[8]

The stock assumptions about the "egregious example" of James Burt and his love surgery are, per the *Dayton Daily News* editorials, that he was "one of a kind," an anomaly, and that profession failed at "policing itself." Hopefully what this book has shown is that framing the Burt story in this way is not only not useful but also not accurate: some local physicians—through the tissue committee at St. Elizabeth, through the local medical society, and individually—did act in response to Burt by questioning what he was doing within review committees, by issuing what were tantamount to warnings regarding love surgery through the language used in the special consent form and in how the local medical society described the surgery, by limiting his practice at area hospitals, by recommending against the surgery as an elective, and by testifying that the surgery was not standard in court. Many physicians did act in line with their responsibilities, although ultimately it was not the actions of physicians but rather the actions of nonmedical actors—of the women who told their story on a national television show—that prompted the process for disciplinary action to be taken against Burt.

Hopefully then, too, this book has illustrated the importance of actions by people other than physicians in medical regulation: the roles of print and broadcast journalists, of formal patient activist groups such as Public Citizen's Health Research Group and the Boston Women's Health Book Collective and of informal ones such as the group of women who met following the appearance of Burt on CBS in the fall of 1988, of patients who brought lawsuits as well as patients who spoke to the media or who filed complaints with the hospital. Indeed, the Burt story strongly points to the importance of patient involvement in the medical regulation process, in patients coming forward to say that something was wrong with the practice of their physician, be it coming forward through a lawsuit, speaking to local or national media, or filing a complaint with the state medical board. Indeed, the Burt story reflects a recent study that found the general public is much more likely to raise a complaint to the state medical board against a physician for professional misconduct than a physician or a medical staff member—66 percent of the time complaints were found to have originated from the general public, compared with 5 percent from physicians and 4 percent from staff members.[9] However, as Marshall Kapp, a bioethicist at Wright State University in Dayton, stated in the months following Phillips's 1991 trial, "It is simply not realistic to expect patients to have the knowledge and the willingness to take on the medical community." Physicians, he said, need to "complain about their peers."[10]

And this is the problem with the Burt story: physicians did "complain about" their peer. In some ways, peer review of Burt worked, if by worked we mean that physicians brought their concerns forward in the expected manner—they told each other of their concerns, they raised issues within relevant committees and societies, they issued a statement critical of an elective surgery, they insisted on a special consent form regarding the surgery as well as data to confirm the surgery did what Burt claimed, and they claimed to have informed the state medical board. But the Burt story also illustrates the problems with the structure of medical regulation and where it fails: the understandable fears doctors have about reporting the actions of another physician, including the worry they could be wrong; that they do not have enough information; that even when correct in their concern, finding patterns showing a particular therapy or intervention has a pattern of poor outcomes is time-consuming; that, even if their concerns are justified, the offending physician could still sue them; that it is difficult to stop an elective surgery wanted by a patient. There is also the issue, again illustrated by the Burt case, of physicians not acting to regulate one of their peers: in this case, because some physicians assumed the women understood what the surgery entailed, assumed the women wanted the surgery, and assumed they consented to the surgery. But, in addition, there is also the issue in this case of physicians not acting despite hearing the persistent rumors of Burt being obsessed with his patients' sex lives and despite, per the recollections of patients who recalled other physicians as recognizing Burt's surgery, also knowing of its complications. As sociologist Ruth Horowitz, in her evaluation of medical licensing and regulation, noted, "democratic governance is complicated" with "no clear blueprint for how to do it right."[11] The Burt story fundamentally illustrates this point.

As a profession, physicians self-regulate, and although other actors, as highlighted in this book, are active participants in medical regulation, ultimately it is physicians who are required, legally and professionally, to ensure they and their peers are practicing competently. According to the 2002 "Medical Professionalism in the New Millennium: A Physician Charter," coauthored by the American Board of Internal Medicine Foundation, the American College of Physicians Foundation, and the European Federation of Internal Medicine and since adopted by more than 108 organizations, professionalism first and foremost demands that physicians place "the interests of the patient above those of the physician" as well as "setting and maintaining standards of competence and integrity." This is the basis for the social contract between physicians and patients, and at its most essential, this contract concerns the "public trust in physicians, which depends on the integrity of both individual physicians and the whole profession."[12] Physicians must uphold their professional responsibilities in return for the privilege to govern themselves.[13]

Medicine enjoys a high degree of autonomy, free of explicit government oversight: the medical profession is able to decide the admission standards to medical school, to determine the curriculum of medical schools, to decide where graduates of medical school will go for their postgraduate medical education (residencies), to decide what continuing medical education should entail, to decide the requirements for practicing in a hospital, and to decide what constitutes a violation of acceptable clinical practice.[14] Self-regulation, however, is a privilege, not a right, and in 2015, in an editorial in *JAMA*, Howard Bauchner, Phil Fontanarosa, and Amy Thompson noted that if "medicine does not self-govern effectively and responsibly," this could change, per the examples of greater governmental oversight of "the banking and accounting industries" that were, because of the 2008 housing crash, "now subject to more federal oversight, at least in part because of their failure to self-regulate."[15]

Bauchner, Fontanarosa, and Thompson's editorial was the lead in a series of editorials in that issue of *JAMA* concerned about "the responsibility and accountability of medicine to self-govern, self-regulate, and ensure the highest degree of professionalism."[16] As Mark Chassin and David W. Baker noted in their editorial as part of the *JAMA* 2015 issue, "medicine's record of self-governance" had not always been "exemplary," as "problematic behaviors have too often been tolerated within health care organizations and by the profession as a whole."[17]

A central aspect of self-governance is that physicians must report unprofessional behavior. In an attempt to address this, in April 2016, the Federation of State Medical Boards (FSMB) adopted a formal statement on the "Duty to Report," which was followed by a one-day summit held in February 2017 on this topic. There, the participants described what this duty entailed—and included more than just physicians who had a duty to report—in their outline: it was, the participants decided, "the responsibility of physicians, hospitals and health organizations, insurers and the public to provide reports to state medical boards of information related to patient safety, physician impairment and professional misconduct." During the summit on this topic, participants focused on two sorts of challenges hindering the duty to report. The first challenge concerned individual behavior: the "impediments that can keep physicians, nurses, office staff—and even patients and families—from stepping forward to report unprofessional conduct." The second challenge concerned system issues: how information was shared from physicians and "physician organizations to hospitals, government agencies and others," including "regulators and law enforcement."[18]

Participants identified several factors keeping individuals from reporting an errant physician within the medical workplace: hierarchical workplaces and power differentials that impede individuals to come forward about actions of someone senior; fear of retribution, including loss of a job, if found out to be the one making the report; fear of being ostracized by colleagues if discovered to be the one who made the report; fear of becoming involved in a time-consuming, or possibly even financially costly, proceeding; difficulties in knowing where and to whom one should file a report; and seeing making a report as being a hostile action as opposed to a chance for correction of the misconduct. Indeed, per this latter point, the FSMB report noted that "the current system of reporting and sharing information, with its strong emphasis on punitive outcomes, tends to disincentivize individuals from stepping forward," with individuals who are perhaps considering making a report seeing "few advantages, but many disadvantages—ranging from professional retaliation from peers to economic cost and emotional stress." Patients, the FSMB report noted, could have similar fears of confronting a figure with authority, as well as being hesitant "to engage in time-consuming and stressful formal complaint process." Regarding the system issues making reporting difficult, the participants outlined multiple barriers, including the complexity of the U.S. health care system and the multiple players, both private and public, within it, all collecting information on physicians; lack of coordination between players and of data they collect; legal restrictions as to what sort of information can be shared, and with whom, regarding a physician; the weaknesses of reporting systems, as well as a lack of a common standard for reporting across systems; a lack of cooperation with law enforcement; and the limited resources of many medical boards.[19] These barriers to reporting existed in the 1970s and 1980s when Burt practiced, and per this report, they remain barriers to reporting forty years later.

The FSMB report concluded with a number of recommendations, including a cultural change in the workplace to be more open and transparent; to raise awareness and visibility regarding how to make a report, emphasizing its ease, clarity, and that it is confidential; to emphasize "prevention and proactivity" by "focusing on identifying smaller issues 'upstream' before they become larger issues"; to change the terms used, since reporting is often seen as meaning assigning fault; and to establish broader partnerships between the many entities in health care. Finally, the report also noted the importance of more information on reporting: "more research is needed on the unique cultural factors that impede transparency and the willingness to report or share information in health care workplaces," as well as more on the "factors that may impede patients and families from reporting or sharing information."[20]

Although, as the FSMB report noted, there are many involved in the process of medical regulation, ultimately all disciplinary actions occur through the state medical board. As three members of the FSMB wrote in *JAMA* in 2015, the "state medical board serves as the ultimate gatekeeper for physicians by issuing licenses and authorizing disciplinary actions when professional misconduct occurs."[21] Some of what are considered gatekeeping activities have changed since the late 1980s. As we saw, sexual assault and misconduct became matters of professionalism in the 1990s, the decade after Burt surrendered his license, and such matters became subject to disciplinary action by state medical boards. And some of these activities have become more public: in 2005, for example, the first national meeting regarding physician self-regulation was held in Texas, with representatives from more than thirty health care organizations, hospitals, and insurance companies, as well as members of the public, in attendance.[22] Moreover, state medical boards have made efforts to increase the public's access to information about physicians; in 2011, for example, Illinois was the first state to make profiles of practicing physicians more easily accessible to the public by placing the information online.[23]

There are seventy medical boards (for both allopathic and osteopathic physicians) within the United States, the District of Columbia, and its territories, and all of them have as part of their publicly available profile of physicians the current license status of a physician and all but one list any actions taken by the state board regarding that physician. However, a little more than half (thirty-nine) of the boards do not share as part of the physician's profile actions other state boards have taken regarding the physician, and the majority (forty-six) do not share hospital disciplinary actions. Finally, thirty-eight do not share criminal convictions and thirty-eight do not share information on medical malpractice. Finally, only four boards publicly provide (not, it should be noted, on their physician profile) complaints or accusations against a physician before an investigation has been conducted and decision of the complaint/accusation has been reached, and only two of these four boards publicly share information about an investigation before a decision and/or an action has been made by the board.[24] As James Thompson and Lee Smith of FSMB wrote in 2006, since medical licensure in the United States "remains state based," there continues to be "wide disparities in the policies and procedures between various states" when it comes to discipline.[25] These differences can be seen in what state boards make publicly available as part of their physician profiles.

But these differences between state medical boards can also be seen regarding disciplinary actions made by medical boards overall. On a national scale, the number of disciplinary actions has been fairly stable between 2008 and 2017, ranging from a low in 2017 of 4,081 physicians with a board action in that year to a high in 2011 of 4,712. Comparing again 2008 with 2017, the 2018 *U.S. Medical Regulatory Trends and Actions* reported actions taken by medical boards remained fairly constant: in 2008, 591 licenses were suspended, 375 were surrendered, and 256 were revoked, compared to 2017 when 656 licenses were suspended, 510 were surrendered, and 248 were revoked.[26] These numbers have stayed fairly similar despite an increase in the number of physicians in the United States; according to the 2016 census, there were 953,695 actively licensed physicians in the United States—an increase of 12 percent from the 2000 census.[27]

However, when one looks at actions made by each medical board, there are striking differences in the number of disciplinary actions taken. In a study that considered the number of disciplinary actions by medical boards between 2010 and 2014, and controlling for the number of physicians in the state and the population of the state, John Alexander Harris and Elena Byhoff found "significant variation" between medical boards regarding major disciplinary actions—defined as revocation, suspension, or surrender of a medical license. Indeed, they found "a fourfold variation in the rate of major physician disciplinary actions between the lowest and highest rates" of disciplinary actions.[28] Different states took—or did not take—different actions regarding when and for what to discipline.

Why were disciplinary actions taken? According to the study by Harris and Byhoff, of the 26,804 unique physician medical board actions, there was no reason given for 5,242 actions, and for another 9,977 (38 percent of the actions), the reason was not specified, or it was listed as for an "other" reason for 3,835 cases (14 percent of the actions). Of the remaining, reasons were illegal activity (8 percent of the actions, or 2,053), unprofessional conduct (4 percent of the actions, or 1,076), negligence (9 percent of the actions, or 2,443), sexual or boundary misconduct (2 percent of the actions, or 430), and because of an "immediate threat to health and safety of public" (1 percent of the actions, or 312).[29]

Looking more narrowly just at Ohio, as of June 30, 2018, according to the State Medical Board of Ohio, there were 42,265 active licenses for allopathic—that is, MD—and 6,676 active licenses for osteopathic—that is, DO—physicians in the state. In fiscal 2018, the board received 5,553 new complaints against practitioners. The board closed 2,700 complaints with no action, as, according to the board's 2018 annual report, "the issue involved profession not regulated by Board," and also closed an additional 2,822 complaints "after investigation as information obtained about allegation did not support Board action." The board acted on 261 complaints, and it took a median of 207 days from receipt of the complaint to closure of the complaint. As a result of the investigations, the board revoked thirty-eight licenses in 2018, down from fifty the year before and forty-seven in 2016. They suspended thirty-one licenses indefinitely and four definitely. The board put thirty licenses on probation, reprimanded twelve practitioners, but placed limits on not a single license. The most common reason for disciplinary action in fiscal 2018 was for impairment, followed by prescribing issues at 32 and 27 percent, respectively; 8 percent of disciplinary actions were for criminal acts/convictions; and 7 percent were for sexual misconduct. Importantly, it is not clear in the annual report how many of these actions regarded *physicians*—the board also regulates the licenses of acupuncturists, anesthesiologist and radiologist assistants, dietitians, genetic counselors, massage and cosmetic therapists, physician assistants, and respiratory care professionals.[30] Probably the majority of the actions involved physicians, however; of the forty-two formal actions—ranging from prehearing suspensions to reinstatement requests to termination of probation to nondisciplinary actions—the state board took in August 2018, thirty-two involved physicians (both MDs and DOs) while the remaining actions involved massage therapists, a physician assistant, or a respiratory care professional.[31]

In the editorial accompanying the study by Harris and Byhoff, Jessica Liu and Chaim Bell emphasized that "there is no overarching federal standard with which each state regulatory board must comply, nor is there a unifying body that compares individual states and their quality standards and policies for physician disciplinary proceedings."[32] What moves forward as a disciplinary action and how it is disciplined is different according to that particular state medical board: how and why Ohio—or Iowa or New York or Alaska—disciplines are different compared to another state. The question raised by Harris and Byhoff's study, Liu and Bell note, is "how physician disciplinary rates could vary so considerably between jurisdictions."[33] To reduce this variation, Harris and Byhoff recommended a move toward standardization of physician discipline for more consistent regulation of physicians among medical boards across the United States.[34]

But one thing that is consistent among the boards, and consistent with how boards operated in the late 1970s when Burt began to be a concern within the medical community in Dayton, is the focus on the physician rather than the protection of the patient. Indeed, although the FSMB mission—appearing on the first page of its website—states that the FSMB supports "America's state medical boards in licensing, disciplining and regulating physicians and other healthcare professionals" with the "end goal: keep patients safe," of the four "Education Modules on Medical Regulation" it offers regarding medical regulation and discipline, not one of them is centered on the duty of the physician to report unprofessional conduct of a peer.[35] The role of the physician to report unprofessional conduct is only touched upon in two of the modules. In the module "Medical Disciplinary Process," under a true or false interactive exercise to see "What You Know Already," one of the prompts asks whether the statement "Most of the complaints against physicians reviewed by a state medical board come from other physicians" is true or false (the correct response is false). The second module that has a component touching on the responsibility of physicians to report unprofessional conduct is titled "Common Reasons Physicians Get in Trouble." In this module appears the statement that per a 2017 study of medical students, 20 percent reported a discrepancy between what they were being taught about professional conduct and what they were actually seeing. The module then tells students that when they witnessed unprofessional conduct, "even as a medical student or resident, you may have an obligation to report what you have observed." There is no mention that this remains true once they are finished with their training.[36] The focus of these modules is on what the process of medical regulation is, rather than on the role of the physician in that regulation. And this parallels the continued focus on the physician, not on the protection of the patient from an unethical or unprofessional physician's actions.

Atul Gawande, whom I quoted in the Introduction, has written that the public expects physicians, when confronted with the unprofessional conduct of one of their peers, to "join forces promptly to remove them from practice and report them to the medical-licensing authorities, who, in turn, are supposed to discipline them or expel them from the profession." But, as Gawande further wrote, "it hardly ever happens that way." The Burt story demonstrates Gawande's point that medical regulation is not as direct, not as simple, and certainly not as transparent or as quick as what Gawande called the "official line about how the medical profession is supposed to deal with these physicians."

I am a medical historian, and I do not pretend to have the answers on how to make this process more direct, simple, or transparent—in other words, on how to correct the flaws in the current system that date back at least to the time when Holden, Reiling, Busacco, members of the hospital tissue committee, and the local medical society all took actions regarding Burt—a physician who often failed to, at best, note or, at worst, purposely ignored the patterns of problems his patients were experiencing as a result of his surgery. But as I write this conclusion, we are well within what has been termed the #MeToo movement, and I think we also need to keep in mind that the formal regulatory system also failed to stop a physician who regarded women's bodies as anatomically wrong for heterosexual sex and who designed a surgery to correct what he regarded as an underlying problem for his female patients—regardless of what they told him.

The majority of physicians practice in a professional manner and never receive a misconduct complaint. But when a physician violates professional norms, especially grievously so, many—both within and outside medicine—are rightly outraged. But by then patients have probably been harmed; for them, the outrage is too late. Although Burt gave up his medical license under pressure thirty years ago, many of the same concerns raised by this story regarding why, how, and even whether errant physicians are disciplined remain.

Questions to Ask If Considering an Elective Surgery

James Burt performed an innovative surgery on hundreds, perhaps thousands, of women. But an innovative surgery in and of itself, as discussed in chapter 3, is not unethical—nor is it necessarily uncommon—and an innovation can become a part of medical practice before it has been fully tested.[1] However, sometimes therapies—in particular here surgeries—may become part of normative practice only to be shown to be not as effective as had been assumed once a study on their effectiveness occurs; an example of this is the recent research showing that for middle-aged people with meniscal tears, exercise therapy was as effective in improving knee function as surgery.[2]

The continued use of procedures when other, less risky (and less expensive) options are just as effective, as well as the overuse of some tests and procedures, has resulted in actions being taken by a variety of organizations, such as the launching in 2012 of the Choosing Wisely campaign by the American Board of Internal Medicine Foundation (ABIMF), Consumer Reports, and the societies of nine additional medical specialties, to address the problem. As part of the Choosing Wisely campaign, all ten of the medical specialty societies came up with a list of five tests or procedures being performed more often than necessary; because of the success of this initial list, seventeen societies developed new lists the following year.[3] As of September 2018, a fully searchable list, produced by more than 500 specialty society recommendations, exists regarding appropriate tests, treatments, and surgeries on the ABIMF's Choosing Wisely website.[4] Although begun in the United States, it is now part of an international effort to reduce overtreatment.[5] A primary goal for the campaign is, per the

United Kingdom's Choosing Wisely campaign, that "just because we can doesn't always mean we should."[6]

Overtreatment—the use of tests, therapy, or procedures that are unnecessary—is not uncommon in the United States; a 2017 study found that physicians believed 20.6 percent of overall medical care was unnecessary.[7] The concern is not just about the financial costs of running tests, administering therapies, or performing surgeries when they are unneeded; it is also that doing so incurs unnecessary risks.[8] This is particularly true of surgery and the possibility of complications following an unnecessary surgery.[9] Unnecessary surgeries are a perennial concern; they were a concern before Burt, they were a concern during the time he practiced, and they remain a concern. As physician Charles Wilson wrote in 2006, "A surgeon's skill and ability to perform a procedure is unimportant, in fact irrelevant, if the procedure should not be done in the first place."[10]

In addition to unnecessary surgeries, innovative and new surgeries are also a concern, for it remains up to the discretion of the individual surgeon as to how much and what sort of information to provide to patients regarding a new or innovative surgery.[11] Moreover, new does not mean better or even improved—these words are not synonymous.[12] A new surgery does not necessarily mean a patient will have better outcomes or that the new surgery is safer. In addition to those concerns, informed consent for an innovative or new surgery can be difficult because the risks are not fully known, since it has only been done on a small number of patients. The benefits, then, may be surmised, but the risks may be more difficult to assess.[13] Moreover, the physician may have an incentive to perform the surgery that is not centrally about the patient who is to undergo it; surgeons proposing an innovative surgery need to, as physician Peter Angelos wrote, ensure they have separated "the potential benefits to the patient from the potential benefits to the surgeon him- or herself."[14]

When it comes, then, to considering an elective surgery—meaning one you decide to undergo, such as hip replacement—there are questions you should ask before agreeing to undergo the surgery to make sure it is necessary for you, to understand why it is being recommended for you, and to understand what the surgery entails. Importantly, per the Burt story, it is important to know what kind of surgery is being proposed: is it an established, standard surgery or a new and innovative one? Understanding what the surgery entails, if it is different from a standard surgery, and, if so, why it is being recommended are important parts of the discussion.

The following list includes some of the questions to ask a physician before agreeing to a surgery to ensure you understand why the surgery is being suggested, how it could benefit you, what the alternatives to surgery are, the risks of the proposed surgery, what the surgery entails, and what the experience of the physician is in performing it.[15]

- Why do I need this surgery? Why are you recommending it? How will it improve my medical condition?
- How will it be performed? Are there different methods for performing this surgery? If so, why do you favor the one you are proposing?
- Who will perform the surgery? How much experience does the person who will perform the surgery have with this surgery? Does the person who will perform this surgery do so regularly? How many times has the person performed it?
- Is this a new surgery? A standard surgery?
- What anatomical changes will occur from the surgery?
- How often have your patients experienced problems? What problems have they experienced?
- Are there others who perform this surgery too?
- What is your success rate? How is success measured?
- Are you board certified?
- Do you have any additional credentials or experience in doing this surgery?
- Who will be present in the operating room? What are their roles?
- Do you have any financial ties to this surgery—for example, if a device will be implanted, do you have a financial stake in the device company?
- What are the known risks for this surgery? How do my health history and current medications factor into these risks?
- What are the known complications for this surgery? How do my health history and current medications factor into these complications?
- What are the possible side effects? How do my health history and current medications factor into these possible side effects?
- What are the benefits of the surgery? How do my health history and current medications factor into these benefits? How long can I expect these benefits to last? Is there published information about the benefits for this procedure?
- Are there simpler, safer alternatives—such as physical therapy, exercising, a change in diet? What are the risks and benefits of the alternatives?
- Will I need, before the surgery, to undergo any specific preparations—any tests, a change in my medications or diet?

- How long is the recovery?
- What is the postoperative care if I will be staying in the hospital? How long would I be in the hospital?
- If outpatient, when would I leave following the operation?
- What type of care will I need to have when I go home?
- What can I expect for the first few days of recovery following the surgery?
- When will I be able to return to my typical daily activities?
- Will I be prescribed any medications—antibiotics or for pain relief?
- What are some things I should be concerned about following the operation?
- Is the surgical facility accredited? Fully staffed?
- How much does the surgery cost? Are there less expensive options?
- What will happen if I do nothing? What if we take a "wait-and-see" approach? Will my condition worsen? Is there a possibility the problem could resolve on its own?

In addition to asking these questions, you should also ask for a paper copy regarding the proposed procedure's risks and benefits as well as details on alternatives to the proposed surgery. Further, for an elective surgery, see about your options for a second opinion.

Acknowledgments

Like all authors, although I wrote the book, I was not alone during the process, and there are many people I want to thank—and my apologies if, over the time it took me to write, I forget to thank someone here publicly. As I first wrote about Burt as part of my dissertation, I need to thank my committee: Jody Carrigan, Andrew Jameton, Patricia Leuschen, Toby Schonfeld, and especially Sharon Wood, who encouraged me to pursue the Burt story. Thanks to my colleagues who I have bounced ideas off for years at Northwestern, first, those in the Medical Humanities and Bioethics Program—Tod Chambers, Megan Crowley-Matoka, Catherine Belling, Katie Watson, Bryan Morrison, and Myria Knox, as well as the graduate students in the program—for their feedback and support (and in particular Catherine, for her careful and attentive edits of a very near-final draft). In addition, I want to thank my colleagues in Global Health Studies for their support of, and curiosity about, this project. Thank you to Donna Leff for letting me talk to your graduate journalism classes over the years about Burt, for all those lunches afterward, and for being a fantastic and supportive sounding board. I also want to thank Rachel Gross for her help in trying to locate people in the Burt story when she was a graduate student at Northwestern.

I want to thank my reading group colleagues, Sandy Sufian and Sydney Halperin, for their feedback and enthusiasm. I would also like to thank those who commented following talks I gave on this topic over the years at the University of Wisconsin–Madison, especially Judith Walzer Leavitt and Judith Houck, at Michigan State University, especially Alice Dreger, and at the conferences of the American Association for the History of Medicine and the American Society for Bioethics and Humanities. Thank you, Jason Keune, for reading and providing very helpful feedback to chapter 3, and to Harold Braswell for introducing me to Jason. And I am very grateful for the time and information Walter Reiling Jr., Bradley Busacco, Donne Holden, and Sandy Theis shared with me.

Historians can rarely do their work without librarians and archivists, and I first want to thank LaShanda Howard Curry, formerly at Northwestern's medical library, for always coming through to obtain a journal article or book. Thank you, Brett Cimbalik, for taking over the fielding of my requests, and to Natasha Bowman, Ira Hardin, Rodney Jackson, and Cheryl Powell for helping me obtain books from storage, and to the librarians at Northwestern's Charles Deering McCormick Library of Special Collections, who helped me navigate the collection of feminist publications. In addition, I want to thank librarians in Ohio for their helping me learn more about Burt and St. Elizabeth Medical Center: Lynda Kachurek and John Armstrong at the Paul Laurence Dunbar Library, Special Collections and Archives, at Wright State University; Connie Conner at the Ohio Historical Society; and the staff at the Dayton Metro Library Local History Room, especially Elli Bambakidis. Finally, thank you to the Kinsey Institute Library and Special Collections at Indiana University Bloomington.

My research on James Burt was enriched because of the help of Anne Cavanagh, Linda Dillon, and Linda Manning, all with the Montgomery County Common Pleas Court, who provided me with much appreciated direction in finding out more about the various lawsuits and trials involving Burt, as did Ernestine Stevens of the county's Clerk of Courts Office and JoElla Jones at the Supreme Court of Ohio Clerk of Courts Office. Thank you too to those who responded with suggestions following my query for information on H-Ohio in the spring of 2012.

Thank you to the reviewers for the time you took to read this book and the attentive and helpful suggestions you provided. Thank you to Peter Mikulas for his thoughtful suggestions, and infinite patience, as well to Rutgers University Press for all their support publishing this book. I also want to thank the University of Rochester Press for publishing my first book, which included a chapter on Burt (and the writing of which prompted me to complete a manuscript concerning Burt) and thank you to the journal *Archives of Sexual Behavior* for granting me permission to use information from an article I published with them in this book. I am also grateful for the generosity of the Alice Kaplan Institute for the Humanities at Northwestern University for the awarding of a subvention grant for this book.

I also need to thank many friends who, over the years, have patiently listened to me talk and who have asked me questions about Burt. Finally, to my parents (who read drafts and, in the case of my father, suggested I see if the Supreme Court of Ohio still had records on the Burt cases), to my children (whose whole lives so far have been lived as I worked on this book), and to my husband—all of you have had to live, in varying degrees, with this project, and I thank you for being supportive as I wrote it and for being, in no small measure, the reason I so often had to put it down. I am grateful to have you all as a distraction.

Notes

Nearly all of the sources in this book came from materials in the public domain: books; newspaper, magazine, and journal articles; the CBS television show recording and transcript; and documents introduced as part of court cases. I requested several interviews but ultimately only conducted four for this book: one with Walter Reiling Jr., one with Bradley Busacco, one with Donne Holden, and one with Sandy Theis. With the exception of the interview with Holden, with whom I spoke over the phone, I traveled to speak to everyone in person. I asked everyone I interviewed to review what I wrote from our interview by providing them with an opportunity to review their comments before they appeared in the manuscript. Mary Lee Sambol was gracious enough to allow me to visit her at her home and speak with her early on in my research for this book, and she provided background as well as confirmation of what I had pieced together up to that point. As Sambol died before I was at a point to have her review what she told me, I did not use any of her comments in this book. Finally, I sought to speak to Janet Phillips, and, in response to several phone calls and letters, I spoke with her briefly, but I did not interview her. The sections concerning her life and involvement with Burt are constructed entirely from public sources.

Abbreviations

DDN   *Dayton Daily News*
DPL   The Local History Room at the Dayton Public Library in Dayton, Ohio
KI   The Kinsey Institute Library and Special Collections at Indiana University Bloomington
NU   Charles Deering McCormick Library, Special Collections, Northwestern University, Evanston, Illinois
OHS   The Archives Library Division at the Ohio Historical Society in Columbus, Ohio
WSU   The Special Collections and Archives, Paul Laurence Dunbar Library, Wright State University in Dayton, Ohio

Janet Phillips, 1981 (I)

1. Direct examination of Janet Phillips, trial transcript, Appellant's Supplement, vol. 3, *Phillips v. Burt*, Case No. 95-1522, Supreme Court of Ohio, filed February 12, 1996, at 1263–1265, 1267–1268.
2. Claire Safron, "The Gynecologist from Hell," *Woman's Day*, August 15, 1989, 70, 74, 76, 87.
3. Direct examination of Janet Phillips, Appellant's Supplement, vol. 3, *Phillips v. Burt*, at 1269–1273.
4. Safron, "Gynecologist from Hell," 74.
5. Direct examination of Janet Phillips, Appellant's Supplement, vol. 3, *Phillips v. Burt*, at 1274–1277.
6. John C. Burnham, "American Medicine's Golden Age: What Happened to It?" in *Sickness and Health in America: Readings in the History of Medicine and Public Health*,

ed. Judith Walzer Leavitt and Ronald L. Numbers, 2nd ed., rev. (Madison: University of Wisconsin Press, 1985), 248.

7. As quoted in David J. Rothman, *Strangers at the Bedside: A History of How Law and Bioethics Transformed Medical Decision Making* (New York: Basic Books, 1991), 1.

8. Safron, "Gynecologist from Hell," 74.

9. Julia Helgason, "Phillips Doesn't Expect to Collect a Penny from Burt," *DDN*, June 23, 1991.

Introduction

1. AP, "Dayton Gynecologist Gives Up His License," *Plain Dealer*, January 26, 1989.

2. Jeanne Marie Laskas, "A Crime against Nature," *Savvy Woman*, June 1989, 63–66; Claire Safron, "The Gynecologist from Hell," *Woman's Day*, August 15, 1989, 70, 74, 76, 87.

3. Atul Gawande, *Complications: A Surgeon's Notes on an Imperfect Science* (New York: Metropolitan Books, 2002), 89. Burt has also been used as an example of "a bad doctor" in Walt Bogdanich, *The Great White Lie: How America's Hospitals Betray Our Trust and Endanger Our Lives* (New York: Simon and Schuster, 1991); Harvey Rosenfield, *Silent Violence, Silent Death: The Hidden Epidemic of Medical Malpractice* (Washington, D.C.: Essential Books, 1994); and John Robbins, *Reclaiming Our Health: Exploding the Medical Myth and Embracing the Source of True Healing* (Tiburon, CA: H. J. Kramer, 1998), as well as in a book by one of the attorneys who sued him, Harvey Wachsman. Wachsman with Steven Alschuler, *Lethal Medicine: The Epidemic of Medical Malpractice* (New York: Henry Holt and Co., 1993). Alice Adams wrote about Burt as part of a longer history on gynecologists altering women's bodies. Alice Adams, "Molding Women's Bodies: The Surgeon as Sculptor," in *Bodily Discursions: Genders, Representations, Technologies*, ed. Deborah S. Wilson and Christine Moneera Laennec (Albany, NY: State University of New York Press, 1997), 59–80. For other brief mentions of Burt, see also Jennifer Drew, "The Myth of Female Sexual Dysfunction and Its Medicalization," *Sexualities, Evolution, and Gender*, August 2003, 89–96, and Virginia Braun and Sue Wilkinson, "Socio-Cultural Representations of the Vagina," *Journal of Reproductive and Infant Psychology* 19, no. 1 (2001): 17–32.

4. See, for illustration, "The 'Love Surgeon' Was Nothing but a Brutal Butcher," *Medical Bag*, December 27, 2013, http://www.medicalbag.com/despicable-doctors/the-love-surgeon-was-nothing-but-a-brutal-butcher/article/472376/ (accessed May 26, 2016), and Cristen Conger, "Dr. Burt's Infamous Love Surgeries," *Stuff Mom Never Told You*, March 8, 2013, https://www.stuffmomnevertoldyou.com/blogs/dr-burts-infamous-love-surgeries.htm (accessed July 27, 2018).

5. Judith Adler Hennessee, "The Love Surgeon," *Mademoiselle*, August 1989, 206–207, 245–247, quotation on 206; Erin Gloria Ryan, "Creepy 'Love Surgery' Performed on New Moms' Vaginas," *Jezebel*, November 29, 2012, http://jezebel.com/5964294/creepy-love-surgery-performed-on-new-moms-unwitting-vaginas (accessed July 16, 2014).

6. Susan Reverby, "Ethical Failures and History Lessons: The U.S. Public Health Service Research Studies in Tuskegee and Guatemala," *Public Health Reviews* 34, no. 1 (2012): 1–18, quotations on 4, 5.

7. Reverby, "Ethical Failures and History Lessons," 3.

8. Robert Aronwitz, "From Skid Row to Main Street: The Bowery Series and the Transformation of Prostate Cancer, 1951–1966," *Bulletin of the Journal of Medicine* 88, no. 2 (Summer 2014): 287–317, quotation on 316, note 85.

9. Gawande, *Complications*, 94.

10. Susan M. Reverby, "The Fielding H. Garrison Lecture: Enemy of the People/Enemy of the State: Two Great(ly Infamous) Doctors, Passions, and the Judgment of History," *Bulletin of the History of Medicine* 88, no. 3 (Fall 2014): 403–430, quotation on 415.

1. The One in the White Coat, 1921–1978

1. Julia Helgason and Dave Davis, "'Media Has Accepted Lies as Truth,' Says Burt," *DDN*, November 20, 1988; "Obituary—Lucretia Helen (Perry) Burt," *DDN*, March 11, 2012.

2. Helgason and Davis, "'Media Has Accepted.'"

3. Helgason and Davis, "'Media Has Accepted.'"

4. Direct examination of Janet Phillips, Appellant's Supplement, vol. 3, *Phillips v. Burt*, Case No. 95-1522, Supreme Court of Ohio, filed February 12, 1996, at 1684–1685.

5. Ohio License Center, License and Registration, search for Dr. James C. Burt, n.d., https://license.ohio.gov/Lookup/SearchDetail.asp?ContactIdnt=2998932&DivisionIdnt=78 . . . (accessed January 11, 2007), copy in author's possession.

6. Editorial, "St. Elizabeth Not Fully to Blame," November 20, 1988, clipping from Burt, Dr. James C., Co-Author "Love Surgery," Chairman—Department of Obstetrics, St. Elizabeth Hospital, WSU.

7. Helgason and Davis, "'Media Has Accepted.'"

8. Helgason and Davis, "'Media Has Accepted.'"

9. Helgason and Davis, "'Media Has Accepted.'"

10. Jeanne Marie Laskas, "A Crime against Nature," *Savvy Woman*, June 1989, 63–66, quotation on 64; Mark Holoweiko, "Why Was the Love Surgeon Allowed to Keep Cutting?" *Medical Economics*, July 17, 1989, 125–128, 131–133, 136–138, quotation on 132.

11. Montgomery Brower, "James Burt's 'Love Surgery' Was Supposed to Boost Pleasure, but Some Patients Say It Brought Pain," *People*, March 27, 1989, 97–98, 100, quotation on 100.

12. Holoweiko, "Why Was the Love Surgeon," 132.

13. Helgason and Davis, "'Media Has Accepted'"; Barbara Demick, "Love Surgery: Sexual Panacea or Mutilation for Profit?" *The Real Paper*, August 26, 1978, 18–21.

14. Walter Reiling Jr., interview with author, August 24, 2015.

15. Holoweiko, "Why Was the Love Surgeon," 126; Judith Adler Hennessee, "The Love Surgeon," *Mademoiselle*, August 1989, 206–207, 245–247, quotation on 207.

16. Nicholas J. Eastman, *Williams Obstetrics*, 11th ed. (New York: Appleton-Century-Crofts, 1956), 450.

17. Judith Walzer Leavitt, *Make Room for Daddy: The Journey from Waiting Room to Birthing Room* (Chapel Hill: University of North Carolina Press, 2009); Barbara Bridgman Perkins, *The Medical Delivery Business: Health Reform, Childbirth, and the Economic Order* (New Brunswick, NJ: Rutgers University Press, 2004).

18. According to a 1977 obstetric nursing text, the "patient is forewarned when the episiotomy is done," not that she was asked if it should be done. Joy Princeton Clausen, Margaret Hemp Flook, and Boonie Ford, *Maternity Nursing Today*, 2nd ed. (New York: McGraw-Hill, 1977), 473. See also Sheila Kitzinger, *Some Women's Experiences of Episiotomy* (London: National Childbirth Trust, 1981).

19. Margot Edwards and Mary Waldorf, *Reclaiming Birth: History and Heroines of American Childbirth Reform* (Trumansburg, NY: Crossing Press, 1984).

20. Nicholas J. Eastman and Louis H. Hellman, *Williams Obstetrics*, 12th ed. (New York: Appleton-Century-Crofts, 1961), 458.

21. William S. Kroger and S. Charles Freed, *Psychosomatic Gynecology: Including Problems of Obstetrical Care* (Philadelphia: W. B. Saunders, 1951), 308.

22. Jayne F., quoted in Leavitt, *Make Room for Daddy*, 42–43.

23. Holoweiko, "Why Was the Love Surgeon," 126; Demick, "Love Surgery," 18.

24. James C. Burt and Joan Burt, *Surgery of Love* (New York: Carlton Press, 1975), 11–12, 68, 260–261.

25. William H. Masters and Virginia E. Johnson, *Human Sexual Response* (Boston: Little, Brown, 1966), 11–13, 20–21.

26. Vern L. Bullough, *Science in the Bedroom: A History of Sex Research* (New York: Basic Books, 1994), 200–202.

27. Masters and Johnson, *Human Sexual Response*, 63–65.

28. Masters and Johnson, *Human Sexual Response*, 45, 47–50, 56, 66–67.

29. Paul Robinson, *The Modernization of Sex: Havelock Ellis, Alfred Kinsey, William Masters and Virginia Johnson* (New York: Harper & Row, 1976).

30. Janice M. Irvine, *Disorders of Desire: Sex and Gender in Modern American Sexology* (Philadelphia: Temple University Press, 1990).

31. For more on this idea, see Jacqueline H. Wolf, *Deliver Me from Pain: Anesthesia and Birth in America* (Baltimore: Johns Hopkins University Press, 2009) and William Ray Arney, *Power and the Profession of Obstetrics* (Chicago: University of Chicago Press, 1982). Alice Adams also places his surgery within the idea that he sought to "cure" women of their inability to have an orgasm during missionary position sex and thus enable them to "conform to traditional heterosexual values." Alice Adams, "Molding Women's Bodies: The Surgeon as Sculptor," in *Bodily Discursions: Genders, Representations, Technologies*, ed. Deborah S. Wilson and Christine Moneera Laennec (Albany: State University of New York Press, 1997), 59–80, quotation on 64.

32. Demick, "Love Surgery," 18–21.

33. Surgeons, as Rachel Prentice wrote, "make the surgical body" by "wielding particular kinds of instruments in the operating room," enabling them to "create a body that is mechanical, a body that can be fixed by opening it up, patching, replacing, and rerouting its pieces." Rachel Prentice, *Bodies in Formation: An Ethnography of Anatomy and Surgery Education* (Durham, NC: Duke University Press, 2013), 16. In some sense, then, whenever a surgeon operates, the body is seen, by necessity, as pathological.

34. Demick, "Love Surgery," 18.

35. James C. Burt, "Surgical Improvement of Vaginal Response by Female Coital Area Reconstruction: A New Modality of Treatment," unpublished paper, p. 4, Stacks 528.3, KI.

36. Demick, "Love Surgery," 18.

37. Burt and Burt, *Surgery of Love*, 264–265.

38. Demick, "Love Surgery," 18.

39. Demick, "Love Surgery,"18.

40. Salee Berman and Victor M. Berman, "A Guide to a Healthy Pubococcygeus Muscle: Kegling, Not Cutting," in *Contemporary Obstetric and Gynecologic Nursing*, ed. Leota Kester McNall (St. Louis, MO: C. V. Mosby, 1980), 216–228.

41. Demick, "Love Surgery," 18.

42. Walter Reiling Jr., interview with author, August 24, 2015.
43. Although Busacco did think it was possible Burt could have operated on perhaps 2,000 women. Bradley Busacco, interview with author, August 25, 2015. Christopher Baughman, "Doctor Testifies Surgeon Secretly Circumcised Woman," *The Advocate* (Baton Rouge, LA), October 30, 1996.
44. Holoweiko, "Why Was the Love Surgeon," 132.
45. Helgason and Davis, "'Media Has Accepted.'"
46. Demick, "Love Surgery,"18.
47. Brower, "James Burt's 'Love Surgery,'" 97, 98.
48. Helgason and Davis, "'Media Has Accepted.'"
49. Wolf, *Deliver Me from Pain.*
50. Brower, "James Burt's 'Love Surgery,'" 97.
51. Laurie Abraham, "Ohio Medical Groups Hit for Not Exposing MD's 'Love Surgery,'" *American Medical News*, January 27, 1989, 1, 9–10, quotation on 9.
52. Burt, *Surgery of Love*, 20.
53. Brower, "James Burt's 'Love Surgery,'" 98.
54. Burt, *Surgery of Love*, 266.
55. Sally Wilde and Geoffrey Hirst, "Learning from Mistakes: Early Twentieth-Century Surgical Practice," *Journal of the History of Medicine and Allied Sciences* 64, no. 1 (2008): 38–77.
56. Burt, *Surgery of Love*, 260.
57. Joseph B. DeLee, "The Prophylactic Forceps Operation," *American Journal of Obstetrics and Gynecology* 1, no. 1 (1920), 34–44, quotation on 43.
58. Later research proved this assumption incorrect. See Katherine Hartmann, Meera Viswanathan, Rachel Palmieri, Gerald Garthehner, John Thorpe, and Kathleen N. Lohr, "Outcomes of Routine Episiotomy: A Systematic Review," *JAMA* 293, no. 17 (May 4, 2005): 2141–2148.
59. DeLee, "The Prophylactic Forceps Operation," 43.
60. Suzanne Arms, *Immaculate Deception: A New Look at Women and Childbirth*, 2nd ed. (New York: Bantam, 1979), 100.
61. See J. Donald Woodruff, Rene Genadry, and Steven Poliakoff, "Treatment of Dyspareunia and Vaginal Outlet Distortions by Perineoplasty," *Obstetrics and Gynecology* 57, no. 6 (June 1981): 750–754.
62. Wallace B. Shute, "Episiotomy: A Physiologic Appraisal and a New Painless Technic," *Obstetrics and Gynecology* 14, no. 4 (October 1959): 467–472, quotation on 468.
63. J. P. Greenhill, *Office Gynecology*, 9th ed., revised and enlarged (Chicago: Year Book Medical Publishers, 1971), 118. There is little evidence to show that vaginal size affects sexual activity or function, however. See Megan O. Schimpf, Heidi S. Harvie, Tola B. Omotosho, Lee B. Epstein, Marjorie Jean-Michel, Cedric K. Olivera, Kristin E. Rooney, Sunil Balgobin, Okechukwu A. Ibeanu, Rajiv B. Gala, and Rebecca C. Rogers, "Does Vaginal Size Impact Sexual Activity and Function?" *International Urogynecology Journal* 21 (2010): 447–452.
64. James J. Ryan, "Surgical Intervention in the Treatment of Sexual Disorders," in *Clinical Management of Sexual Disorders*, ed. Jon K. Meyer (Baltimore: Williams and Wilkins, 1976), 238.
65. "Anterior and Posterior Repair (Colporrhaphy)," Obstetrics and Gynecology, Baylor College of Medicine, https://www.bcm.edu/healthcare/care-centers/obstetrics-gynecology/procedures/minimally-invasive-gynecologic-surgery/anterior-posterior-repair (accessed September 1, 2015).

66. David Reuben, *How to Get More Out of Sex* (New York: David McKay, 1974), 16–17.

67. Seymour Isenberg and L. Melvin Elting, "A Guide to Sexual Surgery," *Cosmopolitan*, November 1976, 104, 108, 110, 164, quotations on 108, 110, 164. Isenberg and Elting reiterated this information in their book, *The Consumer's Guide to Successful Surgery* (New York: St. Martin's, 1976), 283–284.

68. Victoria Andrews, "The Little Operation That Saved My Sex Life," *Ladies Home Journal* 91 (1974): 18, 138.

69. Sarah B. Rodriguez, *Female Circumcision and Clitoridectomy in the United States: A History of a Medical Treatment* (Rochester, NY: University of Rochester Press, 2014).

70. A. S. Waiss, "Reflex Neuroses from Adherent Prepuce in the Female," *Chicago Clinical School* 9 (1900), 279, 282–283.

71. Rodriguez, *Female Circumcision and Clitoridectomy in the United States.*

72. Rodriguez, *Female Circumcision and Clitoridectomy in the United States*; Rodriguez, "Rethinking the History of Female Circumcision and Clitoridectomy: Medicine and Female Sexuality in the Late Nineteenth Century," *Journal of the History of Medicine and Allied Sciences* 63 (July 2008): 323–347.

73. Alfred Henry Tyrer, *Sex Satisfaction and Happy Marriage* (New York: Emerson, 1940), 119.

74. Rodriguez, *Female Circumcision and Clitoridectomy in the United States.*

75. Elting and Isenberg, *The Consumer's Guide to Successful Surgery*, 274.

76. Robert W. Taylor, *A Practical Treatise on Sexual Disorders of the Male and Female*, 3rd ed. (New York: Lea Brothers, 1905), 414.

77. Hannah M. Stone and Abraham Stone, *A Marriage Manual: A Practical Guide-Book to Sex and Marriage* (New York: Simon and Schuster, 1935), 198–199.

78. M. F. Smith, "Queries and Minor Notes: Circumcision in Women," *JAMA* 114, no. 8 (February 24, 1940): 680.

79. Robert Latou Dickinson, *Human Sex Anatomy: A Topographical Hand Atlas* (Baltimore: Williams and Wilkins, 1949), 46.

80. Arthur Hale Curtis and John William Huffman, *A Textbook of Gynecology*, 6th ed. (Philadelphia: W. B. Saunders, 1950), 97. For a review on this topic, see Kim Wallen and Elisabeth Lloyd, "Female Sexual Arousal: Genital Anatomy and Orgasm in Intercourse," *Hormones and Behavior* 59 no. 5 (May 2011): 780–792.

81. Helgason and Davis, "'Media Has Accepted.'"

82. Helgason and Davis, "'Media Has Accepted'"; Rob Modic, "Part of Burt's Book Read in Court," *DDN*, June 4, 1991.

83. Holoweiko, "Why Was the Love Surgeon," 128.

84. Burt and Burt, *Surgery of Love*, book jacket.

85. Burt, *Surgery of Love*, 14–15, 67, 74–75.

86. Sara M. Evans, *Born for Liberty: The Roots of the Women's Liberation Movement in America* (New York: Vintage, 1980), 234–236.

87. Joanne Meyerowitz, "Introduction: Women and Gender in Postwar America, 1945–1960," in *Not June Cleaver: Women and Gender in Postwar America, 1945–1960*, ed. Joanne Meyerowitz (Philadelphia: Temple University Press, 1994), 1–16.

88. Burt, *Surgery of Love*, author's autobiographies, 195–197.

89. Burt, *Surgery of Love*, 72, 83, 262.

90. Burt, *Surgery of Love*, 44, 11, 7, 40.

91. Burt, *Surgery of Love*, 40–42.

92. Lois Bird, *How to Be a Happily Married Mistress* (Garden City, NY: Doubleday, 1970).

93. Burt, *Surgery of Love*, 153, 66, 176, 57.
94. Burt, *Surgery of Love*, 153–154, 57, 200–201, 208.
95. John D'Emilio and Estelle B. Freedman, *Intimate Matters: A History of Sexuality in America* (New York: Harper & Row, 1988), 280; John Heidenry, *What Wild Ecstasy: The Rise and Fall of the Sexual Revolution* (New York: Simon & Schuster, 1997), 60, 66.
96. Heidenry, *What Wild Ecstasy*, 60, 66, 68, 87.
97. D'Emilio and Freedman, *Intimate Matters*, 328.
98. D'Emilio and Freedman, *Intimate Matters*, 300.
99. Beth Bailey, *Sex in the Heartland* (Cambridge, MA: Harvard University Press, 1999), 5–9.
100. D'Emilio and Freedman, *Intimate Matters*, 300, 305, 306.
101. Bailey, *Sex in the Heartland*, 5–7.
102. D'Emilio and Freedman, *Intimate Matters*, 336, 340.
103. Demick, "Love Surgery," 21; Frances FitzGerald, *The Evangelicals: The Struggle to Shape America* (New York: Simon & Schuster, 2017).
104. Burt, *Surgery of Love*, 196, 15.
105. D'Emilio and Freedman, *Intimate Matters*, 330–333.

2. Dayton Doctor Develops Corrective Surgery, 1975–1978

1. Curt Dalton, *Dayton through Time* (Mt. Pleasant, SC: America through Time, 2015; Kenneth M. Keisel, *Dayton Aviation: The Wright Brothers to McCook Field* (Charleston, SC: Arcadia Publishers, 2012); Rebecca Goodman and Barrett J. Brunsman, *This Day in Ohio History* (Cincinnati, OH: Emmis Books, 2005); Kevin F. Kearn and Gregory S. Wilson, *Ohio: The History of the Buckeye State* (Malden, MA: Wiley Blackwell, 2014); and Bruce W. Ronald and Virginia Ronald, *Dayton: The Gem City* (Tulsa, OK: Continental Heritage Press, 1981).
2. Virginia Ronald and Bruce Ronald, *The Land between the Miamis: A Bicentennial Celebration of the Dayton Area* (Dayton, OH: Landfall Press, 1996), 334–335; Teresa Zumwald, *For the Love of Dayton: Life in the Miami Valley, 1796–1996* (Dayton, OH: Dayton Daily News, 1996); Andrew R. L. Cayton, *Ohio: The History of a People* (Columbus: The Ohio State University Press, 2002). Only *The Land between the Miamis* noted the Burt scandal. Ronald and Ronald, *The Land between the Miamis*, 346.
3. Dalton, *Dayton through Time*; Keisel, *Dayton Aviation*; Goodman and Brunsman, *This Day in Ohio History*; Ronald and Ronald, *Dayton: The Gem City*.
4. Kearn and Wilson, *Ohio: The History of the Buckeye State*, 407, 460.
5. Ronald and Ronald, *The Land between the Miamis*, 344; Lester A. Reingold, *Dayton: On the Wings of Progress* (Encino, CA: Chebro Publishing, 2005), 58; Zumwald, *For the Love of Dayton*, 231; Tom Dunham, *Dayton in the 20th Century* (Bloomington, IN: Author House, 2005).
6. Edward D. Berkowitz, *Something Happened: A Political and Cultural Overview of the Seventies* (New York: Columbia University Press, 2006).
7. His ex-wife, Linda Burt, estimated Burt's gross earnings in 1973 were $435,000. Dave Davis, "Burt Asset List Omitted Property," *DDN*, December 16, 1988.
8. Jo Ann Knout, "Local Doctor Develops Corrective Surgery," *DDN*, September 3, 1975.
9. Barbara Demick, "Love Surgery: Sexual Panacea or Mutilation for Profit?" *The Real Paper*, August 26, 1978, 18–21, quotations on 18, 20; "Selected Recent Court Decisions: Advertising by Doctors—*American Medical Association v. Federal Trade Commission*," *American Journal of Law and Medicine*, March 1, 1982, 87–88.

10. "Selected Recent Court Decisions," 87–88.

11. Nancy Tomes, *Remaking the American Patient: How Madison Avenue and Modern Medicine Turned Patients into Consumers* (Chapel Hill: University of North Carolina Press, 2016), 295.

12. Demick, "Love Surgery," 21; Julia Helgason and Dave Davis, "'Media Has Accepted Lies as Truth,' Says Burt," *DDN*, November 20, 1988; Diane K. Shah with Frank Maier, "Heeere's . . . Donahue!" *Newsweek*, March 13, 1978, 85; Mark Holoweiko, "Why Was the Love Surgeon Allowed to Keep Cutting?" *Medical Economics*, July 17, 1989, 125–128, 131–133, 136–138, 141, quotation on 132; Judith Sealander and Dorothy Smith, "The Rise and Fall of Feminist Organizations in the 1970s: Dayton as a Case Study," *Feminist Studies* 12, no. 2 (Summer 1986): 320–341; Laura Grindstaff, *The Money Shot: Trash, Class, and the Making of TV Talk Shows* (Chicago: University of Chicago Press, 2002), 49.

13. Demick, "Love Surgery," 20–21.

14. Linda Murray, "Building a Better Vagina: Changing the Shape of Things to Come," *Playgirl*, November 1977, 96, 102, 104, quotations on 102.

15. Demick, "Love Surgery," 18.

16. James C. Burt and Joan Burt, *Surgery of Love* (New York: Carlton Press, 1975), 269.

17. Demick, "Love Surgery," 20.

18. Helgason and Davis, "'Media Has Accepted Lies as Truth.'"

19. "Furor over Vaginal Surgery for Anorgasmy," *Medical World News*, April 17, 1978, 15–16.

20. Shere Hite, *The Hite Report: A Nationwide Survey of Female Sexuality* (New York: Macmillan, 1976), 58–59, 134, 232.

21. Hite, *The Hite Report*, 58–59, 134, 232.

22. Carol Tavris and Susan Sadd, *The Redbook Report on Female Sexuality: 100,000 Married Women Disclose the Good News About Sex* (New York: Delacorte Press, 1975), 20, 76, 79; emphasis in original.

23. Burt, *Surgery of Love*, 41.

24. Ira M. Reiss with Harriet M. Reiss, *Solving America's Sexual Crises* (Amherst, NY: Prometheus Books, 1997), 174.

25. Reiss with Reiss, *Solving America's Sexual Crises*, 177.

26. Reiss with Reiss, *Solving America's Sexual Crises*, 176, 190.

27. Testimony of Arthur Schramm, Appellant's Supplement, vol. 3, *Phillips v. Burt*, Case No. 95-1522, Supreme Court of Ohio, filed February 12, 1996, at 1141.

28. Testimony of Schramm, Appellant's Supplement, vol. 3, *Phillips v. Burt*, at 1141.

29. Demick, "Love Surgery," 20.

30. Holoweiko, "Why Was the Love Surgeon," 132.

31. Holoweiko, "Why Was the Love Surgeon," 131.

32. "Furor over Vaginal Surgery," 16.

33. Plaintiff's Expert Witnesses, Appellant's Supplement, vol. 1, *Phillips v. Burt*, Case No. 95-1522, Supreme Court of Ohio, filed February 12, 1996, at 0480; Plaintiff's Exhibit List, Appellant's Supplement, vol. 1, *Phillips v. Burt*, at 0492; "Frederick P. Zuspan, M.D.," at Perinatal Resources, http://perinatalresources.org/Zuspan.htm (accessed May 29, 2008).

34. Demick, "Love Surgery," 18.

35. Plaintiff's Exhibit List, Appellant's Supplement, vol. 1, *Phillips v. Burt*, at 0492; "Mary Calderone," C250 Celebrates Columbians Ahead of Their Time, http://c250.columbia.edu /c250_celebrates/remarkable_columbians/mary_calderone.html (viewed May 29, 2008).

36. Plaintiff's Exhibit List, Appellant's Supplement, vol. 1, *Phillips v. Burt*, at 0492–0493; "Luigi Mastroianni, Jr., M.D.," http://www.med.upenn.edu/crrwh/faculty/Mastroianni /Mastroianni.html (accessed May 29, 2008).

37. "Furor over Vaginal Surgery," 16.

38. Letter, Burt to Masters, August 23, 1977, Masters and Johnson Collection, letters, Box 1, Folder 21, Burt, James, MD, KI.

39. James C. Burt, "Surgical Improvement of Vaginal Response by Female Coital Area Reconstruction: A New Modality of Treatment," unpublished paper, pp. 2–3, Stacks 528.3, KI.

40. Burt, "Surgical Improvement of Vaginal Response," 28.

41. Burt, "Surgical Improvement of Vaginal Response," 23–24.

42. Dr. Manford M. Oliphant, Denver, Colorado, Letter to William Masters, December 15, 1977, Masters and Johnson Collection, Box 1, Folder 21, Burt, James, MD, KI.

43. Masters, Letter to Oliphant, December 20, 1977, Masters and Johnson Collection, Box 1, Folder 21, Burt, James, MD, KI.

44. Memo from W to William Masters, March 9, 1978, Masters and Johnson Collection, Box 1, Folder 21, Burt, James, MD, KI.

45. "Dr. James Burt," Memo from Chris to William Masters, March 14, 1978, Masters and Johnson Collection, Box 1, Folder 21, Burt, James, MD, KI.

46. James Burt, Letter to William Masters, March 13, 1978, Masters and Johnson Collection, Box 1, Folder 21, Burt, James, MD, KI.

47. "Furor over Vaginal Surgery," 15.

48. "Furor over Vaginal Surgery," 16.

49. "Furor over Vaginal Surgery," 16.

50. Dr. W. Kenneth Holbrook, Letter to William Masters, April 24, 1978, Masters and Johnson Collection, Box 1, Folder 21, Burt, James, MD, KI.

51. William Masters, Letter to Dr. W. Kenneth Holbrook, May 5, 1978, Masters and Johnson Collection, Box 1, Folder 21, Burt, James, MD, KI.

52. Demick, "Love Surgery," 18.

53. Barbara Demick, email to author, June 22, 2006.

54. Demick, "Love Surgery," 18–19.

55. Chris, Memo to William Masters, July 25, 1978, Masters and Johnson Collection, Box 1, Folder 21, Burt, James, MD, KI.

56. Note on top of July 25, 1978 Memo, from Virginia Johnson, July 25, 1978, Masters and Johnson Collection, letters, Box 1, Folder 21, Burt, James, MD, KI.

57. Demick, "Love Surgery," 19.

58. Demick, "Love Surgery," 19.

59. Demick, "Love Surgery," 19.

60. Demick, "Love Surgery," 19.

61. Demick, "Love Surgery," 19–20.

62. Demick, "Love Surgery," 19.

63. Demick, "Love Surgery," 19–20.

64. Demick, "Love Surgery," 18–21.

65. Burt, *Surgery of Love*, 265, 269.

66. Holoweiko, "Why Was the Love Surgeon," 132; U.S. Bureau of the Census, *Statistical Abstract of the United States: 1980*, 101st ed. (Washington, D.C.: U.S. Department of Commerce, 1980), 112, 458.

67. Holoweiko, "Why Was the Love Surgeon," 132.

68. Demick, "Love Surgery," 19.

69. Demick, "Love Surgery," 20.
70. Demick, "Love Surgery," 20. I asked the Ohio Civil Rights Commission if they still possessed the appeal from the Burts on this matter, but the commission only keeps records for two years, and I asked in 2006. Mark Kautzmann, Chief of Compliance, Ohio Civil Rights Commission, letter to author, December 12, 2006, Re: Request for Records Involving Dr. James Burt, letter in author's possession.
71. *Burt v. Blue Shield of Southwest Ohio*, D.C. Ohio, 1984, 591 F. Supp. 755, 1985–1 Trade Cases P 66, 599.
72. *Burt v. Blue Shield of Southwest Ohio.*
73. Jane E. Brody, "Blue Shield Acts to Curb Payment on Procedures of Doubtful Value," *New York Times*, May 19, 1977; Sarah Rodriguez, *Female Circumcision and Clitoridectomy in the United States: A History of a Medical Treatment* (Rochester, NY: University of Rochester Press, 2014).
74. Sandra Morgen, *Into Our Own Hands: The Women's Health Movement in the United States, 1969–1990* (New Brunswick, NJ: Rutgers University Press, 2002), 71–72, 120–121.
75. Demick, "Love Surgery," 21.
76. Ruth Horowitz, *In the Public Interest: Medical Licensing and the Disciplinary Process* (New Brunswick, NJ: Rutgers University Press, 2012).
77. In the fall of 2011, I examined twenty-five feminist publications published between 1977 and 1981 held in Special Collections at Northwestern University's Deering Library. Of these, only five ran stories on Burt. The dates given after the name of the publication indicate the years I looked through; if the years do not cover 1977 to 1981, this means the collection was either not complete or the publication did not exist for the entirety of these four years. The publications were *Big Mama Rag* (Denver), 1977 to 1979; *Coalition News/Coalition for the Medical Rights of Women* (San Francisco), February 1977 to March/April 1979; *Committee for Abortion Rights and against Sterilization Abuse, CARASA Newsletter* (New York City), 1978 to 1980; *Everywoman* (Amherst, MA), 1977 to June 1978; *HealthRight* (New York City), 1978 to 1980; *HerSay* (San Francisco), August 21, 1978, to July 1979; *Heresies: A Feminist Publication on Art and Politics* (New York City), 1977 to 1981; *The Majority Report* (New York City), 1977 to March 20, 1979; *The Monthly Extract: An Irregular Periodical* (Stamford, CT), May 1977 to April 1978 (final issue); *National NOW Times* (Washington, D.C.), 1977 to January 1980; *National Women's Health Network News* (Washington, D.C.), 1977 to 1980; *New Women's Times* (Rochester, NY), February 1978 to 1979; *Quest: A Feminist Quarterly* (Washington, D.C.), Winter 1976 to 1981; *Rapport* (Evanston, IL), 1977 to 1979; *Right NOW* (Columbus, OH), April 1977 to 1980; *Second Opinion—Coalition for the Medical Rights of Women* (San Francisco), April 1979 to 1980; *The Second Wave* (Cambridge, MA), 1977 to 1981; *Sister* (New Haven, CT), 1977 to 1979; *Sojourner: A Third World Women's Research Newsletter* (Detroit), November 1977 to May 1981; *The Spokeswoman* (Chicago and Washington, D.C.), 1977 to 1980; *WEAL—Women's Equity Action League* (Washington, D.C.), February 1977 to December 1979; *Women against Violence in Pornography and Media Newspage* (Berkeley, CA), 1977 to 1980; *Women and Health* (Binghamton, NY), 1978 to 1979; and *Women's Liberation Union of Rhode Island* (Providence, RI), 1977 to 1980. Additionally, I searched *off our backs* for stories about Burt in the 1970s using the database GenderWatch. I also attempted to look through the National Black Feminist Organization newsletter, Chicago chapter, but Northwestern has only one

issue from 1975; the National Black Feminist Organization national chapter, out of New York City, newsletter, but Northwestern has only one issue from 1975; *Woman-Wise: The New Hampshire Feminist Health Center Quarterly*, but Northwestern has only the winter 1979 issue; and *Women against Pornography Newsreport*, but Northwestern's collection has only four issues from the 1980s.

78. Tacie Dejanikus, "Vaginal Mutilation American Style," *off our backs*, July 31, 1978, 13.

79. "In Brief," *National NOW Times*, October 1978, 2.

80. "More Genital Mutilation," *Big Mama Rag*, July/August 1978, 6. The Northwestern University's library's collection of *HerSay* starts with the August 21, 1978, issue, so I did not have access to the original story in *HerSay*.

81. *What She Wants*, January 1975 to January 1980, NU.

82. Judith Ezekiel, *Feminism in the Heartland* (Columbus: The Ohio State University Press, 2002), 66–67.

83. Both *The Cleveland Feminist* and the Dayton *Women's Liberation Newsletter* are at NU.

84. See Sarah B. Rodriguez, "Female Sexuality and Consent in Public Discourse: James Burt's 'Love Surgery,'" *Archives of Sexual Behavior*, April 2013, 343–351.

85. Carolyn Bronstein, *Battling Pornography: The American Feminist Anti-Pornography Movement, 1976–1986* (New York: Cambridge University Press, 2011), 2.

86. Susan Brownmiller, *Against Our Will: Men, Women, and Rape* (New York: Simon and Schuster, 1975); Christine Stansell, *The Feminist Promise: 1792 to the Present* (New York: The Modern Library, 2010), 288, 344–346.

87. Jane Gerhard, *Desiring Revolution: Second-Wave Feminism and the Rewriting of American Sexual Thought, 1920–1982* (New York: Columbia University Press, 2001), 87.

88. Bronstein, *Battling Pornography*.

89. Beverly LaBelle, "Snuff—The Ultimate in Woman-Hating," in *Take Back the Night: Women on Pornography*, ed. Laura Lederer (New York: William Morrow and Co., 1980), 272–278.

90. Laura Lederer, "Introduction," in *Take Back the Night: Women on Pornography*, ed. Laura Lederer (New York: William Morrow and Co., 1980), 15, 19–20, quotations on 19–20.

91. Segal, "Introduction," 4.

92. Lederer, "Introduction," 15, 19–20.

93. Bronstein, *Battling Pornography*.

94. Fran Hosken, *The Hosken Report* (Lexington, MA: Women's International Network News, 1979), 10. I have been unable to find anything about the publication *Science for the People*.

95. Gena Corea and Cynthia de Wit, "Current Developments and Issues: A Summary," *Reproductive and Genetic Engineering* 2, no. 2 (1989): 153.

96. "Robin Morgan: Love Surgery," *Big Mama Rag*, November 1979, 20.

97. Rodriguez, "Female Sexuality and Consent in Public Discourse."

98. Sealander and Smith, "The Rise and Fall of Feminist Organizations in the 1970s," 324.

99. Ezekiel, *Feminism in the Heartland*.

100. Ezekiel, *Feminism in the Heartland*.

101. Demick, "Love Surgery," 18–21.

Janet Phillips, 1981 (II)

1. Direct examination of Janet Phillips, Appellant's Supplement, vol. 3, *Phillips v. Burt*, Case No. 95-1522, Supreme Court of Ohio, filed February 12, 1996, at 1258–1259.
2. James Burt's medical notes for Janet Phillips, October 23, 1981, Appellant's Supplement, vol. 2, *Phillips v. Burt*, Case No. 95-1522, Supreme Court of Ohio, filed February 12, 1996, at 0933.
3. Direct examination of Phillips, Appellant's Supplement, vol. 3, *Phillips v. Burt*, at 1258–1259.
4. James Burt's medical notes for Janet Phillips, March 25, 1981, Appellant's Supplement, vol. 2, *Phillips v. Burt*, Case No. 95-1522, Supreme Court of Ohio, filed February 12, 1996, at 0993; direct examination of Phillips, Appellant's Supplement, vol. 3, *Phillips v. Burt*, at 1260; Burt's medical notes for Phillips, October 23, 1981, Appellant's Supplement, vol. 2, *Phillips v. Burt*, at 0933; direct examination of Edmund Phillips, Appellant's Supplement, vol. 2, *Phillips v. Burt*, Case No. 95-1522, Supreme Court of Ohio, filed February 12, 1996, at 1249.
5. Affidavit of Janet Phillips, Appellant's Supplement, vol. 1, *Phillips v. Burt*, Case No. 95-1522, Supreme Court of Ohio, filed February 12, 1996, at 52; direct examination of Janet Phillips, Appellant's Supplement, vol. 3, *Phillips v. Burt*, at 1261–1262.
6. Direct examination of Phillips, Appellant's Supplement, vol. 3, *Phillips v. Burt*, at 1261–1262.
7. Burt's medical notes for Phillips, March 25, 1981, Appellant's Supplement, vol. 2, *Phillips v. Burt*, at 0993–0994.
8. Burt's medical notes for Phillips, March 25, 1981, Appellant's Supplement, vol. 2, *Phillips v. Burt*, at 0993–0994; Burt's medical notes for Phillips, August 5, 1981, Appellant's Supplement, vol. 2, *Phillips v. Burt*, at 0996.
9. Burt's medical notes for Phillips, October 23, 1981, Appellant's Supplement, vol. 2, *Phillips v. Burt*, at 0931–0932, 0935.
10. Direct examination of Phillips, Appellant's Supplement, vol. 3, *Phillips v. Burt*, at 1263–1265.
11. Claire Safron, "The Gynecologist from Hell," *Woman's Day*, August 15, 1989, 70, 74, 76, 87, quotation on 74.
12. Direct examination of Phillips, Appellant's Supplement, vol. 3, *Phillips v. Burt*, at 1263–1265.

3. Surgical Development and Regulation

1. "Furor over Vaginal Surgery for Anorgasmy," *Medical World News*, April 19, 1978, 15.
2. "Furor over Vaginal Surgery," 15.
3. Andrew Warwick, "X-rays as Evidence in German Orthopedic Surgery, 1895–1900," *Isis* 96, no. 1 (2005): 1–24, quotation on 3. For two examples of such work, see Sally Wilde, "See One, Do One, Modify One: Prostate Surgery in the 1930s," *Medical History* 48 (2004): 351–366 and Sally Wilde and Geoffrey Hirst, "Learning from Mistakes: Early Twentieth-Century Surgical Practice," *Journal of the History of Medicine and Allied Sciences* 64, no. 1 (2008): 38–77.
4. Christopher Crenner, "Forward," to Marc A. Asher, *Dogged Persistence: Harrington, Post-Polio Scoliosis, and the Origin of Spine Instrumentation* (Traverse City, MI: Chandler Lake Books, 2015), xiii–xiv, quotation on xiii.
5. Barbara Demick, "Love Surgery: Sexual Panacea or Mutilation for Profit?" *The Real Paper*, August 26, 1978, 18–21, quotations on 18.

6. Judith Parsley, "Rethinking the Episiotomy," *Baby Care Forum for the Nursing Professional*, Fall 1990, 1, 3, quotation on 1. M. Gabrielle Myers-Helfgott and Andrew W. Helfgott, "Routine Use of Episiotomy in Modern Obstetrics: Should It Be Performed?" *Obstetrics and Gynecology Clinics* 26, no. 2 (June 1999): 306–325, quotation on 306.

7. Anne M. Weber and Leslie M. S. Meyn, "Episiotomy Use in the United States, 1979–1997," *Obstetrics and Gynecology* 100, no. 6 (December 2002): 1177–1182; Katherine Hartmann, Meera Viswanathan, Rachel Palmieri, Gerald Garthehner, John Thorpe, and Kathleen N. Lohr, "Outcomes of Routine Episiotomy: A Systematic Review," *JAMA* 293, no. 17 (May 4, 2005): 2141–2148; Eugene R. Declercq, Carol Sakala, Maureen P. Corry, and Sandra Applebaum, *Listening to Mothers II: Report of the Second National U.S. Survey of Women's Childbearing Experiences* (New York: Childbirth Connection, 2006), 19, 45.

8. Karis Crawford and Johanne C. Walters, *Natural Childbirth after Cesarean: A Practical Guide* (Cambridge: Blackwell Science, 1996), 69.

9. President's Commission for the Study of Ethical Problems in Medicine and Biomedical and Behavioral Research, *Making Health Care Decisions*, vol. 1 (Washington, D.C.: President's Commission for the Study of Ethical Problems in Medicine and Biomedical and Behavioral Research, October 1982), 64.

10. George J. Annas, Leonard H. Glantz, and Barbara F. Katz, *Informed Consent to Human Experimentation: The Subject's Dilemma* (Cambridge, MA: Ballinger, 1977), 46, 29–31.

11. Nancy Tomes, *Remaking the American Patient: How Madison Avenue and Modern Medicine Turned Patients into Consumers* (Chapel Hill: University of North Carolina Press, 2016), 276–277.

12. Susan E. Lederer, *Subjected to Science: Human Experimentation in American before the Second World War* (Baltimore: The Johns Hopkins University Press, 1995), 16.

13. *Schloendorff v. Society of New York Hospital*, 211 N.Y. 125, 129, 105 N.E. 92, 93 (1914) as quoted in Joseph H. King, *The Law of Medical Malpractice in a Nutshell* (St. Paul, MN: West, 1977), 136.

14. Sylvia Law and Steven Polan, *Pain and Profit: The Politics of Malpractice* (New York: HarperCollins, 1978), 108.

15. Tom L. Beauchamp and Ruth R. Faden, "Informed Consent: History of Informed Consent," in *Encyclopedia of Bioethics*, ed. Warren Thomas Reich, rev. ed., vol. 3 (New York: Simon & Schuster Macmillan, 1995), 1232, 1234–1235.

16. Ruth R. Faden, Catherin Becker, Carol Lewis, John Freeman, and Alan I. Faden, "Disclosure of Information to Patients in Medical Care," *Medical Care* 19 (July 1981): 718–733, quotation on 719.

17. President's Commission for the Study of Ethical Problems in Medicine and Biomedical and Behavioral Research, *Making Health Care Decisions*, 34.

18. Charles Fried, *Medical Experimentation: Personal Integrity and Social Policy* (New York: American Elsevier, 1974), 22.

19. Tomes, *Remaking the American Patient*, 277.

20. Atul Gawande, *Complications: A Surgeon's Notes on an Imperfect Science* (New York: Metropolitan Books, 2002), 210.

21. Tomes, *Remaking the American Patient*, 277. For more on the Tuskegee Syphilis Study, see Susan Reverby, *Examining Tuskegee: The Infamous Syphilis Study and Its Legacy* (Chapel Hill: University of North Carolina Press, 2009).

22. Beauchamp and Faden, "Informed Consent," 1236.

23. Boston Women's Health Book Collective, *Our Bodies Ourselves: A Book by and for Women* (New York: Simon and Schuster, 1973); Boston Women's Health Book Collective, *Our Bodies, Ourselves: A Book by and for Women* (New York: Simon & Schuster, 1979).

24. Francis Hornstein, "Assertiveness in the Dr.'s Office," *The Feminist Women's Health Center Report*, September 1975, 12. L1 Femina Serial Am F32979r, NU.

25. Tomes, *Remaking the American Patient*, 265–266.

26. Edward D. Berkowitz, *Something Happened: A Political and Cultural Overview of the Seventies* (New York: Columbia University Press, 2007), 6.

27. Tomes, *Remaking the American Patient*, 270–271; Beatrix Hoffman, "'Don't Scream Alone': The Health Care Activism of Americans in the 1970s," in *Patients as Policy Actors*, ed. Beatrix Hoffman, Nancy Tomes, Rachel Grob, and Mark Schlesinger (New Brunswick, NJ: Rutgers University Press, 2011), 132–147.

28. Ruth R. Faden and Tom L. Beauchamp, *A History and Theory of Informed Consent* (Oxford: Oxford University Press, 1986), 93–94; Hoffman, "'Don't Scream Alone,'" 132–147; Tomes, *Remaking the American Patient*, 271.

29. Norma Shaw Hogan, "Patient's Rights: Voluntary or Mandatory," *Journal of the American Hospital Association* 52, no. 9 (November 16, 1978): 111–116, quotation on 113.

30. Tomes, *Remaking the American Patient*, 276.

31. Hogan, "Patient's Rights," 114.

32. Hoffman, "'Don't Scream Alone,'" 143.

33. Beatrix Hoffman, *Health Care for Some: Rights and Rationing in the United States since 1930* (Chicago: University of Chicago Press, 2012), 150.

34. "Informed Consent," *Law & Bioethics: Court Cases and Supporting Documents*, http://www.lawandbioethics.com/demo/Main/LegalResources/C5/background01.htm (accessed September 2, 2015).

35. Alan Meisel and Lisa D. Kabnick, "Informed Consent to Medical Treatment: An Analysis of Recent Legislation," *University of Pittsburgh Law Review* 41, no. 3 (1980): 407–564, information found on 409–410.

36. Meisel and Kabnick, "Informed Consent to Medical Treatment," 415, 429.

37. James E. Ludlam, *Informed Consent* (Chicago: American Hospital Association, 1978), 43.

38. Meisel and Kabnick, "Informed Consent to Medical Treatment," 422–423, 526.

39. Faden and Beauchamp, *A History and Theory of Informed Consent*, 91.

40. Ralph J. Alfidi, "Informed Consent: A Study of Patient Reaction," *JAMA* 216 (May 24, 1971): 1325–1329.

41. Jane H. Bergler and Edward D. Freis, "Informed Consent: How Much Does the Patient Understand?" *Clinical Pharmacology and Therapeutics* 27, no. 4 (April 1980): 435–440.

42. James M. Vaccarino, "Consent, Informed Consent, and the Consent Form," *New England Journal of Medicine* 298 (1978): 455.

43. Bradford H. Gray, *Human Subjects in Medical Experimentation: A Sociological Study of the Conduct and Regulation of Clinical Research* (New York: John Wiley and Sons, 1975), 236.

44. Faden and Beauchamp, *A History and Theory of Informed Consent*, 98–99.

45. Jay Katz, *The Silent World of Doctor and Patient* (New York: The Free Press, 1984), 26.

46. Jay Katz, "Informed Consent—A Fairy Tale? Law's Vision," *University of Pittsburgh Law Review* 39, no. 2 (Winter 1977): 137–174.

47. Jane Cleary-Goldman and Julian N. Robinson, "The Role of Episiotomy in Current Obstetric Practice," *Seminars in Perinatology* 27, no. 1 (February 2003): 3–12; V. Kalis, K. Laine, J. W. de Leeuw, K. M. Ismail, and D. G. Tincello, "Classification of Episiotomy: Towards a Standardization of Terminology," *BJOG* 119 (February 2012): 522–526.

48. Wallace B. Shute, "Episiotomy: A Physiologic Appraisal and a New Painless Technic," *Obstetrics and Gynecology* 14, no. 4 (October 1959): 467–472, quotation on 468.

49. James W. Jones, "The Surgeon's Autonomy: Defining Limits in Therapeutic Decision Making," in *Ethical Guidelines for Innovative Surgery*, ed. Angelique M. Reitsma and Jonathan D. Moreno (Hagerstown, MD: University Publishing Group, 2006), 77–92; Daniel J. Riskin, Michael T. Longaker, Michael Gertner, and Thomas M. Krummel, "Innovation in Surgery: A Historical Perspective," *Annals of Surgery* 244, no. 5 (November 2006): 686–693.

50. Joel E. Frader and Donna A. Caniano, "Research and Innovation in Surgery," in *Surgical Ethics*, ed. Laurence B. McCullogh, James W. Jones, and Baruch A. Brody (New York: Oxford University Press, 1998), 216–241.

51. Riskin et al., "Innovation in Surgery: A Historical Perspective"; Clyde F. Barker and Larry R. Kaiser, "Is Surgical Science Dead?" *Journal of the American College of Surgeons* 198, no. 1 (January 2004): 1–19.

52. Myron E. Freund, "Surgical Research," in *Human Subjects Research: A Handbook for Institutional Review Boards*, ed. Robert A. Greenwald, Mary Kay Ryan, and James E. Mulvihill (New York: Plenum, 1982), 169–179, quotation on 173.

53. Walter L. Biffl, David A Spain, Angelique M. Reitsma, Rebecca M. Minter, Jeffrey Upperman, Mark Wilson, Reid Adams, Edward B. Goldman, Peter Angelos, Thomas Krummel, Lazar J. Greenfield, and the Society of University Surgeons Surgical Innovations Project Team, "Responsible Development and Application of Surgical Innovations: A Position Statement of the Society of University Surgeons," *Journal of the American College of Surgeons* 206, no. 6 (June 2008): 1204–1209, quotation on 1204.

54. Norman Fost, "Ethical Dilemmas in Medical Innovation and Research: Distinguishing Experimentation from Practice," *Seminars in Perinatology* 22, no. 3 (June 1998): 223–232, quotation on 227.

55. Grant Gillett, "Ethics of Surgical Innovation," *British Journal of Surgery* 88 (2001): 897–898; Martin F. McKneally, "Ethical Problems in Surgery: Innovation Leading to Unforeseen Complications," *World Journal of Surgery* 23, no. 8 (August 1999): 786–788.

56. Curtis Margo, "When Is Surgery Research? Towards an Operational Definition of Human Research," *Journal of Medical Ethics* 27 (2001): 40–43.

57. Francis D. Moore, "Therapeutic Innovation: Ethical Boundaries in the Initial Clinical Trials of New Drugs and Surgical Procedures," in *Experimentation with human Subjects*, ed. Paul A. Freund (New York: George Braziller, 1970), 358–378, quotation on 358.

58. Reemtsma quoted in Ruth Macklin, "Ethical Implications of Surgical Experiments," *American College of Surgeons Bulletin* 70, no. 6 (June 1985): 2–5, quotation on 2.

59. Angelique M. Reitsma and Jonathan D. Moreno, "Ethical Regulations for Innovative Surgery: The Last Frontier?" *Journal of the American College of Surgeons* 194, no. 6 (June 2002): 792–801, quotation on 793, emphasis in original.

60. Macklin, "Ethical Implications of Surgical Experiments," 3.

61. Laurence B. McCullough, "Standard of Care, Innovation, and Research in Surgery: A Problem in Research Ethics or in Professional Medical Ethics?" in *Ethical*

Guidelines for Innovative Surgery, ed. Angelique M. Reitsma and Jonathan D. Moreno (Hagerstown, MD: University Publishing Group, 2006), 64.

62. Frader and Caniano, "Research and Innovation in Surgery," 216–241; Grant R. Gillett, "Surgical Innovation and Research," in *The Oxford Textbook of Clinical Research Ethics*, ed. Ezekiel Emanuel, Christine C. Grady, Robert A. Crouch, Reidar L. Lie, Franklin G. Miller, and David D. Wendler (Oxford: Oxford University Press, 2008), 367–374.

63. Michael J. Solomon and Robin S. McLeod, "Clinical Studies in Surgical Journals— Have We Improved?" *Diseases of the Colon and Rectum* 36, no. 1 (January 1993): 43–48.

64. Jonathan Meakins, "Innovation in Surgery: The Rules of Evidence," *American Journal of Surgery* 183 (2002): 399–405; Riskin et al., "Innovation in Surgery: A Historical Perspective."

65. Freund, "Surgical Research," 173.

66. Reemtsma quoted in Macklin, "Ethical Implications of Surgical Experiments," 2.

67. Jeffrey S. Barkun, Jeffrey K. Aronson, Liane S. Feldman, Guy J. Maddern, and Steven M. Strasberg, for the Balliol Collaboration, "Evaluation and Stages of Surgical Innovations," *Lancet* 374 (2009): 1089–1096, quotation on 1092.

68. Angelique M. Reitsma and Jonathan D. Moreno, "Ethics of Innovative Surgery: US Surgeons' Definitions, Knowledge, and Attitudes," *Journal of the American College of Surgeons* 200, no. 1 (January 2005): 103–110, quotation on 103.

69. Barkun et al., "Evaluation and Stages of Surgical Innovations," 1090.

70. Some of this, they believed, was because the terms *innovative, experimental,* and *research* were often applied in a similar manner, resulting in their meanings, rather than being distinct, overlapping. Reitsma and Moreno, "Ethical Regulations for Innovative Surgery," 793.

71. Reitsma and Moreno, "Ethics of Innovative Surgery," 104.

72. Barkun et al., "Evaluation and Stages of Surgical Innovations," 1090.

73. Reitsma and Moreno, "Ethics of Innovative Surgery," 103.

74. Reitsma and Moreno, "Ethics of Innovative Surgery," 104.

75. Herrman L. Blumgart, "The Medical Framework for Viewing the Problem of Human Experimentation," *Daedalus* 98, no. 2 (Spring 1969): 248–274, quotation on 248.

76. Fost, "Ethical Dilemmas in Medical Innovation and Research."

77. National Commission for the Protection of Human Subjects of Biomedical and Behavioral Research, "The Belmont Report," U.S. Department of Health and Human Services, April 18, 1979, http://www.hhs.gov/ohrp/humansubjects/guidance/belmont .html (accessed September 22, 2018).

78. Steven M. Strasberg and Philip A. Ludbrook, "Who Oversees Innovative Practice? Is There a Structure That Meets the Monitoring Needs of New Techniques?" *Journal of the American College of Surgeons* 196, no. 6 (June 2003): 938–948.

79. Reitsma and Moreno, "Ethics of Innovative Surgery."

80. Curtis E. Margo, "When Is Surgery Research? Towards an Operational Definition of Human Research," *Journal of Medical Ethics* 27 (2001): 40–43, quotation on 41.

81. David H. Spodick, "Numerators without Denominators: There Is No FDA for the Surgeon," *JAMA* 232, no. 1 (April 7, 1975): 35–37, quotation on 36.

82. J. P. Bunker, D. Hinkley, and W. V. McDermott, "Surgical Innovation and Its Evaluation," *Science* 200 (May 26, 1978): 937–941, quotation on 937.

83. Jack W. Love, "Drugs and Operations: Some Important Differences," *JAMA* 232, no. 1 (April 7, 1975): 37–38.

84. Reitsma and Moreno, "Ethical Regulations for Innovative Surgery."
85. R. Alto Charo, "Human Subjects Have It Worse Than Guinea Pigs," *Chronicle of Higher Education*, June 25, 1999.
86. Spodick, "Numerators without Denominators," 35–37.
87. Barkun et al., "Evaluation and Stages of Surgical Innovations," 1091.
88. Robert M. Sade, Timothy H. Williams, David J. Perlman, Cynthia L. Haney, and Martha R. Stroud, "Ethics Gaps in Surgery," in *The Ethics of Surgery: Conflicts and Controversies*, ed. Robert M. Sade (Oxford: Oxford University Press, 2015), 19–25.
89. Macklin, "Ethical Implications of Surgical Experiments," 5.
90. Riskin et al., "Innovation in Surgery." As further illustration of the uptake of ethical considerations in surgery more largely in the 1990s, it was not until 1998 that the American College of Surgeons' official journal, the *Journal of the American College of Surgeons*, had a regular section on ethical issues. C. Rollins Hanlon, "Ethics in Surgery," *Journal of the American College of Surgeons* 186, no. 1 (January 1998): 41–49; C. Rollins Hanlon, "Surgical Ethics," *American Journal of Surgery* 187 (2004): 1–2.
91. Reitsma and Moreno, "Ethical Regulations for Innovative Surgery"; Ingrid Burger, Jeremy Sugarman, and Steven N. Goodman, "Ethical Issues in Evidence-Based Surgery," *Surgical Clinic of North America* 86 (2006): 151–168; Committee on Emerging Surgical Technology and Education of the American College of Surgeons, "Statement on Issues to Be Considered before New Surgical Technology Is Applied to the Care of Patients," *American College of Surgeons*, September 1, 1995, https://www.facs.org/about-acs/statements/23-issues-new-tech (accessed October 16, 2014).
92. Reitsma and Moreno, "Ethical Regulations for Innovative Surgery," 797.
93. Biffl et al., "Responsible Development and Application of Surgical Innovations," 1204.
94. As noted in a 2012 article examining the ethical challenges of innovative surgery, the authors stressed, "Patients may not be told that they will be (or in fact have been) exposed to a new technique or procedure. While this may be reasonable if the innovation occurred in response to an emergency, such withholding of information is difficult to justify when innovations are planned. It may be argued that in some cases, such information is of a technical nature (for example, whether a surgeon is using an innovative anatomical approach) and thus beyond the usual bounds of informed consent. However, the information is surely germane to the patient if the innovation, no matter its nature, is associated with increased risks." Jane Johnson and Wendy Rogers, "Innovative Surgery: The Ethical Challenges," *Journal of Medical Ethics* 38, no. 1 (2012): 9–12, quotation on 10.
95. Burger, Sugarman, and Goodman, "Ethical Issues in Evidence-Based Surgery," 164. As Jay Katz, however, noted, "No system of control will affect the unscrupulous investigator." Katz, "The Education of the Physician-Investigator," *Daedalus* 98, no. 2 (Spring 1969): 480–501, quotation on 498.
96. Bernard Barber, John J. Lally, Julia Loughlin Makaruskka, and Daniel Sullivan, *Research on Human Subjects: Problems of Social Control in Medical Experimentation* (New York: Russell Sage Foundation, 1973), 7.
97. Freund, "Surgical Research," 173.
98. Moore, "Therapeutic Innovation," 358–378.
99. Fried, *Medical Experimentation*, 29.
100. Patrick L. Ergina, Jonathan A. Cook, Jane M. Blazeby, Isabelle Boutron, Pierr-Alain Clavien, Barnaby C. Reeves, and Christoph M. Seiler, for the Balliol Collaboration, "Challenges in Evaluating Surgical Innovation," *Lancet* 374 (2009): 1097–1104.

101. Charo, "Human Subjects Have It Worse Than Guinea Pigs," A64.
102. Margo, "When Is Surgery Research?" 41.
103. Barkun et al., "Evaluation and Stages of Surgical Innovations," 1091.
104. Biffl et al., "Responsible Development and Application of Surgical Innovations"; Reitsma and Moreno, "Ethical Regulations for Innovative Surgery."
105. Laskas, "A Crime against Nature," 63; Demick, "Love Surgery," 18.
106. For historical examples and discussion of this diffusion, see Cynthia L. Tang and Thomas Schlich, "Surgical Innovation and the Multiple Meanings of Randomized Control Trials: The First RCT on Minimally Invasive Cholecystectomy (1980–2000)," *Journal of the History of Medicine and Allied Sciences* 71, no. 4 (2016): 1–25; Thomas Schlich, "The Art and Science of Surgery: Innovation and Concepts of Medical Practice in Operative Fracture Care, 1960s–1970s," *Science, Technology, and Human Values* 32, no. 1 (2007): 65–87.
107. H. David Banta, "Embracing or Rejecting Innovations: Clinical Diffusion of Health Care Technology," in *Use and Impact of Computers in Clinical Medicine*, ed. James G. Anderson and Stephen J. Jay (New York: Springer, 1987), 132–160.
108. Tang and Schlich, "Surgical Innovation and the Multiple Meanings of Randomized Control Trials."
109. David S. Jones, *Broken Hearts: The Tangled History of Cardiac Care* (Baltimore: Johns Hopkins University Press, 2013), 19.
110. There are many reasons a clinician may add a new therapy or surgical procedure, including but not limited to the evidence—indeed, often times, "clear evidence about the appropriateness of and conditions for good practice rarely emerges until the innovation has been experimented with for some time." Jean-Louis Denis, Yann Hebert, Ann Langley, Daniel Lozeau, and Louise-Helene Trottier, "Explaining Diffusion Patterns for Complex Health Care Innovations," *Health Care Management Review* 27, no. 3 (Summer 2002): 60–73, quotation on 72.
111. John B. McKinlay, "From 'Promising Report' to 'Standard Procedure': Seven Stages in the Career of a Medical Innovation," *The Milbank Memorial Fund Quarterly. Health and Society*, 59, no. 3 (1981): 374–411, quotations on 377, 387. Additionally, as historian John Pickstone noted, whether a physician makes (or is able to make) an innovation is also politically and socially shaped. John Pickstone, "Introduction," in *Medical Innovations in Historical Perspective*, ed. John Pickstone (New York: St. Martin's, 1992), 1–16.
112. For more on the history of the RCT, see Martin Edwards, *Control and the Therapeutic Trial* (Amsterdam: Rodopi, 2007), and Harry Marks, *The Progress of Experiment: Science and Therapeutic Reform in the United States, 1900–1990* (Cambridge: Cambridge University Press, 1997).
113. McKinlay, "From 'Promising Report' to 'Standard Procedure,'" 375, 392, 395–396, 399. Emphasis in original.
114. There were rumors some physicians did pick up his surgery, but I have been unable to confirm this in the medical literature.
115. Banta, "Embracing or Rejecting Innovations," 132–160.
116. Pickstone, "Introduction." Jennifer Stanton similarly argued that the diffusion of innovations "often rested, not on some abstract notion of 'evidence'" but rather "on assertions of authority by professional alliances, which themselves fluctuated through time." Jennifer Stanton, "Introduction: On Theory and Practice," in *Innovations in Health and Medicine: Diffusion and Resistance in the Twentieth Century* (London: Routledge, 2002), 1–18, quotation on 4.

117. Riskin et al., "Innovations in Surgery."

118. Schlich, "The Art and Science of Surgery," 81.

119. Ann Lennarson Greer, "Scientific Knowledge and Social Consensus," *Controlled Clinical Trials* 15 (1994): 431–436, quotation on 434.

4. The Dayton Medical Community Reacts, 1976–1980

1. Jo Ann Ashley, *Hospitals, Paternalism, and the Role of the Nurse* (New York: Teachers College Press, Columbia University, 1976). In the mid-1970s, women dominated the nursing field, with over 95 percent of nurses being female, compared to physicians, 91 percent of whom were male. Bonnie Bullough and Vern L. Bullough, "Sex Discrimination in Heath Care," *Nursing Outlook* 23, no. 1 (January 1975): 40–45.

2. Thetis M. Group and Joan I. Roberts, *Nursing, Physician Control, and the Medical Monopoly: Historical Perspectives on Gendered Inequality in Roles, Rights, and Range of Practice* (Bloomington: Indian University Press, 2001), 217, xxxvii, xli.

3. Louise Lander, *Defective Medicine: Risk, Anger, and the Malpractice Crisis* (New York: Farrar, Straus and Giroux, 1978), 25.

4. Ashley, *Hospitals, Paternalism, and the Role of the Nurse*, 131; Group and Roberts, *Nursing, Physician Control*, 175, 195, 197–199.

5. Lander, *Defective Medicine*, 23–24.

6. Sylvia Law and Steve Polan, *Pain and Profit: The Politics of Malpractice* (New York: Harper & Row 1978), 210.

7. Barbara Demick, "Love Surgery: Sexual Panacea or Mutilation for Profit?" *The Real Paper*, August 26, 1978, 18–21, quotations on 18–21.

8. Rob Modic, "5-Week Burt Trial Down to Closing Arguments," *DDN*, June 19, 1991.

9. Rob Modic, "St. Elizabeth Asks Judge for Immunity," *DDN*, June 18, 1991.

10. Jeanne Marie Laskas, "A Crime against Nature," *Savvy Woman*, June 1989, 63–66, quotation on 66.

11. Rob Modic, "Former Burt Assistant Says Hospital Knew," *DDN*, May 22, 1991.

12. Rob Modic and Tom Beyerlein, "Judge Allows More Evidence in Burt Case," *DDN*, May 16, 1991.

13. Laurie Abraham, "Ohio Medical Groups Hit for Not Exposing MD's 'Love Surgery,'" *American Medical News*, January 27, 1989, 1, 9–10, quotations on 9–10.

14. Modic and Beyerlein, "Judge Allows More Evidence."

15. Modic, "Former Burt Assistant Says Hospital Knew."

16. "Looking Back: 18 Years of Controversy," *DDN*, August 4, 1991. The state medical board formerly was called the Ohio State Medical Board, but I am using its current name here to be consistent across the decades to help avoid confusion; the only time I do not do this is when the name appears in something I am quoting or when it is part of a title.

17. Laskas, "Crime against Nature," 66.

18. Abraham, "Ohio Medical Groups Hit," 10.

19. Mark Holoweiko, "Why Was the Love Surgeon Allowed to Keep Cutting?" *Medical Economics*, July 17, 1989, 125–128, 131–133, 136–138, quotation on 128. Walter Reiling Jr. informed me the spelling of Kircher's name was Kercher, but according to his obituary, it was Kircher. "Dr. Konrad Kircher," *DDN*, February 16, 2010.

20. Demick, "Love Surgery," 21.

21. American Cancer Society, "Laetrile," http://www.cancer.org/treatment/treatment sandsideeffects/complementaryandalternativemedicine/pharmacologicalandbiological

treatment/laetrile (accessed October 24, 2012); "Questions and Answers about Laetrile /Amygdalin," May 5, 2006, National Cancer Institute, www.cancer.gov.cancertopics /pdq/cam/laetrile/Patient/page2 (accessed December 20, 2007).

22. Demick, "Love Surgery," 18.

23. Demick, Love Surgery," 21.

24. Laskas, "Crime against Nature," 63

25. Demick, "Love Surgery," 21.

26. Abraham, "Ohio Medical Groups Hit," 9.

27. Demick, "Love Surgery," 21.

28. Abraham, "Ohio Medical Groups Hit," 9.

29. Holoweiko, "Why Was the Love Surgeon," 131.

30. Holden did not think the former Burt patients she saw had been circumcised. Holden, interview with author, July 29, 2016.

31. Holden was not the physician who spoke with Demick; when I spoke with Holden, she was sure it was one of the male physicians with whom she worked who did. Holoweiko writes briefly about this young woman and Holden in his article. Holoweiko has her leaving Dayton in 1978, but in our conversation, Holden recalled leaving Dayton in 1977 for Boston. Holden did not follow the Burt story once she moved. Holden, interview with author, July 9, 2016.

32. It is important to note, however, that the definition of, and what constitutes, an elective surgery changes over time (and even among practitioners). Cynthia L. Tang and Thomas Schlich, "Surgical Innovation and the Multiple Meanings of Randomized Control Trials: The First RCT on Minimally Invasive Cholecystectomy," *Journal of the History of Medicine and Allied Sciences* 72, no. 2 (2017): 117–141.

33. There are concerns with consent and elective, cosmetic surgery, but I will just touch on one argument here, that when a person seeks such surgery and it does not violate the "rights of others or the morals of society in general, their right to seek" a cosmetic surgery is ethical—and the physician is within his or her ethical abilities to aid the person, assuming a "serious discussion of risks and benefits" has been held. Michael Van Vliet and Joseph Rosen, "An Argument for Patient Autonomy in Elective Surgery," *Virtual Mentor* 12, no. 5 (May 2010): 373–375, quotation on 374.

34. Holden, interview with author, July 9, 2016.

35. Holoweiko, "Why Was the Love Surgeon," 132.

36. Demick, "Love Surgery," 21. The ability for a physician to sue a hospital because of a denial of staff privileges was a result of the Supreme Court's 1975 ruling in *Goldfarb v. Virginia State Bar*, a ruling that rejected the antitrust exemption for the "learned professions." See Carl F. Ameringer, *State Medical Boards and the Politics of Public Protection* (Baltimore: The Johns Hopkins University Press, 1999).

37. Timothy Stoltzfus Jost, "The Necessary and Proper Role of Regulation to Assure the Quality of Health Care," *Houston Law Review* 25, no. 3 (May 1988): 525–598.

38. Milford O. Rouse, "The Walter L. Bierring Lecture," *Federation Bulletin* 55 (1968): 71–78, quotations on 76.

39. Eliot Freidson, *Profession of Medicine: A Study of the Sociology of Applied Knowledge*, 2nd printing (New York: Dodd, Mead and Co., 1970), xvii, 137.

40. Freidson, *Profession of Medicine*, 148.

41. Freidson, *Profession of Medicine*, 149.

42. Freidson, *Profession of Medicine*, 151; emphasis in original.

43. Demick, "Love Surgery," 21.

44. Freidson, *Profession of Medicine*, 152.

45. Holoweiko, "Why Was the Love Surgeon," 131, 132.

46. Walter Reiling Jr., interview with author, August 24, 2015.

47. Holoweiko, "Why Was the Love Surgeon," 131, 132.

48. Rob Modic and Wes Hills, "Peers Criticized Burt in 1978; Phillips Attorney Says Policy Was a Warning," *DDN*, June 13, 1991.

49. Although Holden did not recall the exact wording of her letter, when I read the county medical society's statement to her, she said it reflected the general tone of her letter to them. Holden, interview with author, July 29, 2016. Holoweiko, "Why Was the Love Surgeon," 131, 132.

50. Holoweiko, "Why Was the Love Surgeon," 131, 132.

51. Moreover, the society had six copies of *Surgery of Love* and made them available to local doctors in the county. Rob Modic, "Peers Criticized Burt in '78," *DDN*, June 13, 1991.

52. "Network Show to Examine Area Doctor's Surgery Claim," *DDN*, October 29, 1988.

53. Ameringer, *State Medical Boards and the Politics of Public Protection*.

54. Ameringer, *State Medical Boards and the Politics of Public Protection*.

55. David A. Johnson and Humayun J. Chaudry, *Medical Licensing and Discipline in America: A History of the Federation of State Medical Boards* (Lanham, MD: Lexington Books 2012).

56. Ameringer, *State Medical Boards and the Politics of Public Protection*, 11. For an early critique on the so-called malpractice crisis, see Law and Polan, *Pain and Profit*. For a detailed look at the rise in authority of state medical boards starting in the 1970s for people outside of medicine to help regulate the profession, see Ruth Horowitz, *In the Public Interest: Medical Licensing and the Disciplinary Process* (New Brunswick, NJ: Rutgers University Press, 2012).

57. Modic and Hills, "Peer Criticized Burt in 1978."

58. Hennessee, "Love Surgeon," 246.

59. Jane E. Brody, "U.S. Doctors: About 5 Percent Are Unfit," *New York Times*, February 1, 1976.

60. John H. Budd, "The 1978 Walter L. Bierring Lecture: Professionalism at Bay," *Federation Bulletin* 65 (1978): 131–139, quotation on 138.

61. Law and Polan, *Pain and Profit*, 37, 31–34, 39.

62. Ameringer, *State Medical Boards and the Politics of Public Protection*, 2.

63. Christine E. Dehlendorf and Sidney M. Wolfe, "Physicians Disciplined for Sex-Related Offenses," *JAMA* 279, no. 23 (June 17, 1998): 1883–1888.

64. Council on Ethical and Judicial Affairs, American Medical Association, "Sexual Misconduct in the Practice of Medicine," *JAMA* 266, no. 19 (November 20, 1991): 2741–2745.

65. Dehlendorf and Wolfe, "Physicians Disciplined for Sex-Related Offenses," 1883. They noted that 39.9 percent of those disciplined retained their license to practice.

66. Ameringer, *State Medical Boards and the Politics of Public Protection*, 83, 93, 94. Ameringer noted that organized medicine did not deal as aggressively with sexual misconduct compared to drug abuse among physicians, in part, he argues, because physicians "found it difficult to protect physicians who deliberately violated the physician-patient relationship" and because "there was no clear evidence that treatment programs for physicians who sexually exploited their patients succeeded in altering their behaviors." Ameringer, *State Medical Boards and the Politics of Public Protection*, 94–95.

67. "Looking Back."

68. Law and Pollan, *Pain and Profit*, 43–44.
69. Modic and Hills, "Peers Criticized Burt in '78."
70. Holoweiko, "Why Was the Love Surgeon," 132.
71. Demick, "Love Surgery," 21. Demick does not provide details about what this meant.
72. Freidson, *Profession of Medicine*, 153.
73. Walter Reiling Jr., interview with author, August 24, 2015.
74. Walter Reiling Jr., interview with author, August 24, 2015.
75. Jane E. Brody, "Audits Reducing Shortcomings of Hospitals," *New York Times*, January 29, 1976.
76. R. Crawford Morris and Alan R. Moritz, *Doctor and Patient and the Law*, 5th ed. (St. Louis, MO: C. V. Mosby, 1971), 358.
77. St. Elizabeth Medical Center Annual Report 1977, St. Elizabeth Hospital/Local History documents, DPL.
78. William P. Isele, *The Hospital Medical Staff: Its Legal Rights and Responsibilities* (Springfield, IL: Charles C Thomas, 1984), 26.
79. St. Elizabeth Medical Center, *Bylaws, Rules and Regulations of the Medical Staff* (Dayton, OH, no pub., 1975), 29, 7. Located in the St. Elizabeth Hospital/Local History documents, DPL.
80. Ameringer, *State Medical Boards and the Politics of Public Protection*, 46; Dinesh Vyas and Ahmed E. Hozain, "Clinical Peer Review in the United States: History, Legal Development and Subsequent Abuse," *World Journal of Gastroentereolgy* 20, no. 21 (June 7, 2014): 6357–6363.
81. Isele, *The Hospital Medical Staff*, 126.
82. Jost, "The Necessary and Proper Role of Regulation," 556–557.
83. Isele, *The Hospital Medical Staff*, 126.
84. Sandy Theis, "His Peers Raised Red Flags: Monitors' Concerns Went Beyond Love Surgery," *DDN*, August 4, 1991.
85. Theis, "His Peers Raised Red Flags."
86. Theis, "His Peers Raised Red Flags."
87. Theis, "His Peers Raised Red Flags."
88. "Looking Back."
89. Ameringer, *State Medical Boards and the Politics of Public Protection*, 46.
90. Theis, "His Peers Waved Red Flags."
91. Theis, "His Peers Raised Red Flags."
92. Theis, "His Peers Raised Red Flags." In her article, Theis refers to Kircher as the hospital's executive director, although elsewhere he is referenced as the chief of staff at this time; I used this latter title, since that was also what Walter Reiling Jr. told me. Walter Reiling Jr., letter to author, September 21, 2016, in author's possession.
93. Ameringer, *State Medical Boards and the Politics of Public Protection*, 46.
94. Abraham, "Ohio Medical Groups Hit," 1, 9–10.
95. Walter Reiling Jr., interview with author, August 24, 2015. Reiling was head of the tissue committee for several years in the 1970s, including in 1977. "SEMC 1977 Medical Staff Officers and Committee Chairmen," *SEMC Medical Staff Bulletin*, January 1977, no. page. Subseries IIIC: Newsletters, 1962–1992, Box 32, File 1. MS-497, St. Elizabeth Hospital Records, WSU.
96. Abraham, "Ohio Medical Groups Hit," 10.
97. "Happy Birthday Year, St. Elizabeth," *SE Centennial Medical Staff Bulletin*, July 1978, 1. Subseries IIIC: Newsletters, 1962–1992, Box 28, File 1. MS-497, St. Elizabeth Hospital Records, WSU.

98. Carol Datt Mattar, "100 Years Old . . . and No One Will Ever Be Turned Away," *Journal Herald* (Dayton), July 28, 1978. Through the early 1980s, the *DDN* was the evening newspaper and the *Journal Herald* was the morning newspaper. In 1982, the two staffs merged, and in 1986, the two papers merged into one paper. Teresa Zumwald, *For the Love of Dayton: Life in the Miami Valley, 1796–1996* (Dayton, OH: Dayton Daily News, 1996), 230, 237.

99. "JCAH Accreditation Received," *SE Centennial Medical Staff Bulletin*, January 1979, 1. Subseries IIIC: Newsletters, 1962–1992, Box 28, File 1. MS-497, St. Elizabeth Hospital Records, WSU.

100. "From the Desk of the Chief of Staff," *SE Centennial Medical Staff Bulletin*, November 1978, 1. Subseries IIIC: Newsletters, 1962–1992, Box 28, File 1. MS-497, St. Elizabeth Hospital Records, WSU.

101. Walter W. Keyes, "Q.A.P. Update," *SE Centennial Medical Staff Bulletin*, January 1979, 1. Subseries IIIC: Newsletters, 1962–1992, Box 28, File 1. MS-497, St. Elizabeth Hospital Records, WSU; "Center's Lamaze Room Gaining Many Compliments," *SEMC Medical Staff Bulletin*, July 1977, no page. Subseries IIIC: Newsletters, 1962–1992, Box 32, File 1. MS-497, St. Elizabeth Hospital Records, WSU.

102. Theis, "His Peers Waved Red Flags."

103. "Looking Back."

104. Letter to James C. Burt from E. J. Leschansky, St. Elizabeth Chief of Staff, July 1, 1979, Appellant's Supplement, vol. 2, *Phillips v. Burt*, Case No. 95-1522, Supreme Court of Ohio, filed February 12, 1996, at 0320–0321.

105. Abraham, "Ohio Medical Groups Hit," 10.

106. "Looking Back"; Theis, "His Peers Waved Red Flags."

107. Holoweiko, "Why Was the Love Surgeon," 132; Abraham, "Ohio Medical Groups Hit," 10. Abraham and Holoweiko disagree on when he delivered this to the committee, with Holoweiko saying it was in 1978 and Abraham saying February 1980; given the timeline of events—with the documentation coming upon the request of the hospital in 1979—I went with Abraham's date.

108. Abraham, "Ohio Medical Groups Hit," 10.

109. Holoweiko, "Why Was the Love Surgeon," 132.

110. Letter to Burt from Leschansky, July 1, 1979, Appellant's Supplement, vol. 2, *Phillips v. Burt*, at 0320–0321.

111. "What's a Form?" *Elizabethan Newsletter*, June 1976, no page. Subseries IIIC: Newsletters, 1962–1992, Box 30, File 3, MS-497, St. Elizabeth Hospital Records, WSU. In addition, this form also had the person signing agree that "during the course of the procedure" that was outlined in a blank space above, "unforeseen conditions may necessitate additional or different procedures than those set forth" above and that they authorize "and request that the above named physician . . . perform such procedures as are in his professional judgment necessary and desirable to my health." Moreover, as part of the consent form, the person signing agreed to the statement that "the practice of medicine is not an exact science, and I acknowledge that no warranties, guarantees, or assurances have been made to me concerning the results of the practice."

112. Tom L. Beauchamp and Ruth R. Faden, "Informed Consent," in *Encyclopedia of Bioethics*, ed. Warren Thomas Reich, vol. 3, rev. ed. (New York: MacMillan Library Reference, 1995), 1232–1237, quotation on 1235.

113. T. M. Grunder, "On the Readability of Surgical Consent Forms," *New England Journal of Medicine* 302, no. 16 (April 17, 1980): 900–902.

114. Grunder, "On the Readability of Surgical Consent Forms," 900–902.

115. Law and Pollan, *Pain and Profit*, 113–114.
116. Freidson, *Profession of Medicine*, 180.
117. Plaintiff's Exhibit 13A, Appellant's Supplement, vol. 3, *Phillips v. Burt*, Case No. 95-1522, Supreme Court of Ohio, filed February 12, 1996, at 0983. That St. Elizabeth asked for evidence in the form of a listing of cases and their outcomes, and not a randomized control trial, was not surprising. As Stephen J. Haines, a physician in the department of neurological surgery at the University of Pittsburgh School of Medicine, who looked at the use of RCTs to evaluate surgeries noted in 1979, the "widespread acceptance of randomized control trials has not been apparent in surgical disciplines." Haines, "Randomized Clinical Trials in the Evaluation of Surgical Innovation," *Journal of Neurosurgery* 51 (1979): 5–11, quotation on 5.
118. Holoweiko, "Why Was the Love Surgeon," 132–133.
119. Alfred Julien and Sybil Shainwald, "Is the Hospital Liable?" *National Women's Health Network Newsletter*, March/April 1982, 4.
120. Holoweiko, "Why Was the Love Surgeon," 133.
121. Jane E. Brody, "Audits Reducing Shortcomings of Hospitals," *New York Times*, January 29, 1976.
122. Law and Polan, *Pain and Profit*, 51–52.
123. Holoweiko, "Why Was the Love Surgeon," 133.
124. Letter from Nancy Houston to Executive Director, St. Elizabeth Medical Center, October 19, 1975, Appellant's Supplement, vol. 3, *Phillips v. Burt*, Case No. 95-1522, Supreme Court of Ohio, filed February 12, 1996, at 0323–0326.
125. Letter from Nancy Houston to Executive Director, St. Elizabeth Medical Center.
126. Letter from Nancy Houston to Executive Director, St. Elizabeth Medical Center. According to Laurie Abraham's 1989 article about Burt, "another physician performed corrective surgery so that Houston could have intercourse without great pain." Abraham, "Ohio Medical Groups Hit," 10.

5. Investigating the Medical Profession in Ohio, 1980–1986

1. Mark Holoweiko, "Why Was the Love Surgeon Allowed to Keep Cutting?" *Medical Economics*, July 17, 1989, 125–128, 131–133, 136–138, 141, quotation on 133.
2. Gary Webb, "Dangerous Doctors Free to Prey on You," *Plain Dealer*, April 7, 1985. Physician impairment as a reason for removing someone's medical license arose as a concern during the 1970s as well. See Thomas M. Johnson, "Physician Impairment: Social Origins of a Medical Concern," *Medical Anthropology Quarterly* 2, no. 1 (March 1988): 17–33.
3. Gary Webb, "Board Ignores Malpractice Suits," *Plain Dealer*, April 11, 1985.
4. Carl F. Ameringer, *State Medical Boards and the Politics of Public Protection* (Baltimore: The Johns Hopkins University Press, 1999), 42, 49.
5. Gary Webb, "Dangerous Doctors Free to Prey on You," *Plain Dealer*, April 7, 1985.
6. Webb, "Dangerous Doctors Free to Prey on You."
7. Ruth Horowitz, *In the Public Interest: Medical Licensing and the Disciplinary Process* (New Brunswick, NJ: Rutgers University Press, 2012), 48.
8. Webb, "Dangerous Doctors Free to Prey on You."
9. Eliot Freidson, *Profession of Medicine: A Study of the Sociology of Applied Knowledge*, 2nd printing (New York: Dodd, Mead and Co., 1970), 181.
10. Webb, "Dangerous Doctors Free to Prey on You."
11. Horowitz, *In the Public Interest*, 73, 81.
12. "Misleading the Public," *Plain Dealer*, April 7, 1985.

13. Gary Webb, "Board Protects Addicted Doctors," *Plain Dealer*, April 8, 1985; Gary Webb, "Dr. Caul: From Junkie to Medical Chief," *Plain Dealer*, April 8, 1985; Gary Webb, "Keeping the Probes at Bay: Board Makes Sure Ex-con, Dope Addict Keeps His License," *Plain Dealer*, April 8, 1985.

14. Webb, "Board Protects Addicted Doctors."

15. Gary Webb, "Board Leave Police Disgusted, Angry," *Plain Dealer*, April 9, 1985.

16. Gary Webb, "Malpractice? What Malpractice?" *Plain Dealer*, April 11, 1985.

17. Webb, "Dangerous Doctors."

18. Ameringer, *State Medical Boards and the Politics of Public Protection*, 80–81.

19. Webb, "Board Ignores Malpractice Suits."

20. Webb, "Board Ignores Malpractice Suits."

21. Webb, "Board Ignores Malpractice Suits."

22. Horowitz, *In the Public Interest*, 49.

23. Horowitz, *In the Public Interest*, 69, 5.

24. Webb, "Board Ignores Malpractice Suits."

25. Gary Webb, "Medical Panelists 'Cringe' at Suit Threat," *Plain Dealer*, April 12, 1985.

26. Gary Webb, "Heal Thyself, Now, Celeste Tells Board," *Plain Dealer*, April 12, 1985; Gary Webb, "Medical Board Chief Quits Job under Fire," *Plain Dealer*, April 18, 1985.

27. Webb, "Heal Thyself, Now."

28. "Thompson Leads Inquiry on Med Board," *Plain Dealer*, April 18, 1985.

29. "Lawmaker Promises Med Board Hard Look," *Plain Dealer*, May 7, 1985.

30. Gary Webb, "Ditch Members, House Advised on Board," *Plain Dealer*, May 23, 1985.

31. "Board Gets Nailed," *Plain Dealer*, June 19, 1985.

32. "Get Tough, Medical Groups Urge Doctor-Watch Board," *Plain Dealer*, June 5, 1985.

33. Gary Webb, "Ohio Med Board Steps Up Secrecy," *Plain Dealer*, June 26, 1985.

34. Mary Anne Sharkey, "Medical Board Begins Setting Discipline Rules," *Plain Dealer*, August 15, 1985.

35. Gary Webb, "Stiff Rules Urged for Errant Doctors," *Plain Dealer*, December 12, 1985.

36. Gary Webb, "Lobbyists Limit Bill to Reform the State Medical Board," *Plain Dealer*, March 3, 1986; Gary Webb, "Medical Board Reform Passes Hurdle," *Plain Dealer*, March 6, 1986.

37. "Medical Board Bill Passes House 95–0," *Plain Dealer*, March 13, 1986; Gary Webb, "Senate Warns State Medical Board as 'Tough' Reforms are Passed 30–0," *Plain Dealer*, November 21, 1986.

Janet Phillips, 1981–1984

1. James Burt's medical notes for Janet Phillips, various dates, Appellant's Supplement, vol. 2, *Phillips v. Burt*, Case No. 95-1522, Supreme Court of Ohio, filed February 12, 1996, at 1000–1005.

2. Burt's medical notes for Phillips, various dates, at 1008, 1012; letter from Janet Tobe, RN, to Dr. Rougradd, October 27, 1983, Appellant's Supplement, vol. 2, *Phillips v. Burt*, Case No. 95-1522, Supreme Court of Ohio, filed February 12, 1996, at 1034.

3. James Burt's medical notes for Janet Phillips, April 10, 1984, Appellant's Supplement, vol. 2, *Phillips v. Burt*, Case No. 95-1522, Supreme Court of Ohio, filed February 12, 1996, at 1018.

4. Affidavit of Janet Phillips, Appellant's Supplement, vol. 1, *Phillips v. Burt*, Case No. 95-1522, Supreme Court of Ohio, filed February 12, 1996, at 54.

5. Affidavit of Carol M. Loechinger, Appellant's Supplement, vol. 1, *Phillips v. Burt*, Case No. 95-1522, Supreme Court of Ohio, filed February 12, 1996, at 46–47.

6. Direct examination of Janet Phillips, Appellant's Supplement, vol. 3, *Phillips v. Burt*, Case No. 95-1522, Supreme Court of Ohio, filed February 12, 1996, at 1684–1687.

7. Affidavit of Phillips, Appellant's Supplement, vol. 1, *Phillips v. Burt*, at 54; emphasis in original.

8. Direct examination of Phillips, Appellant's Supplement, vol. 3, *Phillips v. Burt*, at 1684–1687.

9. Affidavit of Michael Clark, Appellant's Supplement, vol. 1, *Phillips v. Burt*, Case No. 95-1522, Supreme Court of Ohio, filed February 12, 1996, at 49–50.

10. Rob Modic, "Woman Testifies of Trust for Gynecologist Burt," *DDN*, June 1, 1991.

11. Letter from Michael Clark to Carol Loechinger, Appellant's Supplement, vol. 1, *Phillips v. Burt*, Case No. 95-1522, Supreme Court of Ohio, filed February 12, 1996, at 48.

12. Affidavit of Janet Phillips, Appellant's Supplement, vol. 1, *Phillips v. Burt*, Case No. 95-1522, Supreme Court of Ohio, filed February 12, 1996, at 52–57; emphasis in original. Clark may have been the person who recommended she see Mary Lee Sambol; Phillips said she learned about Sambol from him, but when Clark testified, he could not confirm he recommended Sambol. Rob Modic, "St. Elizabeth Asks Judge for Immunity," *DDN*, June 18, 1991.

6. Turn on Your Radio for the Love Surgeon, 1978–1988

1. Rebecca Goodman and Barrett J. Brunsman, *This Day in Ohio History* (Cincinnati, OH: Emmis Books, 2005), 100.

2. Virginia and Bruce Ronald, *The Land Between the Miamis: A Bicentennial Celebration of the Dayton Area* (Dayton, OH: Landfall Press, 1996), 343.

3. Goodman and Brunsman, *This Day in Ohio History*, 37.

4. St. Elizabeth Medical Center Annual Report 1977, in the St. Elizabeth Hospital/Local History documents folder, DPL.

5. Julia Helgason, "Insurers Rejected Love Surgery," *DDN*, December 8, 1988; *Burt v. Blue Shield of Southwest Ohio*, United States District Court, S.D. Ohio, W.D., 591 F Supp., January 27, 1984.

6. Mark Holoweiko, "Why Was the Love Surgeon Allowed to Keep Cutting?" *Medical Economics*, July 17, 1989, 125–128, 131–133, 136–138, 141, quotation on 132.

7. "Sex Surgery Doctor Sues Insurers," article clipping in Burt, Dr. James C. Co-Author "Love Surgery," Chairman—Dept. of Obstetrics, St. Elizabeth Hospital, WSU.

8. *Burt v. Blue Shield of Southwest Ohio*.

9. *LeMonde Art Gallery, Inc., v. James C. Burt*, Case No. CA 6712, Court of Appeals, Second District, Montgomery County, OH, not reported in N.E.2d.

10. Doug Mcinnis, "Burt Seeks Protection from Debts, Court Records Say," *DDN*, November 8, 1988.

11. Holoweiko, "Why Was the Love Surgeon," 136.

12. Bob Schumacher, "Turn on Your Radio for the 'Love Surgeon,'" *Journal Herald* (Dayton), October 22, 1980.

13. Schumacher, "Turn on Your Radio."

14. List of Plaintiff's Exhibits Admitted into Evidence, Appellant's Supplement, vol. 1, *Phillips v. Burt*, Supreme Court of Ohio, Case No. 95-1522, filed February 12, 1996, at 0491. I searched Google and Google Scholar but did not find these titles. Search done on May 2, 2017.

15. Vaginoplasty was described in a 1946 article by Robert Toll as "the art of plastic repair of herniations of the urethra, bladder and rectum into the vaginal sheath." It was, as

Toll described, a surgery meant to alleviate the feeling of "things dropping out." Robert M. Toll, "Vaginoplasty," *American Journal of Surgery* 72, no. 5 (November 1946): 742–743, quotation on 742. Vulvo-vaginoplasty appears in only two articles in PubMed: the one by Burt and Schramm from 1983 and one in Spanish: J. A. Blanco, C. Perez, M. Jimenez, J. Bel, A. Castellvi, R. M. Isnard, and J. M. Casasa, "Usefulness of Transrectal Ultrasonography in the Diagnosis of Anomalies of Intersexual Conditions," *Cirugia Pediatrica* 16, no. 2 (April 2003): 86–89. Search done May 12, 2016.

16. James C. Burt and Arthur R. Schramm, "Plastic Surgical Postero-Lateral Redirection Extension Vulvo-Vaginoplasty," *Annales Chirurgiae* 72, no. 5 (1983): 268–273, quotation on 268.

17. Burt and Schramm, "Plastic Surgical Postero-Lateral," 269.

18. Burt and Schramm, "Plastic Surgical Postero-Lateral," 270–271.

19. Burt and Schramm, "Plastic Surgical Postero-Lateral," 270–272.

20. Holoweiko, "Why Was the Love Surgeon," 136.

21. Julia Helgason, "Burt's 'Love Surgery' Put on Hold During Probe, St. Elizabeth's Says," *DDN*, November 8, 1988.

22. Laurie Abraham, "Ohio Medical Groups Hit for Not Exposing MD's 'Love Surgery,'" *American Medical News*, January 27, 1989, 1, 9–10, quotation on 10.

23. Holoweiko, "Why Was the Love Surgeon," 136.

24. Sandy Theis, "His Peers Waved Red Flags," *DDN*, August 4, 1991.

25. Sandy Theis, "Senator Spurred Burt Probe, Official Says," *DDN*, July 7, 1989.

26. Holoweiko, "Why Was the Love Surgeon," 137.

27. Wes Hills, "Judge Allows Data from Former Burt Home into Evidence," *DDN*, October 19, 1990.

28. Mcinnis, "Burt Seeks Protection from Debts."

29. Judy Grande, "'Love' Doctor under Attack," *Plain Dealer*, October 29, 1988.

30. Nancy Tomes, *Remaking the American Patient: How Madison Avenue and Modern Medicine Turned Patients into Consumers* (Chapel Hill: University of North Carolina Press, 2016), 265–266.

31. Nancy Tomes, *Remaking the American Patient*, 182–185, 302–303, 312.

32. Grande, "'Love' Doctor under Attack." I wrote to Sidney Wolfe in July 2016 requesting a copy of the letter he sent to the state board, but Jennifer Rubio, managing editor at Public Citizen, Health Research Group, who responded, stated she was unable to find the letter in their archives. Jennifer Rubio, letter to author, July 28, 2016.

33. AP, "Physician Accuses Area Gynecologist of Sexual Butchery," *DDN*, October 30, 1988; Grande, "'Love' Doctor under Attack."

34. "Network Show to Examine Area Doctor's Surgery Claim," *DDN*, October 29, 1988.

35. Carol Rini, "Oregon Puts on a Party," *DDN*, October 30, 1988.

36. "TV This Week," *DDN*, October 29, 1988.

7. The Women and the Surgery, 1970–1986

1. Mark Holoweiko, "Why Was the Love Surgeon Allowed to Keep Cutting?" *Medical Economics*, July 17, 1989, 125–128, 131–133, 136–138, 141, quotation on 133; "Looking Back: 18 Years of Controversy," *DDN*, August 4, 1991.

2. *Moore v. Burt*, 645 N.E.2d 749 (Ohio App. 2 Dist. 1994).

3. "Looking Back."

4. Ruby Moore, letter to the editor, *DDN*, August 15, 1991.

5. *Moore v. Burt*.

6. Laurie Abraham, "Ohio Medical Groups Hit for Not Exposing MD's 'Love Surgery,'" *American Medical News*, January 27, 1989, 1, 9–10, quotation on 9.

7. *Yearyean v. Burt*, not reported in N.E.2d, 1994 WL 472097 (Ohio App. 2 Dist.).

8. *Hanks v. Burt*, 99 Ohio App.3d 403, 650 N.E.2d 955.

9. *Kennard v. Burt*, not reported in N.E.2d, 1994 WL 484167 (Ohio App. 2 Dist.).

10. "Local Doctor Sued for 'Love Surgery,'" *DDN*, July 3, 1976, clipping from Burt, Dr. James C. Co-Author "Love Surgery," Chairman—Dept. of Obstetrics, St. Elizabeth Hospital, WSU.

11. *Dresher v. Burt*, not reported in N.E.2d, 1994 WL 527675 (Ohio App. 2 Dist.).

12. *Eiford v. Burt*, not reported in N.E.2d, 1994 WL 470319 (Ohio App. 2 Dist.).

13. *Jeffery v. Burt*, not reported in N.E.2d, 1994 WL 484184 (Ohio App. 2 Dist.).

14. *Ginter v. Burt*, not reported in N.E.2d., 1994 WL 484196 (Ohio App. 2 Dist.).

15. *Chappell v. Burt*, not reported in N.E.2d, 1994 WL 484189 (Ohio App 2. Dist.).

16. Claire Safron, "The Gynecologist from Hell," *Woman's Day*, August 15, 1989, 70, 74, 76, 87, quotations on 74, 76.

17. Keith S. Fineberg, J. Douglas Peters, J. Robert Wilson, and Donald A. Kroll, *Obstetrics/Gynecology and the Law* (Ann Arbor, MI: Heath Administration Press, 1984), 5, 8.

18. Charges of physicians performing physiologically unnecessary surgeries were not new in the 1970s; see Nancy Tomes, *Remaking the American Patient: How Madison Avenue and Modern Medicine Turned Patients into Consumers* (Chapel Hill: University of North Carolina Press, 2016). This concern continues; see Julie Creswell, "A Small Town Scarred by a Trusted Doctor," *New York Times*, October 18, 2015.

19. Tomes, *Remaking the American Patient*, 182–185, 302–303, 312.

20. Victor Cohn, "U.S. Moves to Curb Unneeded Surgery: U.S. Announces Drive to Combat Excess Surgery; Second Opinion for Medical Patients," *Washington Post*, November 12, 1977.

21. Victor Cohn, "No. 1 Operation Now: Hysterectomy," *Washington Post*, May 10, 1977.

22. Tomes, *Remaking the American Patient*, 182–185, 302–303, 312.

23. Jane E. Brody, "Incompetent Surgery Is Found Not Isolated," *New York Times*, January 27, 1976.

24. Sylvia Law and Steven Polan, *Pain and Profit: The Politics of Malpractice* (New York: Harper & Row, 1976), 12.

25. Joseph H. King, *The Law of Medical Malpractice in a Nutshell* (St. Paul, MN: West, 1986), 322–323.

26. King, *Malpractice in a Nutshell*, 323. See also Carl F. Ameringer, *State Medical Boards and the Politics of Public Protection* (Baltimore: The Johns Hopkins University Press, 1999), for more on the rise of malpractice lawsuits in the 1970s as part of larger changes in medicine.

27. Barbara Demick, "Love Surgery: Sexual Panacea or Mutilation for Profit?" *The Real Paper*, August 26, 1978, 18–21, quotation on 21.

28. Louise Lander, *Defective Medicine: Risk, Anger, and the Malpractice Crisis* (New York: Farrar, Straus and Giroux, 1978), 6.

29. "Local Doctor Sued for 'Love Surgery,'" *DDN*, July 3, 1976, clipping from Burt, Dr. James C. Co-Author "Love Surgery," Chairman—Dept. of Obstetrics, St. Elizabeth Hospital, WSU; Judith Adler Hennessee, "The Love Surgeon," *Mademoiselle*, August 1989, 206–207, 245–247, quotation on 246.

30. Safron, "Gynecologist from Hell," 76.

31. R. Crawford Morris and Alan R. Moritz, *Doctor and Patient and the Law* (St. Louis, MO: C. V. Mosby, 1971), 401.

32. Safron, "Gynecologist from Hell," 76.

33. Holoweiko, "Why Was the 'Love Surgeon,'" 131; Montgomery Brower, "James Burt's 'Love Surgery' Was Supposed to Boost Pleasure, but Some Patients Say It Brought Pain," *People*, March 27, 1989, 97–98, 100, quotation on 100.

34. Julia Helgason, "He Hurt Us, Physically and Emotionally, Burt's Ex-Patients Say." Stamped November 6, 1988. Clippings from Burt, Dr. James C. Co-Author "Love Surgery," Chairman—Departments of Obstetrics, St. Elizabeth Hospitals, Special Collections and Archives, WSU.

35. "Looking Back"; "Malpractice Suit Hits St. E.," *Journal Herald* (Dayton), May 31, 1980; Bob Schumacher, "Turn on Your Radio for the 'Love Surgeon,'" *Journal Herald*, October 22, 1980.

36. Schumacher, "Turn on Your Radio."

37. "Malpractice Suit Hits St. E."

38. Schumacher, "Turn on Your Radio."

39. "Looking Back"; "Malpractice Suit Hits St. E."

40. Brower, "James Burt's 'Love Surgery' Was Supposed to Boost Pleasure," 97.

41. Demick, "Love Surgery," 21.

42. Gerry Harness, as told to Judith Kelman, "My Gynecologist Butchered Me!" *Redbook*, July 1989, 22, 26.

43. Carol Tavris and Susan Sadd, *The Redbook Report on Female Sexuality: 100,000 Married Women Disclose the Good News about Sex* (New York: Delacorte Press, 1975), 20, 76, 79.

44. Linda Wolfe, *The Cosmo Report* (New York: Arbor House, 1981), 21, 101, 109, 104, 131; Shere Hite, *The Hite Report: A Nationwide Study of Female Sexuality* (New York: Macmillan, 1976), 58–59, 134, 232, 251.

45. Shere Hite, *Women as Revolutionary Agents of Change: The Hite Reports and Beyond* (Madison: The University of Wisconsin Press, 1994), 185–197.

46. Lilian R. Furst, *Between Doctors and Patients: The Changing Balance of Power* (Charlottesville: University Press of Virginia, 1998).

47. Sue Fisher, *In the Patient's Best Interest: Women and the Politics of Medical Decisions* (New Brunswick, NJ: Rutgers University Press, 1986), 4–5.

48. Furst, *Between Doctors and Patients*.

49. Fisher, *In the Patient's Best Interest*, 4–6, 30; emphasis in original.

Janet Phillips, 1986–1987

1. Direct examination of Janet Phillips, Appellant's Supplement, vol. 3, *Phillips v. Burt*, Case No. 95-1522, Supreme Court of Ohio, filed February 12, 1996, at 1687–1688, 1691.

2. Doug Mcinnis, "Burt Seeks Protection from Debts, Court Records Say," *DDN*, November 8, 1989.

3. Rob Modic and Wes Hills, "Burt Caused Irreversible Damage, Doctor Says" *DDN*, May 24, 1991.

4. Bradley Busacco, interview with author, August 25, 2015.

5. France Griggs, "Breaking Tradition," *Chicago Tribune*, August 25, 1991.

6. Busacco, interview with author, August 25, 2015.

7. Busacco, interview with author, August 25, 2015.

8. Busacco, interview with author, August 25, 2015.

9. Busacco, interview with author, August 25, 2015.

10. Griggs, "Breaking Tradition."

11. Busacco, interview with author, August 25, 2015.

12. Griggs, "Breaking Tradition."

13. Bradly Busacco's deposition, taken March 6, 1987, Appellant's Supplement, vol. 3, *Phillips v. Burt*, Supreme Court of Ohio, Case No. 95-1522, filed February 12, 1996, at 1656.

14. Busacco's deposition, taken March 6, 1987, Appellant's Supplement, vol. 3, *Phillips v. Burt*, at 1649–1663.

8. Tabloid Headlines, 1988–1989

1. John Corry, "TV Review: 'West 57th,' on CBS: Magazine Has Its Debut," *New York Times*, August 13, 1985.

2. Peter J. Boyer, *Who Killed CBS? The Undoing of America's Number One News Network* (New York: Random House, 1988), 179, 273.

3. Teresa Keller, "Trash TV," *Journal of Popular Culture* vol. 26, no. 4 (Spring 1993): 195–206; Alex S. Jones, "'Trash TV' Debated at Editors' Convention," *New York Times*, April 13, 1989.

4. Harry S. Waters et al., "Trash TV: The Industry's Shock Artists Are All over the Dial. They're Lurid and They're Loud and Their Credo Is: Anything Goes as Long as It Gets an Audience," *Newsweek*, November 14, 1988, 72–78.

5. Keller, "Trash TV," 198–199.

6. Judy Grande, "'Love' Doctor under Attack; Women Go Public with Charges against Dayton Surgeon," *Plain Dealer*, October 29, 1988.

7. Julia Helgason, "We Had No Way to Stop Burt, Physicians Say; Strict Rules Govern Complaints, Privileges," *DDN*, November 13, 1988.

8. Ruth Horowitz, *In the Public Interest: Medical Licensing and the Disciplinary Process* (New Brunswick, NJ: Rutgers University Press, 2012), 73, 85.

9. "The Love Surgery: A Sex Scandal," CBS News—West 57th, October 29, 1988, video recording and transcript, possession of author.

10. "The Love Surgery: A Sex Scandal," 1.

11. "The Love Surgery: A Sex Scandal," 1.

12. "The Love Surgery: A Sex Scandal," 1–2.

13. "The Love Surgery: A Sex Scandal," 2.

14. "The Love Surgery: A Sex Scandal," 2.

15. "The Love Surgery: A Sex Scandal," 3.

16. "The Love Surgery: A Sex Scandal," 4.

17. "The Love Surgery: A Sex Scandal," 2–4.

18. "The Love Surgery: A Sex Scandal," 4.

19. AP, "Physician Accuses Area Gynecologist of Sexual Butchery," *DDN*, October 30, 1988.

20. AP, "Doctor Defends Himself; Labels TV Report 'Conspiracy of Lies," *Plain Dealer* November 1, 1988.

21. Mark Fisher, "Hospital Chief Orders Review of Sex Surgery," *DDN*, November 1, 1988.

22. Julia Helgason and Dave Davis, "State Board Looks at 'Love Surgery' Supporting Cast," *DDN*, January 15, 1989.

23. Memo, Paul Goggin to Governor Richard F. Celeste, Re: Ohio State Medical Board (OSMB) Investigation—Dr. Burt, November 1, 1988, Ohio, Office of the Governor, Chief Legal Counsel's General Files, 1983–1991, Box 2480, OHS.

24. Memo, Paul Goggin to Governor Richard F. Celeste, Re: Ohio State Medical Board (OSMB) Investigation—Dr. Burt, November 1, 1988, Ohio, Office of the Governor, Chief Legal Counsel's General Files, 1983–1991, Box 2480, OHS.

25. Memo, Napoleon A. Bell, Counsel to the Governor, to Governor Richard F. Celeste, Re: Ohio State Medical Board/Dr. James Burt Investigation, November 3, 1988, Ohio, Office of the Governor, Chief Legal Counsel's General Files, 1983–1991, Box 2480, OHS.

26. Memo, Napoleon A. Bell, Counsel to the Governor, to Governor Richard F. Celeste, Re: Ohio State Medical Board/Dr. James Burt Investigation, November 3, 1988, Copy with Governor's Initials, Ohio, Office of the Governor, Chief Legal Counsel's General Files, 1983–1991, Box 2480, OHS.

27. Memo, Napoleon A. Bell, Counsel to the Governor, to Governor Richard F. Celeste, November 9, 1988, Re: Dr. James Burt Investigation—For Your Information, Ohio, Office of the Governor, Chief Legal Counsel's General Files, 1983–1991, Box 2480, OHS.

28. Richard F. Celeste, Governor, to Timothy L. Stephens, Chairman, Ohio State Medical Board, November 3, 1988, Ohio, Office of the Governor, Chief Legal Counsel's General Files, 1983–1991, Box 2480, OHS.

29. Sandy Theis, "Board to Ask How Doctors Let Burt Operate," *DDN*, November 4, 1988.

30. Walter Reiling Jr., interview with author, August 24, 2015; Theis, "Board to Ask How Doctors Let Burt Operate."

31. Theis, "Board to Ask How Doctors Let Burt Operate."

32. AP, "Med Society Denies Any Cover-up on 'Love' Doctor," *Plain Dealer*, November 5, 1988.

33. Rosemary Harty, "Letter on Burt Angers Local Medical Society," *DDN*, November 5, 1988.

34. Letter, James B. Makos, Acting President and CEO, to Honorable Richard F. Celeste, Governor, November 4, 1988, Ohio, Office of the Governor, Chief Legal Counsel's General Files, 1983–1991, Box 2480, OHS.

35. Julia Helgason, "He Hurt Us, Physically and Emotionally, Burt's Ex-Patients Say." Stamped November 6, 1988. Clippings from Burt, Dr. James C. Co-Author "Love Surgery," Chairman—Departments of Obstetrics, St. Elizabeth Hospitals, WSU.

36. Helgason, "He Hurt Us, Physically and Emotionally, Burt's Ex-Patients Say."

37. Editorial, "Dr. Burt Wasn't Shut Down Because Too Few Stood Up," *DDN*, November 4, 1988.

38. Monica Kittle Schiffler, Letter to Editor. "Patients Can't Always Trust Their Doctors." Stamped November 21, 1988. Clippings from Burt, Dr. James C. Co-Author "Love Surgery," Chairman—Departments of Obstetrics, St. Elizabeth Hospitals, WSU. But another letter in response to the November 6 article called the reporting "offensive" and asked if it was "necessary to give all the details of the operation—then in the fine print say that teenagers should not read it?" That, Sara Craig concluded, "was stupid!" Sara J. Craig, Letter to Editor. "Offensive Article." Stamped November 21, 1988. Clippings from Burt, Dr. James C. Co-Author "Love Surgery," Chairman—Departments of Obstetrics, St. Elizabeth Hospitals, WSU.

39. Letter, Timothy L. Stephens Jr., President, the State Medical Board, to the Honorable Richard F. Celeste, Governor, November 10, 1988, Ohio, Office of the Governor, Chief Legal Counsel's General Files, 1983–1991, Box 2480, OHS.

40. Agreement, signed by James C. Burt, M.D., Henry G. Cramblett, M.D., and John E. Rauch, D.O., November 10, 1988, Ohio, Office of the Governor, Chief Legal Counsel's General Files, 1983–1991, Box 2480, OHS.

41. "Burt Agrees Not to Perform Surgery in Ohio," *DDN*, November 11, 1988.
42. Laurie Abraham, "Ohio Medical Groups Hit for Not Exposing MD's 'Love Surgery,'" *American Medical News*, January 27, 1989, 1, 9–10, quotation on 9.
43. When I asked for a record of an investigation of Dayton-area physicians and their knowledge about love surgery, I received a letter from the State Medical Board of Ohio stating that "the Medical Board has no public records related to any such possible investigation." Sallie J. Debolt, Executive Staff Attorney, State Medical Board of Ohio, February 13, 2007, letter to author, in author's possession. Nothing apparently ever came of the probe—or at least nothing that was made public. In January 1993, Sandy Theis, reporting for the *DDN*, noted that the board—four years after announcing it would investigate the actions of the Dayton medical community—had taken no actions, although the investigation was still open. Rhine McLin, the state representative for Dayton, found it hard to believe, and unacceptable, and called it a sign of the "arrogance" that the "medical community" had not disciplined any of Burt's peers. AP, "Board Attacked for Not Acting against Dr. Burt's Peers," *Plain Dealer*, January 24, 1993; Theis, "Board Probe of Area Doctors Impotent, McLin Says," *DDN*, January 17, 1993.
44. AP, "Doctors Aware of 'Love Surgery,'" *Plain Dealer*, November 14, 1988.
45. Sandy Theis, "Ex-Investigators: Burt's Peers Mum." Stamped December 18, 1988. Clippings from Burt, Dr. James C. Co-Author "Love Surgery," Chairman—Departments of Obstetrics, St. Elizabeth Hospitals, WSU.
46. Theis, "Board Probe of Area Doctors Impotent."
47. AP, "Doctors Aware of 'Love Surgery' Investigated," *Plain Dealer*, December 12, 1988.
48. Sandy Theis, "Fear of Lawsuits Stifles Doc Snitches, Some Say." Stamped December 25, 1988. Clippings from Burt, Dr. James C. Co-Author "Love Surgery," Chairman—Departments of Obstetrics, St. Elizabeth Hospitals, WSU.
49. Helgason, "We Had No Way to Stop Burt."
50. Helgason, "We Had No Way to Stop Burt."
51. Abraham, "Ohio Medical Groups Hit," 9.
52. Charles M. Johnson, Letter to Editor, "Reasons for Doctors' Silence on Burt Are Many." No date. Clippings from Burt, Dr. James C. Co-Author "Love Surgery," Chairman—Departments of Obstetrics, St. Elizabeth Hospitals, WSU.
53. Abraham, "Ohio Medical Groups Hit," 10.
54. Helgason, "We Had No Way to Stop Burt."
55. AP, "'Snitch' Probe Pressed in 'Love Doctor' Case," *Plain Dealer*, February 24, 1989.
56. Julia Helgason and Dave Davis, "State Board Looks at 'Love Surgery' Supporting Cast," *DDN*, January 15, 1989.
57. Helgason and Davis, "State Board Looks at 'Love Surgery' Supporting Cast." The state medical board announced in late February 1989 that there was a "reasonably good possibility" some Dayton-area physicians who the board had started investigating in November would be charged for failing to alert the board about Burt's questionable surgeries. AP, "'Snitch' Probe Pressed in 'Love Doctor' Case." This investigation, and the threat of charges, however, apparently did not progress much past threats. According to Reiling, the board backed down when learning it had been told to investigate Burt by at least two Dayton physicians—one of those physicians being Reiling's brother. Walter Reiling Jr., interview with author, August 24, 2015. Max Blue lost his privileges at St. Elizabeth in 1989 and resigned them from Good Samaritan Hospital in 1990. It was not clear if the resignation was voluntary, and St. Elizabeth did not

make public whether Blue's loss of privileges was as a result of peer review. When reached by a *DDN* reporter, however, his wife—who refused to give her name— charged St. Elizabeth with not acting fairly toward her husband. Sandy Theis, "Burt Helper Lost St. E Privileges," *DDN*, August 8, 1991.

58. Ray Marcane, "Doctors 30,000, Investigators 12; State Board Sets Standards, Has Power to Suspend or Revoke Licenses," *DDN*, November 13, 1988.

59. "Doctors Aware of 'Love Surgery' Investigated."

60. Julia Helgason and Dave Davis, "'Media Has Accepted Lies as Truth,' says Burt; 'Love Surgery' Doctor Denies Horror Stories," *DDN*, November 20, 1988.

61. "A Statement to the Community from St. Elizabeth Medical Center," advertisement, *DDN*, November 27, 1988.

62. "Women's Group Plans Protest Rally," *DDN*, November 29, 1988.

63. Montgomery Brower, "James Burt's 'Love Surgery' Was Supposed to Boost Pleasure, but Some Patients Say It Brought Pain," *People*, March 27, 1989, 97–98, 100, quotation on 100; Jim Bland, "Burt's Links to Hospital Protested; About 50 Ask Why Surgery Was Allowed," *DDN*, December 4, 1988.

64. Bland, "Burt's Links to Hospital Protested."

65. Jim DeBrosse, "Memories of St. Elizabeth," *DDN*, July 16, 2000. Another vigil was held on January 4, 1989, with about ninety staff, volunteers of St. Elizabeth, former patients, and friends of the hospital in attendance. "Vigil at St. Elizabeth," *DDN*, January 5, 1989.

66. Thus meaning she was ten years older than the Kathy interviewed by Demick in 1978. Roger Snell, "Ohio Woman Sold on 'Love Surgery,'" *Columbus Dispatch*, November 15, 1988. Clipping in Ohio, Office of the Governor, Chief Legal Counsel's General Files, 1983–1991, Box 2480, Government Records, OHS.

67. Roger Snell, "Ohio Woman Sold on 'Love Surgery,'" *Columbus Dispatch*, November 15, 1988. Clipping in Ohio, Office of the Governor, Chief Legal Counsel's General Files, 1983–1991, Box 2480, Government Records, OHS.

68. Jeanne Marie Laskas, "A Crime against Nature," *Savvy Woman*, June 1989, 63–66, quotation on 64.

69. Abraham, "Ohio Medical Groups," 9.

70. Laskas, "Crime against Nature," 63–66, quotation on 64.

71. Jeanne L. Johnson, Letter to Editor, "May Burt Find Peace Away from Media Glare," February 21, 1989, clipping from Burt, Dr. James C. Co-Author "Love Surgery," Chairman—Department of Obstetrics, St. Elizabeth Hospital, Special Collections and Archives, WSU.

72. State of Ohio, The State Medical Board, Letter for James C. Burt, December 8, 1988, 12/08/1988 Citation. Based on alleged performance of experimental and medically unnecessary surgical procedures, in some instances without proper patient consent— notice of opportunity for hearing, Ohio License Center, http://license.ohio.gov (accessed January 11, 2007), copy in author's possession.

73. State of Ohio, The State Medical Board, Letter for James C. Burt, December 8, 1988.

74. Napoleon A. Bell, Memo to Governor Richard F. Celeste, December 8, 1988, Re: Dr. James Burt Investigation—Four Your Information, Ohio, Office of the Governor, Chief Legal Counsel's General Files, 1983–1991, Box 2480, Archives Library Division, OHS.

75. Julia Helgason and Sandy Theis, "State Board Accuses Burt of 41 Offenses against His Patients," *DDN*, December 8, 1988.

76. Helgason and Theis, "State Board Accuses Burt of 41 Offenses against His Patients."

77. AP, "Doctor Is Accused of 'Immoral' Tests," *New York Times*, December 9, 1988; Beth Grace, "Ohio Doctor Charged with Immorality," *Mesa Tribune/Tempe Daily News/ Chandler Arizonan Tribune*, December 9, 1988; "'Surgery of Love' Doctor Faces Medical Charges," *San Jose Mercury News*, December 9, 1988.

78. Teresa Zumwald, *For the Love of Dayton: Life in the Miami Valley, 1796–1996* (Dayton, OH: Dayton Daily News, 1996), 241.

79. Mark Holoweiko, "Why Was the Love Surgeon Allowed to Keep Cutting?" *Medical Economics*, July 17, 1989, 125–128, 131–133, 136–138, quotation on 138.

80. "Bankruptcy Judge OKs Lawsuits against Dr. Burt," *DDN*, November 19, 1988.

81. AP, "'Love Doctor' Seeks Hearing on Charges," *Plain Dealer*, January 5, 1989.

82. AP, "Hospital Won't Act against 'Love Doctor,'" *Plain Dealer*, January 25, 1989; Ray Marcano, "Burt Did 170 'Love Surgeries' at St. Elizabeth," *DDN*, January 25, 1989.

83. Editorial, "St. E's Running from the Truth," *DDN*, January 28, 1989; emphasis in original.

84. AP, "Doctor Loses Practice over Genital Surgery," *New York Times*, January 26, 1989.

85. Staff and Wire Reporters, "Dr. Burt Offers to Quit," *DDN*, January 18, 1989; AP, "Ohio Doctor Offers to Quit," *New York Times*, January 20, 1989.

86. Napoleon A. Bell, Counsel to the Governor, Memo to Richard F. Celeste, Governor, January 18, 1988, Re: Closure of Dr. James Burt/Love Doctor File FYI, Ohio, Office of the Governor, Chief Legal Counsel's General Files, 1983–1991, Box 2480, OHS.

87. Sandy Theis, "Burt Bid to Resign Rejected," *DDN*, January 19, 1989.

88. Sandy Theis, "Burt Quits Medicine; No Hearing," *DDN*, January 26, 1989.

89. Letter from James Burt, 01/25/1989: Voluntary surrender—Permanent revocation; ineligible to apply for licensure or practice medicine anywhere in the United States, Ohio License Center, http://license.ohio.gov (accessed January 11, 2007), copy in author's possession. I contacted the State Medical Board of Ohio in April 2012 requesting any public documents relating to its investigation of Burt but was told the only ones available were those posted on its website; all others did not constitute public records. Sallie J. Debolt, General Counsel, State Medical Board of Ohio, letter to author, April 16, 2012, in author's possession.

90. Julia Helgason, "'Love Surgery' Might Be Allowed in Future, St. E President Says," *DDN*, January 27, 1989.

91. Theis, "Burt Quits Medicine"; AP, "Dayton Gynecologist Gives Up His License," *Plain Dealer*, January 26, 1989.

92. AP, "Doctor Loses Practice"; "Doctor Gives Up License 'Love Surgery' Drew Charges," *Akron Beacon Journal*, January 26, 1989; "'Love Doctor' Loses License," *Philadelphia Daily News*, January 26, 1989.

93. Theis, "Burt Quits Medicine."

94. Helgason, "'Love Surgery' Might be Allowed."

95. AP, "Dayton Hospital Removes Privileges of 'Love Doctor,'" *Plain Dealer*, January 27, 1989.

96. Helgason, "'Love Surgery' Might be Allowed."

97. Editorial, "When a Doctor Harms, That Shouldn't be Secret," *DDN*, August 6, 1991.

98. Wes Hills, "Bank Employee: Burt Never Asked to Enter Home," *DDN*, September 15, 1990; Editorial, "St. Elizabeth Did the Right Thing," *DDN*, February 27, 1989, clipping from Burt, Dr. James C. Co-Author "Love Surgery," Chairman—Department of Obstetrics, St. Elizabeth Hospital, WSU.

99. AP, "Hospital Keeping Records"; "'Love Doctor' Patients Worried," *Plain Dealer*, February 13, 1989.

100. ". . . and the Medical Organizations Froze," *DDN*, February 27, 1989, clipping from Burt, Dr. James C. Co-Author "Love Surgery," Chairman—Department of Obstetrics, St. Elizabeth Hospital, WSU.

101. AP, "Hospital Keeping Records"; "'Love Doctor' Patients Worried."

102. "Court Limits Access to Burt Records," article clipping in Burt, Dr. James C. Co-Author "Love Surgery," Chairman—Department of Obstetrics, St. Elizabeth Hospital, Special Collections and Archives, WSU.

103. "Court Limits Access to Burt Records," and Editorial, "Trustee Has Records; Patients Need Them," *DDN*, February 27, 1989, article clippings from Burt, Dr. James C. Co-Author "Love Surgery," Chairman—Department of Obstetrics, St. Elizabeth Hospital, WSU.

104. Gerry Harness, as told to Judith Kelman, "My Gynecologist Butchered Me!" *Redbook*, July 1989, 22, 26.

105. Laskas, "Crime against Nature," 64.

106. *Chappell v. Burt*, not reported in N.E.2d, 1994 WL 484189 (Ohio App. 2 Dist.).

107. *Eiford v. Burt*, not reported in N.E.2d, 1994 WL 470319 (Ohio App. 2 Dist.).

108. *Tripoli v. Burt*, not reported in N.E.2d, 1994 WL 483505 (Ohio App. 2 Dist.).

109. *Peters v. Burt*, not reported in N.E.2d, 1994 WL 567436 (Ohio App. 2 Dist.).

110. *Eiford v. Burt*.

111. *Jeffery v. Burt*, not reported in N.E.2d, 1994 WL 484184 (Ohio App. 2 Dist.).

112. *Hopkins v. Burt*, not reported in N.E.2d, 1994 WL 484202 (Ohio App. 2 Dist.).

113. *Roberts v. Burt*, not reported in N.E.2d, 1994 WL 567435 (Ohio App. 2 Dist.).

114. Abraham, "Ohio Medical Groups," 9.

115. AP, "'Love Doctor' Sued by 3 Former Patients," *Plain Dealer*, February 9, 1989.

116. Holoweiko, "Why Was the Love Surgeon," 141.

117. Transcript testimony of Janet Phillips, December 18, 1990, *State of Ohio v. Janet Phillips*, Common Pleas Court of Montgomery County, Ohio, Case No. CR-2161, filed May 3, 1991, at 51–52. Most of the women who attended the Cambridge Inn meeting were also Sambol's clients. Rob Modic, "Reporter: Break-in Not in Plan," *DDN*, December 13, 1990.

118. Kathleen Hopson, Letter to Editor. "Burt's Practices, Catholic Teaching Collide." Stamped February 4, 1989. Clippings from Burt, Dr. James C. Co-Author "Love Surgery," Chairman—Departments of Obstetrics, St. Elizabeth Hospitals, WSU.

119. Laura Lee Frye, Letter to Editor. "Informed Consent?" Stamped February 4, 1989. Clippings from Burt, Dr. James C. Co-Author "Love Surgery," Chairman—Departments of Obstetrics, St. Elizabeth Hospitals, WSU.

120. Nancy Grisby, Letter to Editor. "Destructive Myth." Stamped February 4, 1989. Clippings from Burt, Dr. James C. Co-Author "Love Surgery," Chairman—Departments of Obstetrics, St. Elizabeth Hospitals, WSU.

121. Suzanne Rosen, Letter to Editor. "The Real Problem." Stamped February 4, 1989. Clippings from Burt, Dr. James C. Co-Author "Love Surgery," Chairman—Departments of Obstetrics, St. Elizabeth Hospitals, WSU.

122. "'The Reporters' Plans Burt Segment," *DDN*, February 25, 1989.

123. Ira M. Reiss with Harriet M. Reiss, *Solving America's Sexual Crises* (Amherst, NY: Prometheus, 1997), 265. Transcripts do not exist for the shows in the 1980s. Despite numerous attempts to contact Harpo Productions, no one ever responded to my requests to view this show or to obtain transcripts of it.

124. Brower, "James Burt's 'Love Surgery,'" 97–98, 100.

125. Brower, "James Burt's 'Love Surgery,'" 97–98, 100.

126. Safran, "The Gynecologist from Hell," 76.

127. Laskas, "Crime against Nature," 66.

128. Holoweiko, "Why Was the Love Surgeon," 141.

129. Martin Gottlieb, "Jury Hears Horror Story Over and Over," *DDN*, May 24, 1991; Holoweiko, "Why Was the Love Surgeon," 141, 127; Julia Helgason, "Huge 'Love Surgery' Lawsuit Filed," *DDN*, May 5, 1989.

130. Holoweiko, "Why Was the Love Surgeon," 141, 127.

131. Holoweiko, "Why Was the Love Surgeon," 141, 127.

132. AP, "N.Y. Lawyer to Sue Hospitals, Others Over 'Love' Surgery," *Plain Dealer*, May 4, 1989.

133. Helgason, "Huge 'Love Surgery' Lawsuit Filed."

134. Holoweiko, "Why Was the Love Surgeon," 141, 127.

135. Helgason, "Huge 'Love Surgery' Lawsuit Filed."

136. Holoweiko, "Why Was the Love Surgeon," 141, 127.

137. Helgason, "Huge 'Love Surgery' Lawsuit Filed."

138. Dave Davis, "Burt May Lose Real-Estate License," *DDN*, February 9, 1989; Brower, "James Burt's 'Love Surgery,'" 98.

139. AP, "Default Judgment Granted in Dayton 'Love Doctor' Suit," *Plain Dealer*, February 4, 1989.

140. "Burt Clinic Becoming Insurance Offices," February 4, 1989, article clipping in Burt, Dr. James C. Co-Author "Love Surgery," Chairman—Department of Obstetrics, St. Elizabeth Hospital, WSU.

141. The revocation came two weeks after Burt surrendered his license as a result of the real estate board investigating whether Burt misrepresented himself when he applied for the license during the summer of 1988. AP, "'Love' Doctor Loses Real Estate License," *Plain Dealer*, July 20, 1989.

142. Julia Helgason, "Burt to Undergo Surgery for Cancer, Attorney for Ex-Gynecologist Says." Stamped March 8, 1989. Clippings from Burt, Dr. James C. Co-Author "Love Surgery," Chairman—Departments of Obstetrics, St. Elizabeth Hospitals, WSU; AP, "'Love Surgeon' Faces Prostate Cancer Surgery," *Plain Dealer*, March 9, 1989.

143. AP, "Former Gynecologist Gets Out of Hospital." Stamped April 8, 1989. Clippings from Burt, Dr. James C. Co-Author "Love Surgery," Chairman—Departments of Obstetrics, St. Elizabeth Hospitals, WSU.

144. AP, "Judge Throws Out Portion of 'Love Doctor' Suit against CBS," *Plain Dealer*, September 25, 1990.

145. AP, "Dayton Gynecologist Refiles Suit against CBS," *Plain Dealer*, October 21, 1990.

146. *Burt v. CBS, Inc.,* United States District Court, S.D. Ohio, W.D., 769 F. Supp. 1012, Opinion on Motion for Summary Judgment, April 17, 1991; Jim Dillon, "Judge: Letter Can't Be Used in Burt Lawsuit," *DDN*, October 12, 1990.

147. Dillon, "Judge: Letter Can't Be Used in Burt Lawsuit."

148. Testimony of Janet Phillips, *State of Ohio v. Janet Phillips*, Case No. 90-CR-2161, Common Pleas Court of Montgomery County, Ohio, at 11.

149. Sandy Theis, "Board Probe of Area Doctors Impotent, McLin Says," *DDN*, January 17, 1993; Napoleon A. Bell, Counsel to the Governor, Memo to Richard F. Celeste, Governor, March 8, 1989, Re: Follow-up on Dr. James Burt/Love Doctor/For Your Information, Ohio, Office of the Governor, Chief Legal Counsel's General Files, 1983–1991,

Box 2480, OHS. In his memo to Celeste, Bell suggested the governor support this legislation.

150. Mitch Weiss, "Lawmakers Bill Would Protect Patients," *Plain Dealer*, March 7, 1989. Clipping in Ohio, Office of the Governor, Chief Legal Counsel's General Files, 1983–1991, Box 2480, Government Records, OHS.

151. Daniel W. van Heeckeren, "Board Should Get MD's Fees," *Plain Dealer* March 20, 1989. Clipping in Ohio, Office of the Governor, Chief Legal Counsel's General Files, 1983–1991, Box 2480, Government Records, OHS.

152. Sandy Theis, "Board Probe of Area Doctors Impotent, McLin Says," *DDN*, January 17, 1993. Announcement of Committee Meeting, January 10, 1990, House Health and Retirement Committee files, State Archives Series 2361, Box 3275, Folder 18, OHS.

153. "Empowering the Medical Board," *Plain Dealer*. Clipping in Ohio, Office of the Governor, Chief Legal Counsel's General Files, 1983–1991, Box 2480, Government Records, OHS.

154. Sandy Theis, "Board Probe of Area Doctors Impotent, McLin Says," *DDN*, January 17, 1993. Announcement of Committee Meeting, January 10, 1990, House Health and Retirement Committee Files, State Archives Series 2361, Box 3275, Folder 18, OHS. This legislation was the first major bill proposed by McLin, who was appointed to fill the term of her father after he died. "McLin Details Plan to Give Medical Board More Power," *DDN*, March 7, 1989. Clipping in Ohio, Office of the Governor, Chief Legal Counsel's General Files, 1983–1991, Box 2480, Government Records, OHS.

155. Theis, "Legislators Allot More Money, Muscle to Medical Board." Clippings from Burt, Dr. James C. Co-Author "Love Surgery," Chairman—Departments of Obstetrics, St. Elizabeth Hospitals, WSU.

156. Health and Retirement Committee Minutes, February 6, 1990, House Health and Retirement Committee Files, State Archives Series 2361, Box 3275, Folder 18, OHS. A week later, Carol Rolfes and Timothy Jost, board members of the state medical boards, and Ray Bumgarner, executive director of the medical board who also appeared as a representative for the board, came as interested parties to the legislation. They were joined by state senator Linda Furney who testified in favor of the legislation. Health and Retirement Committee Meeting Minutes, February 14, 1990, House Health and Retirement Committee Files, State Archives Series 2361, Box 3275, Folder 18, OHS. Health and Retirement Committee Meeting Minutes, February 21, 1990, House Health and Retirement Committee Files, State Archives Series 2361, Box 3275, Folder 18, OHS; Health and Retirement Committee Meeting Minutes, February 28, 1990, House Health and Retirement Committee Files, State Archives Series 2361, Box 3275, Folder 18, OHS. The testimony from these committee hearings was not archived.

157. Sandy Theis, "Burt Patients Tell of 'Love Surgery,'" *DDN*, February 7, 1990.

158. Sandy Theis, interview with author, August 26, 2015.

159. Theis, "Burt Patients Tell of 'Love Surgery.'"

160. Theis, interview with author, August 26, 2015. Theis ended up interviewing many of the women upon whom Burt operated and getting to know some of them fairly well. She recalled, when she and I spoke, the women as being angry at Burt and embarrassed about what happened to them and embarrassed that they allowed it to happen to them. Often, she said, the women would break down and cry, telling her their stories and the ramifications of the surgery on their lives. Though working in Columbus, because the state medical board was part of her beat, she ended up covering some Burt stories as well.

161. McLin's 1989 bill was unsuccessful. In the fall of 1991, after the Phillips trial concluded, McLin announced she planned to introduce her bill again in the upcoming
session. Despite the opposition of the Ohio State Medical Association to her identi-
cal 1990 bill and with this opposition the bill's certain failure again, something McLin
readily acknowledged, she planned on reintroducing it in 1993, although she doubted
it would be passed because of the resistance by the medical association, what she
called "one of the strongest lobbying associations." Said McLin, "If Dr. Burt isn't
enough to change the law, what does it take?" AP, "Board Rapped for No Action against
Dr. Burt's Peers," *Plain Dealer*, January 24, 1993. Sandy Theis, "McLin after Inept
Doctors—but Not Optimistic about Changing Law," *DDN*, August 26, 1991.

9. Love Surgery on Trial

1. Eliot Freidson, *Profession of Medicine: A Study of the Sociology of Applied Knowledge*, 2nd printing (New York: Dodd, Mead and Co., 1970), 180.
2. Timothy Stoltzfus Jost, "The Necessary and Proper Role of Regulation to Assure the
Quality of Health Care," *Houston Law Review* 25 (1988): 525–598, quotation on 572.
3. This first lawsuit against Burt had been scheduled to start in August 1990, but it was
delayed. This delay was in no small part because of a break-in that occurred in early
1989 and the accusation of burglary leveled against (and by) several of the people in
the Burt story, including Janet Phillips, Mary Lee Sambol, Cheryl Sexton, Linda Cook,
and *DDN* reporter Dave Davis. The information about what happened is confusing—
and altogether not clear within the available public documents—regarding exactly
who broke in, whose idea it was to do so, who took what if anything, and if anything
that was taken was used in the Burt malpractice trial. I will give a general overview
of what was reported within the local newspaper as to what happened, but I decided
not to include this in the main section of the book because it deviated and distracted
too much away from the main narrative—just as it deviated and distracted from the
malpractice lawsuits against Burt at the time.
    Sometime between January and the end of March 1989, the Burt home, which
the Burts were no longer living in, at 7152 Paragon Road, was broken into at least
once. Rob Modic, "'Love Surgeon' Was Burglary Victim," *DDN*, June 22, 1990; Modic,
"Burt's Lawyer Seeking Source of Evidence," *DDN*, June 30, 1990; Modic, "Phillips
Once Denied Entering," *DDN*, December 18, 1990. Sambol and/or other attorneys
working with her may have taken documents from the house that may have been
used or at least may have been seen. Modic, "Judge Orders Lawyers to Hand Over
Any 'Love Doctor' Records," *DDN*, July 26, 1990. Davis, who had been reporting on
the Burt story and was working on a book about it, was asked to resign by the *DDN*
when he told the editor he had been on the property after saying he had not. Modic,
"'Love Surgeon' Was Burglary Victim."
    On Thursday, July 12, 1990, Phillips was charged with one count of burglary
and also that an unidentified man, labeled as "John Doe," had also been charged by
the county prosecutor's office with burglary. George Patricoff, an assistant county
prosecutor, declined to say what items Phillips had allegedly taken from the Burt
home. Wes Hills, "Woman Suing 'Love Doctor' Charged as Burglar," *DDN*, July 7,
1990. On August 22, a grand jury indicted Phillips on one count of burglary. The
indictment charged Phillips with breaking into Burt's home at least once between
January 1 and March 31, 1989. The jury based their decision on statements made by
people that she had entered the house and upon recovery and identification of a lapel

pin as Joan Burt's. In his statement to reporters about the grand jury's indictment, Patricoff also said that although the Burt house was vacant that spring and had been sold at the sheriff's auction, Joan Burt held the deed to the house until May 1989, months after the home had been sold. Although the grand jury indicted Phillips, they did not indict "John Doe," revealed now as Dave Davis. Modic, "Burt's Accuser Indicted," *DDN*, August 22, 1990.

On September 11, 1990, Phillips pleaded not guilty to burglarizing Burt's home. "Burt's Accuser Pleads Not Guilty to Burglary," *DDN*, September 12, 1990. On December 19, a jury deliberated for two hours and acquitted Phillips of burglary but convicted her of trespassing, a misdemeanor. The jury, however, said they reached that verdict because they felt they never heard the whole truth from any of the key witnesses. "Who was being truthful and who was not—that was the hardest thing for us to decide," Ken Reilly, the jury foreman said. "I don't think we believed anybody was being totally truthful." Modic, "Woman Acquitted of Burt Burglary," *DDN*, December 20, 1990.

In his opinion column for the *DDN* the following day, Martin Gottlieb compared the burglary trial of Janet Phillips to a "Lewis Carroll world without humor, in which everything is the opposite of what a normal person would expect—upside down, crazy." Under the headline "The Burt Story Just Gets More Bizarre," Gottlieb wrote that such an "upside down, crazy" world just played out in Dayton as "Janet Phillips gets put on trial for victimizing James Burt." That trial, Gottlieb continued, "stands as a perfect symbol of the larger haunting story of the breakdown of the American system in the case of James Burt." Phillips, Gottlieb contended, simply got too zealous, entering her doctor's former house more than once, but, he continued, who cares? "She walked into a house Burt had abandoned and took stuff he had abandoned. So what? Why is the system suddenly getting vigilant now? Why does it move first against the victim?" he demanded. Indeed, Gottlieb wondered why the trial occurred at all. Martin Gottlieb, "The Burt Story Just Gets More Bizarre," *DDN*, December 21, 1990.

Phillips ending up receiving a $100 fine and was required to pay the court costs of the burglary trial. Following the announcement of the sentence in early January 1991, Phillips said the matter had "cost a lot of money" but that she was satisfied with the outcome. "I was honest up front," she told the *DDN*, "I didn't take anything off the property." "Burt-Home Trespasser Fined $100, Court Costs," *DDN*, January 15, 1991.

4. "Area Digest," *DDN*, January 31, 1991.
5. Medical Expenses of Janet Phillips, Appellant's Supplement, vol. 1, *Phillips v. Burt*, Supreme Court of Ohio, Case No. 95-1522, filed February 12, 1996, at 0483, 0487; Plaintiff's Exhibits Admitted into Evidence, Appellant's Supplement, vol. 1, *Phillips v. Burt*, Supreme Court of Ohio, Case No. 95-1522, filed February 12, 1996, at 0487.
6. "Lawsuit Against Dr. Burt Might Be Heard in Toledo," *DDN*, March 10, 1991.
7. "Love-Surgery Case Lawyers Fined," *DDN*, April 29, 1991.
8. Sandy Theis, "Burt Must Go to Trial in 'Love Surgery,'" *DDN*, May 3, 1991.
9. Sandy Theis, "Burt Begs to Skip Love-Surgery Trial," *DDN*, May 3, 1991.
10. Theis, "Burt Begs to Skip."
11. Rob Modic, "Burt's Trial Monday; Judge Again Nixes Request to Default," *DDN*, May 4, 1991.
12. James Hannah, "'Love Surgeon' Faces Jail," *Plain Dealer*, June 21, 1991.
13. Editorial, "Burt Can't Keep Running from Court," *DDN*, May 6, 1991.

14. Modic, "Burt's Trial Monday."
15. Rob Modic, "Lawyers Grill Burt Jury Prospects—Query: Can You Spare 5 Weeks?" *DDN*, May 7, 1991.
16. Rob Modic, "Judge Uses Summons to Get More Burt Jurors," *DDN*, May 9, 1991.
17. "Trial Begins This Morning in Burt Case," *DDN*, May 14, 1991.
18. "Trial Begins This Morning in Burt Case."
19. Dodge was reportedly disappointed with this outcome, something attorneys for St. Elizabeth later charged showed him as biased against them. Rob Modic, "St. E's Says Judge Biased in Civil Trial," *DDN*, January 9, 1993.
20. Rob Modic, "Hospital's Role at Issue as Burt Trial Opens," *DDN*, May 15, 1991.
21. Rob Modic, "Judges to Rule if Phillips Filed in Time," *DDN*, June 5, 1991; Modic, "Witness: Phillips Knew," *DDN*, June 6, 1991.
22. Rob Modic and Tom Beyerlein, "Nurse Testified She Complained about Dr. Burt," *DDN*, May 16, 1991.
23. Modic and Beyerlein, "Nurse Testifies She Complained about Dr. Burt."
24. Testimony of Nancy Goodman, Appellant's Supplement, vol. 3, *Phillips v. Burt*, Supreme Court of Ohio, Case No. 95-1522, filed February 12, 1996, at 1146–1150.
25. Rob Modic, "Former Burt Assistant Says Hospital Knew," *DDN*, May 22, 1991.
26. Rob Modic, "5-Week Burt Trial Down to Closing Arguments," *DDN*, June 19, 1991.
27. Testimony of Yvonne Curington, Appellant's Supplement, vol. 3, *Phillips v. Burt*, Supreme Court of Ohio, Case No. 95-1522, filed February 12, 1996, at 1212, 1215–1218.
28. Rob Modic and Wes Hills, "Burt Caused Irreversible Damage, Doctor Says," *DDN*, May 24, 1991.
29. Rob Modic and Raymond Hernandez, "'Love Surgery' Defied Norms, Expert Testifies; Procedure Hurt Woman, Court Told," *DDN*, May 17, 1991.
30. Plaintiff's Expert Witnesses, Appellant's Supplement, vol. 3, *Phillips v. Burt*, Supreme Court of Ohio, Case No. 95-1522, filed February 12, 1996, at 0481; Rob Modic, "Only Burt's Patients Had to Sign Form, Officials Say," *DDN*, May 29, 1991.
31. Rob Modic, "Burt Kept 2 Sets of Records, Witness Says," *DDN*, May 21, 1991; Rob Modic and Tom Beyerlein, "Judge Rebukes 'Tired' Lawyer in Burt Trial," *DDN*, May 31, 1991.
32. Modic, "Burt Kept 2 Sets of Records."
33. Modic and Beyerlein, "Judge Rebukes 'Tired' Lawyer in Burt Trial."
34. Rob Modic, "Aides Deny Nurses Made Complaints," *DDN*, June 14, 1991.
35. Modic, "Only Burt's Patients Had to Sign Form."
36. Tom Beyerlein, "Expert Had Said Burt Surgery Unnecessary," *DDN*, June 15, 1991.
37. James Hannah, "Jury Told Surgical Forms Okay," *Plain Dealer*, June 15, 1991.
38. Modic and Hernandez, "'Love Surgery' Defied Norms."
39. Modic, "Only Burt's Patients Had to Sign Form."
40. Rob Modic, "Secretary: Phillips Gave Okay," *DDN*, June 11, 1991.
41. James Hannah, "Witness Says Plaintiff Knew about Surgery," *Plain Dealer*, June 6, 1991.
42. Hannah, "Witness Says Plaintiff Knew about Surgery."
43. James Hannah, "Patient Tells Court of 'Love Surgery,'" *Plain Dealer*, June 1, 1991.
44. Editorial, "Burt Non-Appearance Leaves Gap," *DDN*, June 14, 1991.
45. Modic, "5-Week Burt Trial Down to Closing Arguments."
46. Modic, "Burt Kept 2 Sets of Records."
47. Martin Gottlieb, "Jury Hears Horror Story Over and Over," *DDN*, May 24, 1991.
48. Rob Modic and Wes Hills, "Burt Caused Irreversible Damage, Doctor Says," *DDN*, May 24, 1991.

49. Martin Gottlieb, "Trial Victimizes the Victim—Again," *DDN*, May 31, 1991.
50. Modic and Hills, "Burt Caused Irreversible Damage"; Gottlieb, "Trial Victimizes the Victim—Again."
51. Dodge stopped this particular cross-examination and suggested Moore speak with the attorneys for St. Elizabeth regarding his tactics. Rob Modic, "Phillips' Lawyers Build Their Case on Emotion," *DDN*, June 9, 1991.
52. Julia Helgason, "Phillips Doesn't Expect to Collect a Penny from Burt," *DDN*, June 23, 1991.
53. Modic and Beyerlein, "Judge Rebukes 'Tired' Lawyer in Burt Trial."
54. Helgason, "Phillips Doesn't Expect to Collect a Penny from Burt."
55. Gottlieb, "Trial Victimizes the Victim—Again."
56. Modic and Hernandez, "'Love Surgery' Defied Norms."
57. Rob Modic, "Woman Testifies of Trust for Gynecologist Burt," *DDN*, June 1, 1991.
58. Modic and Hernandez, "'Love Surgery' Defied Norms."
59. Modic and Beyerlein, "Judge Rebukes 'Tired' Lawyer in Burt Trial."
60. Modic, "Secretary: Phillips Gave Okay."
61. Modic and Beyerlein, "Judge Rebukes 'Tired' Lawyer in Burt Trial."
62. Gottlieb, "Trial Victimizes the Victim—Again."
63. Modic, "5-Week Burt Trial Down to Closing Arguments."
64. Rob Modic, "Doctor or 'Devil': Jurors to Deliberate," *DDN*, June 20, 1991.
65. Editorial, "Trial Part Handled Well in Case of Burt-St. E's," *DDN*, June 21, 1991.
66. Editorial, "Trial Part Handled Well in Case of Burt-St. E's."
67. Modic, "5-Week Burt Trial Down to Closing Arguments."
68. Tom Hopkins, "WDTN-TV Invisible—Just ask WHIO-TV," *DDN*, June 22, 1991.
69. AP, "Million Awarded to Woman Who Said Doctor Maimed Her," *New York Times*, June 22, 1991.
70. Modic, "Doctor or 'Devil.'"
71. Hannah, "'Love Surgeon' Faces Jail."
72. Editorial, "Trial Part Handled Well in Case of Burt-St. E's."
73. Hannah, "'Love Surgeon' Faces Jail"; Dwayne Bray, "Florida Won't Honor Warrant for James Burt," *DDN*, June 26, 1991. The Supreme Court of Ohio ruled this warrant legal in 1992. Tim Miller, "Warrant for Burt Ruled Legal," *DDN*, October 22, 1992.
74. It was not publicly clear why this amount was determined. Rob Modic, "Phillips' Lawyers Build Their Case on Emotion," *DDN*, June 9, 1991.
75. Rob Modic, "Burt Case Judge: 'Grueling' Trial Was Memorable," *DDN*, June 22, 1991; Modic, "A Mixed Verdict: Burt: Pay $5 Million, Jury Says; St. E.'s: Off Hook on Technicality," *DDN*, June 22, 1991.
76. Modic, "A Mixed Verdict."
77. Editorial, "Limitations Law Dubious," *DDN*, June 25, 1991.
78. Modic, "A Mixed Verdict."
79. AP, "Million Awarded to Woman Who Said Doctor Maimed Her."
80. Modic, "A Mixed Verdict: Burt."
81. Helgason, "Phillips Doesn't Expect to Collect a Penny from Burt."
82. Editorial, "Phillips Story a Marvel of Medicine—and Law," *DDN*, June 22, 1991.
83. James Hannah, "'Love Surgery' Doctor Can't Pay Damages," *Plain Dealer*, July 9, 1991.
84. Mizell Stewart III, "Juror Regrets Burt Verdict Did Not Penalize Hospital," *DDN*, June 23, 1991.
85. AP, "Appeal Says Hospital Liable in 'Love Surgery,'" *Plain Dealer*, July 3, 1991.

86. Rob Modic, "Appeals Court Puts Hospital Back in Cases," *DDN*, August 21, 1991.
87. *Browning et al., Appellees, v. Burt; Blue et al.*, Appellants, 66 Ohio St.3d 544, 613 N.E.2d 993.
88. Trial transcript, *Mitchell v. Burt and St. Elizabeth Medical Center*, vol. 1, Case No. 91-2121, Supreme Court of Ohio, filed March 2, 1991, at 50, 62, 64, 71.
89. Editorial, "Appeals Court Changes Rules in Dr. Burt Cases," *DDN*, August 25, 1991.
90. AP, "Hospital Denies Blame in 'Love Surgery,'" *Plain Dealer*, August 26, 1991.
91. Rob Modic, "Judges' Change of Mind May Force New Look at Hospital in Burt Case," *DDN*, August 30, 1991.
92. "Burt Case Decision Due within Week," *DDN*, August 17, 1992.
93. "Women Seek High Court's Aid," *DDN*, January 17, 1993.
94. Tim Miller, "Court: Ex-Patients of Burt Can Sue St. E's," *DDN*, July 1, 1993.
95. Rob Modic, "Insurer: We're Not Liable in Burt Suits," *DDN*, March 12, 1994.
96. AP, "Hospital Faces Love Doc Suits," *Plain Dealer*, February 23, 1994; "Cases against Burt," *DDN*, September 7, 1997.
97. Rob Modic, "Burt's Patients Get Time: Suits Can Proceed against Hospital," *DDN*, February 23, 1994.
98. Jim Dillon, "Former 'Love Surgery' Doctor Optimistic," *DDN*, February 24, 1994.
99. Rob Modic, "Patients Quit Burt Claim, Eye Hospital," *DDN*, March 2, 1994.
100. Rob Modic, "25 Seeking Lawsuit in 'Love Doctor' Case," *DDN*, June 21, 1994.
101. Rob Modic, "Appeals Court: 5 'Love Doctor' Suits Can Proceed," *DDN*, September 3, 1994.
102. Rob Modic, "7 More Win Court OK to Seek Burt Case Trials," *DDN*, September 10, 1994.
103. Modic, "Patient of Burt Gets New Trial."
104. Wes Hills, "Court Oks Suit Against St. E.'s," *DDN*, June 15, 1995.
105. Wes Hills, "Supreme Court to Review Lawsuit against Hospital over Burt Work," *DDN*, November 23, 1995.
106. Jim DeBrosse, "Court Hears Woman's Case," *DDN*, November 14, 1996.
107. Debra Jasper, "Records Not Public, Court Rules," *DDN*, January 23, 1997.
108. Jim DeBrosse, "Attorney Eyes Settlement," *DDN*, January 24, 1997.
109. Wes Hills and Rob Modic, "St. E's Offers to Settle Burt Cases for $2.4 Million—Lawyer Assails Move as 'Sleazeball Tactic,'" *DDN*, November 9, 1991; Wes Hills, "Attorney Says St. Elizabeth's Holding Out," *DDN*, November 14, 1991; Ellen Belcher, "Burt Victims Suffer While Lawyers Fight," *DDN*, November 14, 1991.
110. "Cases against Burt," *DDN*, September 7, 1997.
111. Jim DeBrosse, "Attorney Eyes Settlement," *DDN*, January 24, 1997.
112. Modic, "Most Burt Suits Settled," *DDN*, September 7, 1997.
113. Modic, "Most Burt Suits Settled."
114. Kevin Lamb, "Franciscan Hospital to Close," *DDN*, July 14, 2000.
115. Editorial, "Franciscan Did Right by Many," *DDN*, July 14, 2000.
116. Editorial, "Franciscan Did Right by Many"; Jim DeBrosse, "Hands-On Hospital," *DDN*, July 16, 2000.

Conclusion

1. Susannah Breslin, "Designer Vaginas," *Harper's Bazaar*, November 1998, 130.
2. Michael P. Goodman, "Female Genital Cosmetic and Plastic Surgery: A Review," *Journal of Sexual Medicine* 8 (2011): 1813–1825.
3. Simone Weil Davis, "Loose Lips Sink Ships," *Feminist Studies* 28, no. 1 (Spring 2002): 7–35; Virginia Braun, "In Search of (Better) Sexual Pleasure: Female Genital

'Cosmetic' Surgery," *Sexualities* 8, no. 4 (2005): 407–424; Cristen Conger "'Designer Vaginas': A Brief Timeline of Labiaplasty," February 6, 2014, HowStuffWorks.com, https://www.stuffmomnevertoldyou.com/blogs/designer-vaginas-timeline-labia plasty.htm (accessed August 10, 2018).

4. Virginia Braun, "Female Genital Cosmetic Surgery: A Critical Review of Current Knowledge and Contemporary Debates," *Journal of Women's Health* 19, no. 7 (2010): 1393–1407, quotation on 1393.

5. James Apesos, Roy Jackson, John R. Miklos, and Robert D. Moore, *Vagina Makeover and Rejuvenation: Vaginal/Vulval Procedures, Restored Femininity* (MWP Media, 2008), v.

6. Editorial, "Ohio's Doctors Learn Nothing from Burt Fiasco," *DDN*, August 16, 1991.

7. Editorial, "Ohio's Doctors Learn Nothing."

8. Editorial, "When a Doctor Harms, That Shouldn't Be Secret," *DDN*, August 6, 1991.

9. Amir A. Khaliq, Hani Dimassi, Chiung-Yu Huang, Lutchmie Narine, and Raymond A. Smego Jr., "Disciplinary Actions against Physicians: Who Is Likely to Get Disciplined?" *American Journal of Medicine* 118, no. 7 (July 2005): 773–777.

10. Tim Miller, "Regulation Shrouded in Secrecy," *DDN*, August 4, 1991.

11. Ruth Horowitz, *In the Public Interest: Medical Licensing and the Disciplinary Process* (New Brunswick, NJ: Rutgers University Press, 2012), 192.

12. ABIM Foundation, "The Physician Charter," 2018, http://abimfoundation.org/what -we-do/physician-charter (accessed September 8, 2018). Importantly, the charter stresses three points to professionalism: patient welfare, autonomy, and social justice.

13. Daniel Wolfson, John Santa, and Lorie Slass, "Engaging Physicians and Consumers in Conversations about Treatment Overuse and Waste: A Short History of the Choosing Wisely Campaign," *Academic Medicine* 89, no. 7 (July 2014): 990–995.

14. Jordan J. Cohen, "Tasking the 'Self' in the Self-Governance of Medicine," *JAMA* 313, no. 18 (May 12, 2015): 1839–1840.

15. Howard Bauchner, Phil B. Fontanarosa, and Amy E. Thompson, "Professionalism, Governance, and Self-Regulation of Medicine," *JAMA* 313, no. 18 (May 12, 2015): 1831–1836, quotation on 1831. These regulations were, however, weakened. Erica Werner, "Trump Signs Law Rolling Back Post-Financial Banking Rules," *Washington Post*, May 24, 2018.

16. Bauchner, Fontanarosa, and Thompson, "Professionalism, Governance, and Self-Regulation of Medicine," 1831.

17. Mark R. Chassin and David W. Baker, "Aiming Higher to Enhance Professionalism: Beyond Accreditation and Certification," *JAMA* 313, no. 18 (Mau 12, 2015): 1795–1796, quotation on 1795.

18. Federation of State Medical Boards, "Duty to Report: Protecting Patients by Improving the Reporting and Sharing of Information about Health Care Practitioners, a Summit Meeting of Health Care Stakeholders, Held February 7, 2017, University Club, Washington, D.C.," http://www.fsmb.org/globalassets/advocacy/publications/duty-to -report-summary.pdf (accessed September 11, 2018), 1–5, 8.

19. FSMB, "Duty to Report," 1–5, 8.

20. FSMB, "Duty to Report," 10–12; emphasis in original.

21. Humayun J. Chaudhry, J. Daniel Gifford, and Arthur S. Hengerer, "Ensuring Competency and Professionalism through State Medical Licensing," *JAMA* 313, no. 18 (May 12, 2015): 1791–1792, quotation on 1791.

22. James N. Thompson and Lee E. Smith, "Medical Licensure and the Federation of State Medical Boards," *Archives of Facial Plastic Surgery* 8 (September/October 2006): 338–340.
23. Chaudhry, Gifford, and Hengerer, "Ensuring Competency and Professionalism through State Medical Licensing."
24. Federation of State Medical Boards, *2018 U.S. Medical Regulatory Trends and Actions*, December 2018, https://www.fsmb.org/siteassets/advocacy/publications/us-medical-regulatory-trends-actions.pdf (accessed April 20, 2019), 74, 76. Only sixty-nine boards appear in these data.
25. Thompson and Smith, "Medical Licensure," 338.
26. FSMB, *2018 U.S. Medical Regulatory Trends and Actions*, 20–21.
27. Aaron Young, Humayun J. Chaudhry, Xiaomei Pei, Katie Arnhart, Michael Dugan, and Gregory B. Snyder, "A Census of Actively Licensed Physicians in the United States, 2016," *Journal of Medical Regulation* 103, no. 2 (2017): 7–21.
28. John Alexander Harris and Elena Byhoff, "Variations by State in Physician Disciplinary Actions by US Medical Licensure Boards," *BMJ Quality and Safety* 26 (2017): 200–208, quotation on 202.
29. Harris and Byhoff, "Variations by State," 202.
30. State Medical Board of Ohio, *Annual Report Fiscal Year 2018*, July 31, 2018, 8, 12, 14, 16, http://www.med.ohio.gov/Portals/0/Publications/Annual%20Reports/State%20Medical%20Board%20of%20Ohio%20FY18%20annual%20report.pdf (accessed September 4, 2018).
31. State Medical Board of Ohio, Formal Action Report—August 8, 2018, http://www.med.ohio.gov/Portals/0/Publications/Monthly%20Formal%20Action%20List/August%202018%20MFAL.pdf (accessed September 10, 2018).
32. Jessica J. Liu and Chaim M. Bell, "Disciplined Doctors: Learning from the Pain of the Past," *BMJ Quality and Safety* 26 (2017): 174–176, quotation on 174.
33. Liu and Bell, "Disciplined Doctors," 174.
34. Harris and Byhoff, "Variations by State," 200.
35. FSMB, "Protecting the Public," 2018, https://www.fsmb.org/ (accessed September 21, 2018); FSMB, "Educational Modules on Medical Regulation," 2018, https://www.fsmb.org/education/ (accessed on September 21, 2018).
36. FSMB, "Education Modules on Medical Regulation," https://www.fsmb.org/education/ (accessed December 2, 2019).

Appendix

1. H. David Banta, "Embracing or Rejecting Innovations: Clinical Diffusion of Health Care Technology," in *Use and Impact of Computers in Clinical Medicine*, ed. James G. Anderson and Stephen J. Jay (New York: Springer, 1987), 132–160.
2. "Surgery No Benefit to Patients with Meniscal Tears," *JAMA* 326, no. 12 (September 27, 2016): 1250.
3. Daniel Wolfson, John Santa, and Lorie Slass, "Engaging Physicians and Consumers in Conversations About Treatment Overuse and Waste: A Short History of the Choosing Wisely Campaign," *Academic Medicine* 89, no. 7 (July 2014): 990–995.
4. Choosing Wisely, "Our Mission," Choosing Wisely: An Initiative of the ABIM Foundation (2018), http://www.choosingwisely.org/our-mission/ (accessed September 5, 2018).
5. Academy of Medical Royal Colleges Press Release, "Forty Treatments That Bring Little or No Benefit to Patients," Academy of Royal Colleges, October 24, 2016,

https://www.aomrc.org.uk/wp-content/uploads/2016/10/Choosing_wisely_PR _211016-3.pdf (accessed September 8, 2018).

6. Academy of Medical Royal Colleges, "Questions to Ask Your Doctor or Nurse," Choosing Wisely UK (2018), http://www.choosingwisely.co.uk/i-am-a-patient-carer /questions-ask-doctor/ (accessed September 6, 2018).

7. Heather Lyu, Tim Xu, Daniel Brotman, Brandan Mayer-Blackwell, Michol Cooper, Michael Daniel, Elizabeth C. Wick, Vikas Saini, Shannon Brownlee, and Martin A. Makary, "Overtreatment in the United States," *PLoS One*, September 6, 2017, https:// www.ncbi.nlm.nih.gov/pmc/articles/PMC5587107/pdf/pone.0181970.pdf (accessed September 8, 2018); see also Daniel J. Morgan, Sanket S. Dhruva, Scott M. Wright, and Deborah Korenstein, "2016 Update on Medical Overuse: A Systematic Review," *JAMA Internal Medicine* 176, no. 11 (November 2016): 1687–1692; Daniel J. Morgan, Sanket S. Dhruva, Eric R. Coon, Scott M. Wright, and Deborah Korenstein, "2017 Update on Medical Overuse: A Systematic Review," *JAMA Internal Medicine* 178, no. 1 (January 2018): 110–115.

8. Another concern is when there is a question regarding who benefits from the tests, therapies, or surgeries—the patient or the physician who, by accepting payments from pharmaceutical and/or medical device companies, potentially undermines a patient's trust that the physician has the patient's best interests in mind. Noam N. Levey, "Medical Professionalism and the Future of Public Trust in Physicians," *JAMA* 313, no. 18 (May 12, 2015): 1827–1828. Stories questioning whether physicians have the best interest of their patients instead of perhaps their own financial interests predate and postdate Burt; for example, as I write this conclusion, an article appearing on the front page of the *New York Times* on September 9, 2018, noted that Jose Baselga, the chief medical officer at Memorial Sloan Kettering Cancer Center in New York and a major breast cancer doctor, "failed to disclose millions of dollars in payments from drug and health care companies in recent years, omitting his financial ties from dozens of research articles in prestigious publications like the *New England Journal of Medicine* and *The Lancet*." Charles Ornstein and Katie Thomas, "A Top Doctor Didn't Disclose Corporate Ties: Sloan Kettering Chief Was Paid Millions," *New York Times*, September 9, 2018. Baselga resigned later that week following the *New York Times* story—again highlighting the role of the media in medical regulation. Editorial, "Medicine's Financial Contamination," *New York Times*, September 16, 2018.

9. Lyu et al., "Overtreatment in the United States."

10. Charles B. Wilson, "Adoption of New Surgical Technology," *BMJ* 332 (January 14, 2006): 112–114, quotation on 114.

11. Ingrid Burger, Jeremy Sugarman, and Steven Goodman, "Ethical Issues in Evidence-Based Surgery," *Surgical Clinics of North America* 86, no. 1 (February 2006): 151–168, quotation on 164.

12. David A. Grimes, "Technology Follies: The Uncritical Acceptance of Medical Innovation," *JAMA* 269, no. 23 (June 16, 1993): 3030–3033.

13. Peter Angelos, "When the Evidence Isn't There—Seeking Informed Consent for New Procedures," *Virtual Mentor* 13 (January 2011): 6–9.

14. Angelos, "When the Evidence Isn't There," 7.

15. Questions adapted from Academy of Medical Royal Colleges, "Questions to Ask Your Doctor or Nurse," Choosing Wisely UK (2018), http://www.choosingwisely.co.uk /i-am-a-patient-carer/questions-ask-doctor/ (accessed September 6, 2018); Choosing Wisely: An Initiative of the ABIM Foundation, "5 Questions to Ask Your Doctor Before

You Get Any Test, Treatment, or Procedure," 2016, http://www.choosingwisely.org/wp
-content/uploads/2018/03/5-Questions-Poster_8.5x11-Eng.pdf (accessed September 7,
2018); Husam Abed, Rebecca Rogers, Deborah Helitzer, and Teddy D. Warner,
"Informed Consent in Gynecological Surgery," *American Journal of Obstetrics and
Gynecology* (December 2007): 674.e1–e5; American College of Surgeons, "10 Questions to Ask before Having an Operation," https://www.facs.org/education/patient
-education/patient-resources/prepare/10-questions (accessed September 6, 2018);
Johns Hopkins Medicine Health Library, "Questions to Ask before Surgery," https://
www.hopkinsmedicine.org/healthlibrary/conditions/surgical_care/questions_to_ask
_before_surgery_85,P01409 (accessed September 7, 2018); Orly Avitzur, "Before You
Have Surgery, Read This," *Consumer Reports*, March 30, 2017, https://www.consumer
reports.org/surgery/before-you-have-surgery-read-this/ (accessed September 6, 2018).

Index

A and P repair, 16–18, 20
ABC interview with Burt, 174
ABIMF (American Board of Internal
 Medicine Foundation), 186, 193–196
Abraham, Laurie, 142
Abramson, William, 86–87
Abromowitz, Herman, 104
abuse of spouse, Burt's, 7–8
activism, antipornography, 42, 43–44
activism, feminist health, 122
Against Our Will: Men, Women, and Rape
 (Brownmiller), 43
AHA (American Hospital Association), 54
alcohol and drug problems, physicians
 with, 98–99, 101, 103, 104, 105
Alfidi, Ralph, 56
American Board of Internal Medicine
 Foundation (ABIMF), 186, 193–196
American College of Physicians Founda-
 tion, 186
American College of Surgeons, 63, 65, 84, 122
American Hospital Association (AHA), 54
*American Journal of Obstetrics and
 Gynecology* (Ed. Zuspan), 31, 33–34
American Medical Association (AMA), 28,
 75, 80, 101, 133, 142
American Psychiatric Association, 80
American Surgical Association, 122
Ameringer, Carl, 100
Andrews, Victoria, 18
Angelos, Peter, 194
Annas, George, 158
anterior and posterior repair, 16–18, 20
antifeminism, 43
antipornography activism, 42, 43–44
Apesos, James, 183, 184
Arms, Suzanne, 16
Aronwitz, Robert, 4–5
arrest warrant for Burt, 174
"Assertiveness in the Dr.'s Office," *Feminist
 Women's Health Center Report* (Horn-
 stein), 53–54

Bailey, Beth, 25
Baker, David W., 186
Baker, Jennifer, 170
bankruptcy, Burt's attempts to file for, 112,
 115, 151
Bauchner, Howard, 186
Beauchamp, Tom, 56
bedside manner, Burt's, 13–14, 29, 38
Bell, Chaim, 190–191
Bell, Napoleon, 138–139, 150, 152
Belmont Report, 60–61
Big Mama Rag, 42
Bird, Lois, 23
Bland, Jim, 148
Blue, Max, Jr., 144–145, 176, 177
Board, Ohio State Medical. *See* Ohio State
 Medical Board
Boston Feminists Working against Violence
 against Women, 43–44
Boston Women's Health Book Collective, 41,
 42, 53
Boyles, John H., Jr., 95, 120
Braun, Virginia, 183
Brewer, Carol, 70
Brody, Jane, 79–80, 122
Bronstein, Carolyn, 42
Browning, Jimmie Dean, 176–177,
 178–179
Brownmiller, Susan, 43
Budd, John, 80
Bumgarner, Ray, 104, 146
Bunker, John, 121
Burnes, Karen, 133–137
Burt, Benjamin, 7
Burt, Gerre, 7, 9
Burt, James C., III, 175, 179, 181
Burt, Joan, 9, 13, 27–28, 40–42, 91, 111–112,
 160. See also *Surgery of Love* (James Burt,
 Joan Burt)
Burt, Linda, 9
Burt, Lucretia, 7
Burt, Stella, 7

About the Author

Sarah B. Rodriguez is a medical historian at Northwestern University in the Global Health Studies Program, the Department of Medical Education, and the Graduate Program in Medical Humanities and Bioethics. Her teaching and research focus on the history of reproduction, clinical practice, and research ethics. Her publications include the book *Female Circumcision and Clitoridectomy in the United States: A History of a Medical Practice.*

Available titles in the Critical Issues in Health and Medicine series: